'Kicker Dancin'
Texas Style

How to Do the Top Ten
Country-Western Dances

Shirley Rushing
Trinity University

and

Patrick McMillan
McMillan and Company

 Hunter Textbooks Inc.

> **Dedicated to**
> Frank, Rachel, Mike, Laura, Will,
> LeeAnn, Craig, Bill, Glen, Pat, John
> and all of our students
> through the years.

A videotape, *Kicker Dancin' Texas Style*, is designed to accompany this text. The 50-minute tape features the authors, Shirley Rushing and Patrick McMillan, demonstrating the top ten country-western dances included in this text. Orders or requests for information should be addressed to: Rushing Productions, 7254 Blanco Rd., Suite 114-341, San Antonio, TX 78216.

Inquiries should be addressed to the publisher:

Hi Hunter Textbooks Inc.

823 Reynolda Road
Winston-Salem, North Carolina 27104

PREFACE

The purpose of this book is to teach the non-dancer how to dance and to teach the novice dancer how to improve his/her skills. "The Introduction" explains the fundamentals applicable to all dancing. Becoming familiar with this section will enhance your dance skills as you learn the footwork of different dances. "The Dances" contains step analyses for ten different dances with a cumulative total of 95 variations. You should master the footwork and timing of the basic step at the beginning of each section before attempting to learn the variations. The man and lady should learn to execute their steps individually before attempting to dance them together. "Dance Fundamentals" and "Dance Positions," discussed in the Introduction, should be referred to frequently as you begin to dance with a partner.

Each section of "The Dances" begins with a brief history of the dance and rhythmical analysis of the basic step. Linear notation is used to analyze the music for each basic step. Amalgamations of variations that make desirable combinations are found at the end of each section. Suggested musical selections are also listed at the end of each dance.

Dance terms with brief definitions may be found at the end of the Introduction for quick reference. More thorough explanations are found when the term is used within the book. Footnotes are listed at the end of the "History of Dance" section. "Bootnotes" are suggestions which enhance the learning and performance of the dances. They are listed on the pages with the individual steps to which they apply.

The videotape, *Kicker Dancin' Texas Style*, contains the same step patterns as this book. Each may be used independently, but they will be more effective when used as companions.

ACKNOWLEDGMENTS

Students featured in the photographs are members of the "McMillan and Company" Country-Western Performing Company: Beth Burgeson, Howard Clift, Tim Ferguson, Christi Jo Ferguson, Shiela Garcia Galindo, Luana Johnson Garcia, Eric Hopper, Tom Litzinger, Janet Moore, Kris Moore, Christi Nall, Robert Reich, Ralph Rodriguez, Will Veal, Brenda Walker, Andy Williams, and Kim Wrightsman.

We extend our appreciation to Richard Crowther, photographer, for his diligent work in helping to articulate each step.

Our grateful appreciation also goes to Jane Blake for typing, re-typing, and assisting us in checking the details of each step.

Table of Contents

The Dances

HISTORY OF COUNTRY-WESTERN DANCE

Introduction

Dance is as old as humankind and its desire for expression. County-Western dance has a heritage derived from primitive times and influenced by our ancestors from every continent and through every generation. Hieroglyphics carved on cave walls show that people danced before there was any evidence of a written language. As a form of communication used to express joys and sorrows, worship and sacrifice, they utilized the only instrument at their disposal—their bodies.

The dance has often been defined as "the mother of the arts." Noted dance historian Curt Sachs states that "the dance, inherited from savage ancestors as an ordered expression in motion of the exhiliration of the soul, develops and broadens into the search for God, into a conscious effort to become a part of those powers beyond the might of man which controls our destinies. The dance becomes a sacrificial rite, a charm, a prayer, and a prophetic vision. It summons and dispels the forces of nature, heals the sick, links the dead to the chain of their descendants; it assures sustenance, luck in the chase, victory in the battle; it blesses the fields and the tribe. It is creator, preserver, stewart, and guardian." (1)

Primitive (The Stone Age): Circle, Chain, and Processional Dances

Primitive men and women danced for all occasions — worship, sacrifice, initiations, weddings, funerals, and attempts to entreat the gods on various occasions. One of the inspirations for the dance of primitive people was the dancelike movements of animals. Many insects, birds, animals, and fish perform movement patterns that appear similar to our conception of dance. Bees perform dancelike movements to make other bees aware of the newly found location of nectar, fish dance a "slow waltz" during their courtship, while ants form perfect lines to march to and fro in search of a chosen destination. (2)

Further evidence of the influence of insects and animals describes the male-female roles in dance. "Male birds don brilliant colors and dance during the mating season; the peacock spreads his tail and struts before the female. Antelopes often dance during mating time; the moose jumps with rhythmic steps about the female he is wooing. The horse was trained to dance after he was domesticated, and the original 'horse ballets' were performed for the Romans and Arabs. Anthropoid apes dance, sometimes forming circles and parading around a tree or post. Chimpanzees have been known to bedeck themselves with string, vines, and rags which swing in the air as they move." (3)

Many dance historians agree that religious dance, as depicted by our primitive cultures, is the foundation of all forms of dance. From these religious dances were derived three separate forms of dance: the Circle, the Chain, and the Processional. The closed circle is the oldest form of the three and is believed to symbolize the rotation of the sun. To break the circle would let good or bad spirits either in or out, depending upon the culture's belief. The Chain derived from the closed circle and was used to travel and carry good luck along the way. The processional form of dance utilized a double line of dancers with men and women dancing in separate lines or a single line with everyone dancing together. The Processional is also known as a march or promenade. Originally a complete dance, it later developed into an opening activity for an evening of festivities. (4) These three forms of ritual and religious dance that presented patterns used to interweave the dancers exerted a great influence on our present-day folk dances.

Medieval (The Middle Ages, 330-1350): Folk and Peasant Dances—The Round, the Square, and the Long-Way

The folk dances of today are the original social dances of the Middle Ages. The more complex the culture became, the more complex were the dances. Dance provided both a universal language and an image of the people. Ritual and religious dances depicted the educated class throughout the world, while in the folk dances the common or country people expressed their feelings on birth, life, and death. Although the movements differed from one area to another, the dances themselves strongly overlapped at some points. The distinguishing characteristics of costumes, music, religion and dance movements often identified the proper origin of each folk dance.

Medieval European peasant dances are still found throughout Europe today and are believed to be much the same as they were a thousand years ago. England was a country without any great natural hazards or barriers; therefore, in English dances the essential element of design was large and open, and the preferred movement patterns were free, light running steps. "The Germans stamped and slapped; the Russians squatted, spun, and leaped; the Spaniards clacked, clicked, and tapped. From country to country steps varied, but they maintained certain European characteristics: the body was upright, the arms were extended, the legs and feet covered space. The dance was outgoing, vigorous and free." (5)

Country or peasant dances, primarily in England, were the dances of the people, performed first at festivals and later on any occasion whenever the opportunity presented itself. Characterized by the use of flirtation or coquetry by the females, these dances easily identified geographical regions by the costumes worn. Descendants of the primitive Circle, Chain, and Processional, they appeared in three basic forms: the Round, the Square Eight, and the Long-way. Such dances became forerunners of our social Round Dancing, American Square Dance, and the ever-popular Contras, coming to the United States with the first American immigrants.

Renaissance (1350-1650): Court Dances

The processional dances influenced the court dances which were popular during the Renaissance. The court dances promoted the birth of social dance that is practiced today. Dance masters were hired by the courts of Europe to dignify many of the peasant dances and teach them to the aristocracy. Exquisite dress and manners were in vogue among the ladies and gentlemen of the court as they competed with other courts for the most elaborate ball. The same social graces are found today at our formal dances, debutante balls, cotillions, and military functions.

The court dances, although taken from the peasant-style patterns, developed into elegant forms that discarded any rough steps or movements. Court dances were concerned almost exclusively with pageantry or courtship. The arts of high coquetry were used in their dances, including handkerchiefs, fans, veils, and long trailing skirts and cloaks. (6)

The princes of Italy encouraged art and learning and created a brilliant court in an effort to increase their prestige and impress their neighbors. Dance was especially well-suited to this and it was utilized to the fullest degree. (7)

Costumes of the dancer often indicated status, prestige, and wealth. The peasants, being of a poor nature, wore lightweight material in their shirts, vests, skirts, and trousers. Their shoes were of soft leather or they danced barefooted. Thus the dances of the peasant or country folk, influenced by their clothing and footwear, were very free-spirited and unlimited in movement. In contrast, the Renaissance lady wore heavy-cut velvets, brocades and jewel-encrusted silks. These dresses had long trains, so the dance steps were restricted to gliding, tapping, or posing. (8) The heavy clothing did not permit exuberant movement, but what the dance of the nobility lost in vitality, it gained in pomp and pageantry.

Pierre Beauchamps, the leading dance master of the early 1700s, developed the Minuet, named for the small (menu) steps of the dance. The tiny precise steps and constrained movements were executed in staged precision, making it unsurpassed in its blend of dignity and charm. The Minuet lasted more than a hundred years, dying during the French Revolution.

In the early 1800s Europe was enraptured by a new dance sweeping the country, the Waltz. A voluptuous turning dance with an intoxicating rhythm, the Waltz was considered indecent and promiscuous because, for the first time, the man held his partner in closed dance position and even placed his hand on her back. Europe became a "breeding ground for dances that involved turnings, glidings, leapings and stampings. In Italy, the most common dance of this type was called the Volta; in France, the Volte; in Germany, the Walzen; and in Austria, the Landler. All these originally were round dances in which the dancers broke into couples and continued to whirl around. Dance historians have credited the Landler as the forerunner of the Waltz." (9)

Following the Waltz in the 1800s was the Polka, originally a Czechoslovakian peasant dance which was developed in Bohemia. Historians believe that it was invented by a peasant girl for her own amusement. A village dance teacher saw her, noted the dance and the music, and later performed it at the village festival. The name of the dance (pulka) is Czech for "half-step," referring to the rapid weight-shift on the first two steps. Like the Waltz, the Polka was characterized by the closed dance position, the constant turning, and the exuberant tempo and enthusiasm with which it was performed.

From the Waltz and the Polka originated ballroom dance as it is known today. Each moved from peasant dance improvisation through the renown dance masters of Europe and onto the dance floors of the aristocracy where they were performed for the nobility.

Colonial Period (1600-1900)

The basic need to survive and the Puritan work ethic created a void in dance during early Colonial America. By the time crops had been planted and harvested, trees had been cut down and shlelters built, and other physical expenditures had been made for family protection and welfare, there was little time left for recreation. Religious attitudes shaped by Calvinism prohibited any sort of play. The early Puritans did not permit "mixed dancing" of men and women, nor was it permissable to dance in local taverns, especially for women. They even opposed dancing that accompanied any type of feast or festival.

The Puritans, however, could not keep the inevitable from happening. Such educators as Roger Ascham in *The Schoolmaster,* John Locke in *Some Thoughts Concerning Education,* and John Playford in *The English Dancing Master,* emphasized the values of dance and appealed to the educated colonists. People began to appreciate the concomitant values of dance, such as good manners and posture, graceful movements and social graces. Country dances of Europe, in which a number of people danced together, became very popular in New England; even the Puritans approved while frowning on other forms. The dancers formed figures or patterns, sometimes executing intricate steps and requiring choreographed movement of the entire group. Dancing served an important role in social amusement and gradually gained acceptance as a vital part of education. It came to be perceived as one of the accomplishments proper for a gentleman; not having a knowledge of dance showed a lack of adequate education. Although a gentleman was expected to dance well, he was never to become so proficient that he rivaled the dancing master. (10) The dances favored by the colonists were the Country Dances, Clogs, Cotillions, Minuet, Courante, Galliard, Rigadoon, and Gavotte.

The popularity of social dancing flourished at the beginning of the nineteenth century throughout the United States. In the cities, where dancing masters conducted regular classes and where education in dance had become a mark of aristocratic upbringing, instruction was formal and disciplined. But on the frontier and in rural areas, where life was rougher, there were few dancing masters and no formal cotillions or rules of etiquette. Girls and women were scarce and often the action was rough and ready. The men and women of the frontier loved to dance the

Virginia Reels, Country Jigs, and Shakedowns, and this soon became the favorite form of entertainment in frontier settlements.

Adding a unique and original contribution to American dance lore were the Shakers, a group that had broken off from the Quaker faith. Using dance in their religious ceremonies, they created one of the most unusual exhibitions of their time. Originally from England, they migrated as far south as Kentucky. Their dance followed the basic square and line dance patterns and consisted of shaking—a strenuous exercise which they believed would "shake sin out of their bodies." The Shakers contributed nothing new to the field of dance, but they kept alive the idea of dance as a basic part of religion—an idea that has perhaps made our society a little more tolerant than it otherwise might have been. People outside the sect adopted some of the dances and games of the Shakers for their own entertainment. One such children's dance was the Lobby-Lou, which is still a present-day favorite. This children's game later inspired a popular community dance favorite which gained adult favor under the name "Hokey Pokey." (11)

Some religious sects discouraged dancing to instrumental music but permitted the use of games performed to songs or vocal recitations. Quadrilles and square dances were tolerated under the guise of Play Party games. So classified along with Lobby-Lou are such favorites as Shoo Fly, Ringo, Old Dan Tucker, and Coming Through the Rye.

The western migration in the United States was largely due to the continuous flow of immigrants arriving from England, Germany, Poland, France, Ireland, Scandinavia, Czechoslovakia, and Russia. The Square Dance followed the westward migration and became an important part of the communal barn raisings, quilting bees, and corn huskings. Some of the dances varied from their European originals because of the less sophisticated environment in which they were performed. Dancing floors of packed earth or rough-hewn timber as opposed to polished hardwood and baroque ballroom necessitated changes in styling. (12)

People of the westward migration gathered everywhere when it came time to dance—on ranches, in barns, outside under the stars. The dances popular at this time were the American Square Dance; the Varsouvianna, which is now recognized as Put Your Little Foot; and contra dances such as Sir Rodger de Coverly, which later became simplified under the more familiar name of Virginia Reel. The other dance favorites which have stood the test of time are the Waltz, with its intoxicating spinning movement, and the Polka, which has the intimacy of the Waltz and the vivacity of the Irish Jig.

After the Civil War and with the rise of the booming cattle industry, the cowboy made his appearance. America welcomed him with open arms, and the cowboy became a legend. It was during this era that he found the enticing saloons and the incomparable dance legacy from France—the Can-Can. Developed in the cafes of France by the leisure class in the 1840s, the Can-Can was a protest of the stately dances of the aristocracy. These dances followed the western migration and served as entertainment for the wandering men on horseback and the tired, rugged cowboy. The Can-Can consisted of high-kicking, the raising of skirts, and a jump into the splits, behavior totally unacceptable to ladies and gentlemen of that era.

When the cowboy himself took to the dance floor, "It was a rompin', stompin', affair," wrote western historian Ramon Adams, as quoted in Peter Livingston's *The Complete Book of Country and Western Dance.* "The feet of the dancers pounded the floor so hard that no matter how clean it had been scrubbed, they brought the dirt up from under the boards that had been there since the shack was built." (13) Joseph McCoy, the great cattle baron for whom the phrase "the real McCoy" was coined, wrote in 1874 that the cowboy "usually enters the dance with a peculiar zest, his eyes lit up with excitement, liquor and lust. He stomps in without stopping to divest himself of his sombrero, spurs or pistols." (14)

The cowboy expressed his individualistic character while developing his own style of dancing. The heavy boots and spurs influenced his using small steps and the shuffle movement is still characteristic of Country-Western Dance today. The fiddle replaced the violin, and the cowboy danced until dawn to the tune of the fiddle, banjo, and guitar. Various dance movements closely resembled the patterns used by the cowboy in his daily work. "The habitual swing of the leg when dismounting from a horse became a mighty polka gallop. The 'double arms over' move was reminiscent of the final 'tying off' of a calf's legs prior to branding. The basic 'push pull' position recaptured the rhythm of grasping the reins, and in the Bronco Baile the partners reeled to and fro as if riding a bucking bronco." (15) Another favorite which developed later and was highly frowned upon by the moralists was the Texas Tommy. "Tommy" meant prostitute and, true to its namesake, this innovative dance was overtly seductive and sexual.

Paralleling the emergence of the booming cattle industry in the west was the introduction into American social life of the newly freed slaves in the south. America's original contribution to dance came from rhythmic patterns of the American Blacks. Using drums, gourds, banjos, and cymbals, they effected a musical accompaniment that would later influence "swing" both in ballrooms and country-western dance halls. Minstrel shows developed as a form of entertainment on the plantation. The minstrels later began to perform in theaters and their steps finally became integrated into the mainstream of American dance. The Cake Walk, Strut, and the Two-Step became the popular dance favorites, and the terms "ragtime" and "jazz" were coined to identify the new and distinct musical style.

Twentieth Century: Social and Popular Dance

Exhibition dancing evolved at the turn of the century as a result of the new "ragtime" rhythm. These dances included names like the Turkey Trot, Grissly Bear, Bunny Hug, Camel Walk, Ballin' the Jack, and other novelty types inspired by Black rhythm. Fast, gyrating, and acrobatic, the dancers separated from each other, turned and twirled, and experienced the joy of improvisation and spontaneous movement. These movements were very much against the accepted standards of the former European dances, not to mention the moralists of the era. European dances which retained popularity were the Three Step, the Rye Waltz, and various interpretations of the Schottische.

In the 1920s exhibition dance teams began to emerge. Vernon and Irene Castle, Fred Astaire (first with sister Adele and later with Ginger Rogers), and Arthur and Kathryn Murray introduced exhibition ballroom dancing. Although it was designed for theatre entertainment, it was possible for the average person to emulate and imitate. Arthur and Kathryn Murray made a very successful career of standardizing, simplifying, and teaching ballroom dance in studios throughout the United States. Rudolph Valentino became the heartthrob of movie-going Americans as he introduced the sensuous Argentine Tango. The radio prompted an explosion of interest as it began to broadcast current musical hits. The syncopated rhythms of jazz were discovered, and flapper dances of the Charleston, Shimmy, Lindy Hop, Black Bottom, and Varsity Drag dominated this freedom-loving postwar period.

The depression years of the thirties ushered in the Big Band sound. Benny Goodman's jazz dominated the musical scene as the Lindy Hop gave birth to the Jitterbug. The fad dances were the Big Apple, Susie Q, and Trucking; the Rhumba and Conga emigrated from our neighbors to the south; Fred Astaire and Ginger Rogers popularized the Carioca; and Bob Wills and his Texas Playboys developed a style of music that became the cornerstone of "Country Swing."

In the 1940s the Lindy, Shag, and Jitterbug merged into "Swing" as our servicemen carried American dances into USOs all over the world. The Andrews Sisters harmonized on "Boogie Woogie Bugle Boy of Company B," and the dancing reflected the frenzied feeling of wartime insecurity. The Fox Trot continued to be the dance of the masses, and the teenagers began to "Boogie." The Mambo and Cha-Cha grew from Afro-Cuban forms, and Carmen Miranda, under her marvelous banana hat, introduced us to the Samba.

The 1950s reflected a Caribbean Island influence as American tourists returned with the Calypso, Merengue, Cha-Cha, and Mambo. The Jitterbug, Bop, and Fox Trot continued to dominate popular dance for the masses. Students on college campuses were doing the Bunny Hop and Hokey Pokey while many of the "Big Bands" were giving way to smaller "combos." Bill

Haley, formerly of the Four Aces of Western Swing, and his Comets changed Rock-a-Billy to Rock and Roll as they ushered in the era of Rock with their smash hit "Rock Around the Clock." Classical Ballet had its first rival in the theatre as Americans began to appreciate the works of Martha Graham, Charles Weldman, Doris Humphrey, and Hanya Holm, and Modern Dance took its place alongside Ballet as "dance as an art form."

The dance of the sixties reflected the attitude of the era when everyone was protesting something—the Viet Nam War, social injustices, civil rights, and basic philosophies of education. The protests manifested a "do your own thing" attitude which was highly reflected in the dance. Partners separated and danced along with improvised and sometimes frenzied movements. For the first time since primitive times, it was socially acceptable to dance without knowing any formal dance steps—one could participate merely by shaking, twisting, or imitating the movements of animals. Popular imitations were the Monkey, Pony, Dog, and for the more adventuresome, the Dirty Dog and the Alligator. Dances patterned after familiar activities were the Swim, the Surfer, and the Hitchhiker. The Twist, Bump, Frug, Watusi, Boogaloo, Hully Gully and the Stroll completed the picture.

Couple dancing was revived in the seventies with Disco, a dance that was influenced by the Black American and popularized for the masses by the movie "Saturday Night Fever." An amalgamation of movements from Lindy, Jitterbug, Western Swing, and Rock 'n' Roll, Disco was characterized by flashing strobe lights, flashy attire, and very loud music. The Latin Hustle was patterned after the West Coast Swing; the Swing Hustle was similar to the Jitterbug; and the Manhattan Hustle used the single step of the Merengue. Although studios taught basic step patterns, the masses seemed to ignore the footwork and concentrate primarily on the complicated arm movements. The popularity of the Disco was short-lived, and in the late seventies, all over the country Disco Clubs became Country-Western Dance Halls overnight. The interest in Disco generated by "Saturday Night Fever" was surpassed when the movie "Urban Cowboy" skyrocketed the popularity of Country-Western dance.

Always popular in such states as Texas, Oklahoma and Colorado, the Country-Western craze swept the United States in the late 1970s. Its appeal was reflected in dance, music, and wearing apparel. Specialty stores as well as department stores stocked full lines of western wear, and the Lone Star Cafe opened in the midst of Greenwich Village in the largest metropolitan area in the United States. "Cotton-Eyed Joe" became the national anthem of country music, and every drugstore cowboy owned a pair of western boots. Classes in Country-Western dance flourished and people stood in line to get into overcrowded dance halls.

As we moved into the eighties, Country-Western Dance continued to dominate the dance scene. Ballroom dance continued to flourish through colleges, universities, cotillions, and high society. "Turning Point" brought ballet to the movie-going masses and jazz was rejuvenated by "Staying Alive" and "Flashdance." We find tap, clogging, folk, round and square dance being enjoyed by thousands of people throughout the nation. The street gangs of New York introduced break and pop dancing, which gained popularity through music videos and movies such as "Breaking." Music Television (MTV) brings current Rock and Roll into millions of households daily, while the Nashville Station through its videos keeps its viewers abreast of the latest County and Western stars. These two forms of dance are riding the crest of popularity of all dance throughout the world.

The music of such stars as Bob Wills (the king of western swing), the immortal Hank Williams, and Texas' own Willie Nelson have inspired Country-Western dance through the years. Dance halls such as Gilley's in Houston, Billy Bob's in Fort Worth, and Bluebonnet Palace in San Antonio have dwarfed the size of traditional dance halls throughout the country.

Country-Western Dance has been a part of the culture of our country since the westward migration of the early settlers. As we have seen the popularity of different forms of dance rise and fall in this country, there has always been a nucleus of people who have kept alive the dance of the cowboy. The attraction to Country-Western dance and music appears to be as enduring as the image of the cowboy. As long as we have ranches, farms, horses, country music, and free spirits, we will always have Country-Western dance.

NOTES

1. Curt Sachs, *World History of the Dance.* (New York: W.W. Norton & Company, Inc., 1937), 4.
2. Richard Kraus and Sarah Chapman, *History of the Dance.* (Englewood Cliffs: Prentice-Hall, Inc., 1980), 21.
3. Richard Stephenson and Joseph Saccarino, *The Complete Book of Ballroom Dancing.* (Garden City: Doubleday & Company, Inc., 1980), 3.
4. Jane Harris, Ann Pittman, and Marlys Waller, *Dance a While.* (Minneapolis: Burgess Publishing Company, Fifth Ed., 1978), 3.
5. Agnes de Mille, *The Book of the Dance.* (New York: Golden Press, 1963), 46-47.
6. Agnes de Mille, *America Dances.* (New York: MacMillan Publishing Company, Inc., 1980), 4-5.
7. Jack Anderson, *Dance.* (New York: Newsweek Books, 1974), 12.
8. De Mille, *The Book of the Dance,* 60.
9. Aurora Villacorta, *Step by Step to Ballroom Dancing.* (Danville, Illinois: The Interstate Printers & Publishers, Inc., 1974), 13.
10. Kraus and Chapman, *History of the Dance,* 91.
11. Virgil L. Morton, *The Teaching of Popular Dance.* (New York: J. Lowell Pratt & Company, 1966), 3.
12. Morton, *Popular Dance,* 3.
13. Peter Livingston, *The Complete Book of Country Swing and Western Dance.* (New York: Doubleday & Company, Inc.), 41.
14. Livingston, *Country Swing and Western Dance,* 33.
15. Livingston, *Country Swing and Western Dance,* 39-41.

MUSIC AND THE DANCE

One must be able to recognize the basic underlying beat and to identify the accent in order to know which dance should be done to the music. The meter, or time signature, of the music tells you how many notes are in a measure and what kind of note gets one beat. This is expressed in a fraction with the numerator indicating how many notes are in the measure and the denominator indicating the type of notes.

The *underlying beat* is the steady pulsation heard throughout the music underneath the melody. The *accent* is the stress placed on the note at the beginning of each measure. If you will pat your foot to the underlying beat and begin to count in chronological order, you will soon recognize a rhythm pattern emerge reflecting the accented and unaccented beats. If the strong accent occurs every fourth beat, it is 4/4 rhythm. (You may have a secondary accent on the third note of the measure in 4/4 time.) An accent every third beat will be a 3/4 rhythm and an accent every other beat will be a 2/4 rhythm.

Dances to be executed to the rhythms are:

4/4   (slow to medium tempo) Western Two-Step

4/4   (medium tempo) Western Swing

4/4   (medium to fast tempo) Texas Two-Step, Texas Two-Step Swing

3/4   Western Waltz

2/4   Western Polka

DANCE FUNDAMENTALS

There are fundamentals that are applicable to all forms of dancing. One should be cognizant of them as he/she is learning to execute the steps. It is easier, however, to really perfect these fundamentals after one has developed some confidence in executing the basic step patterns.

Posture

Since country-western attire is less formal than the attire worn in ballroom dance, you will also find the dance posture more relaxed. A proper alignment of body parts (shoulder, hip, knee, ankle) should be assumed with a feeling of relaxation. Knees should be slightly flexed, never hyperextended. Each person should support his/her own weight, never imposing on the partner to support dead weight from the arms and upper body.

Leading

In order to execute an effective lead to advanced variations, fundamentals of leading correctly should begin as you are learning to dance. Many dance holds in closed position do not allow an effective lead to be transmitted to the lady. Different parts of the hand initiate the proper lead into various directives. In closed dance position, the *heel* of the hand leads the lady directly backward. The *fingers* lead the lady into a forward moving patttern. To move the lady to his left (her right) pressure is exerted by the *palm* of the hand. A directional pull with his *fingertips* will lead her to his right (her left). The entire *hand* is used to strengthen the lead in many movements, such as an underarm turn or holding the lady in place.

Although approximately 90% of the lead comes from the man's right hand, some variations require additional lead from the man's left hand. Added pressure in a forward movement, circling the lady's head for an underarm turn, and the turning of the wrist to hold the lady in conversation position are examples of the lead coming from the man's left hand.

In addition to leads from the right and left hand, a natural lead comes from the right arm and shoulder by assuming correct dance position. The lead should be firm enough to direct your partner but light enough so that it cannot be detected by anyone watching.

Following

From different dance positions the man will execute a variety of leads transmitted to his partner through body movements. As the man moves forward, backward, or sideways, the lead will be transmitted primarily from his right shoulder and through his right arm and hand. In order to receive his lead, the lady must offer a proper amount of resistance. This resistance involves the entire body, but it is received primarily through her left arm and shoulder. The proper amount of resistance varies among couples. A stronger lead will demand a stronger resistance, and a softer lead will demand less resistance. Resistance may be developed by the following exercises:

1. **Facing Position:** Man and lady stand facing each other with his hands on her shoulders and her hands on his shoulders. Both have elbows slightly bent. As the man moves forward, backward, or sideward, he exerts pressure and his partner resists, yielding enough to cause her to move with him. He then should remove his hands from her shoulders and let his arms hang by his sides, giving her total responsibility for the resistance as he repeats moving in all directions.

2. **Battle Position:** The man and lady stand facing each other with arms bent at a 90-degree angle, his palms facing up and her palms facing down. Each grasps the other's forearms. The

man may move in a forward, backward, sideways, or turning pattern. If the lady gives enough resistance with her arms and shoulders, she should be able to follow his lead.

To be able to exert the proper amount of resistance differentiates between a good dancer and a great dancer. The fastest way to learn the proper amount comes from a critique while dancing with an instructor, but concentration and practice while talking with your partner will enhance your skill.

Footwork

Footwork in Country-Western Dance consists of small steps with a toe lead. The toe lead is executed by stepping forward with the ball of the foot remaining in contact with the floor. This movement results in a small step called the shuffle step, which is also the basic step in square dancing.

In ballroom dance the heel or toe lead is determined by the tempo of the music, with slow music dictating a heel lead with long reaching steps and faster music dictating a toe lead with shorter steps. In Country-Western Dance, styling takes precedence and dictates a toe lead regardless of the tempo of the music.

The tempo of the music will determine whether the length of each step is small or medium. The size of steps taken by the man should also be influenced by the height of his partner. The size of a step may feel comfortable to a man whose normal walking step is longer than the lady's, but he should always consider the comfort of his partner. Long reaching steps with a heel lead are used in ballroom dance such as the Fox Trot, Waltz, and Tango. Because of the Cuban motion, Latin dances such as Rumba, Cha Cha, and Merengue use short steps. Country-Western Dance steps, depending on the tempo of the music, range in size from small to medium.

In different dance forms foot positions are defined as 1st, 2nd, 3rd, 4th and 5th. In Country-Western Dance only 1st, 2nd and 3rd are utilized. In 1st position, the feet are parallel and together. In 2nd position, the feet are parallel and separated to approximately shoulder-width. In third position, one foot is in front of the other with the back foot in contact with the instep of the front foot at approximately a 45-degree angle.

Feet Positions

| 1st Position | 2nd Position | 3rd Position
Left Foot Forward | 3rd Position
Right Foot Forward |

Some of the footwork remains the same in several different dances while the hand/arm movements and positions change. The most prevalent example is the "Triple Step," found in Cotton-Eyed Joe, Western Polka, and Ten-step Polka. An illustrated explanation of the "Triple Step" follows.

Left Triple Step:
Step L foot directly forward
Step R foot forward bringing feet together
(3rd position, L foot forward)
Step L foot directly forward.

Left Triple Step

| 1st Step | 2nd Step | 3rd Step |

Right Triple Step:
Step R foot directly forward
Step L foot forward bringing feet together
(3rd position, R foot forward)
Step R foot directly forward.

Right Triple Step

| 1st Step | 2nd Step | 3rd Step |

Hand/Arm Movements

Some of the hand/arm movements remain the same in several different dances while the footwork changes. These movements are explained in detail in each section. Examples of such movements are:

Hand/Arm Movements	Dance
1. Lasso	Cotton-eyed Joe Ten Step Polka Texas Two-Step Swing
2. Pretzel	Texas Two-Step Swing Western Polka Western Swing
3. String-a-long	Texas Two-Step Swing Western Polka Western Swing
4. Sweetheart	Texas Two-Step Swing Western Polka Western Swing
5. Sweetheart to Wringer	Texas Two-Step Swing Western Polka Western Swing
6. Twin Cities into Continuous Layover	Texas Two-Step Swing Western Swing
7. Underarm Turn	Texas Two-Step Western Polka Western Swing Western Two-Step Western Waltz
8. Whip (Alternate Underarms)	Texas Two-Step Swing Western Polka Western Swing
9. Wringer	Texas Two-Step Swing Western Polka Western Swing
10. Weave-the-Basket	Cotton-eyed Joe Ten Step Polka Texas Two-Step Swing Western Polka

Turns (Step patterns in closed position)

In different dances involving a complete turn clockwise, the person who steps with the left foot usually takes a larger step than the person who steps with the right. As the man/lady steps around his/her partner, the person stepping around makes a larger step and the person stepping in place makes a smaller step. For both partners the basic turning steps will be alternately large and small. Turns may be executed in a stationary pattern or a progressive pattern. Stationary turns are dance patterns that are executed in place even though the dance may be designed to progress around the dance floor in the line of direction. Progressive turns are a series of turning patterns that the dancers execute as they progress down the line of dance.

Stationary patterns are used in the following dances:

1. Western Two-Step

    A. Basic step turning left (counterclockwise)
    B. Basic step turning right (clockwise)

2. Texas Two-Step

    A. Basic step turning left (counterclockwise)
    B. Basic step turning right (clockwise)

3. Western Swing

    A. Basic step turning right (clockwise)

Progressive patterns are used in the following dances:

1. Polka—Advanced turns right (clockwise)

2. Waltz—Advanced left turns (counterclockwise)

3. Texas Two-Step—Advanced turns right (clockwise)

Although the turns in all dances may be executed clockwise or counterclockwise, one direction is usually more comfortable than the other. The direction that is easiest to execute in each dance has consistently been chosen for this book. Advanced dancers may wish to experiment with turns in the opposite direction.

For turns in the opposite direction, the person who begins the movement with the right foot will make a larger step and the person who begins the movement with the left foot will make a smaller step in place.

DANCE POSITIONS

You can see many different dance positions in country and western dance halls, ranging from the man's hand around the lady's neck to the lady's forefinger in the man's belt loop. These fad positions may be comfortable and adequate for the basic movements but they do not contribute to an effective lead in the more advanced variations. **A strong lead with the right hand is absolutely essential in executing the basic step and even more important in executing the variations.**

Closed Position

The man's right hand (steering wheel) is placed with the hand under the lady's left shoulder blade. The heel of his right hand is placed under the lady's left arm with his wrist held higher than his hand. His fingers are pointed slightly downward, causing his elbow to rise.

The lady's left hand should rest on the man's right shoulder with her entire arm in contact with his right arm. Her fingers will be on the back part of his shoulder and her thumb will rest in front of his shoulder. If her partner is much taller than she, the hand should rest further down his right arm, still maintaining contact between their arms.

The man's left hand holds the lady's right hand in a comfortable position extended to the side with elbows slightly bent.

Open Position

Man and lady face each other with shoulders parallel. Arm positions may vary in the following ways:

A. Double hand hold, his left holding her right, his right holding her left.

B. Single hand hold, his left holding her right.

C. Single hand hold, his right holding her left.

D. Double hand hold, right hands over left. To assume a single hand hold (right hand to right hand), his left hand releases her left hand.

E. Double hand hold, left hands over right. To assume a single hand hold (left hand to left hand), his right hand releases her right hand.

Conversation Position

The man and lady stand side by side facing the same direction with his right shoulder adjacent to her left shoulder. His right hand remains on her shoulder blade and her left hand rests on his right shoulder. He holds her right hand with his left in front at waist level.

Left Parallel

Arms remain in closed position as partners stand side by side with left shoulders adjacent.

Right Parallel

Arms remain in closed position as partners stand side by side with right shoulders adjacent.

Sweetheart Position

Man and lady are side-by-side, lady on the man's right, both facing the same direction. Man's right arm is behind the lady's shoulder and his right hand holds her right hand in front of her right shoulder. Left hand hold is extended diagonally to the man's left at waist level.

Reverse Sweetheart Position

Man and lady are side-by-side, lady on the man's left, both facing the same direction. Man's left arm is behind the lady's shoulder and his left hand holds her left hand in front of her left shoulder. Right hand hold is extended to the man's right at waist level.

Sweetheart Wrap Position

Man and lady are side-by-side, lady on the man's right, both facing the same direction. His left hand holds her right hand in front of her at waist level. Her left arm reaches across her body and wraps around her waist, his right hand reaching around her back holds her left hand at waist level.

Reverse Sweetheart Wrap

Man and lady are side-by-side, lady on the man's left, both facing the same direction. His right hand holds her left hand in front of her at waist level. Her right arm reaches across her body and wraps around her waist, his left hand reaching around her back holds her right hand at waist level.

Lasso Positions

Position # 1. Man and lady are side-by-side, lady on the man's right, both facing the same direction. Man's right arm is behind the lady's shoulder and his right hand holds her right hand in front of her right shoulder. Left hand hold is extended diagonally to the man's left at waist level (same as sweetheart position).

Position #2. Man and lady are side-by-side, lady on the man's left, both facing same direction. Lady's right arm is behind man's shoulder with his right hand holding her right hand in front of his right shoulder. Left hand hold is extended diagonally to the man's left at waist level.

Position #3. Man and lady are side-by-side, lady on the man's right, both facing the same direction. Lady's left arm is behind the man's shoulder with his left hand holding her left hand in front of his left shoulder. Right hand hold is extended diagonally to the man's right at waist level.

Wringer

Man and lady stand side-by-side facing opposite directions with right shoulder to right shoulder. With lady's right arm extended to the right in front of the man, his left hand holds her right hand at chest level. Her left hand is behind her back at waist level and the man holds her left hand with his right hand.

Reverse Wringer

Man and lady stand side-by-side facing opposite directions with left shoulder to left shoulder. With the lady's left arm extended to the left in front of the man, his right hand holds her left hand at chest level. Her right hand is behind her back at waist level and the man holds her right hand with his left hand.

DANCE TERMINOLOGY

Amalgamation: Combining two or more variations is called amalgamation. Certain steps combine with other step patterns more easily than others. When applicable, suggested amalgamations may be found at the end of each section.

Beat: A time unit — a continuous pulse that is heard throughout the measure.

Broken Rhythm: Broken rhythm occurs when more than one measure of music is needed to complete a basic dance step. Broken rhythm is found in the Texas Two-Step, Texas Two-Step Swing, Western Two-Step and the Western Swing.

Clockwise: Movement that flows in the direction of the hands on a clock (to the right).

Even Rhythm: Even rhythm occurs when each step gets the same note value. The rhythm may be fast, medium, or slow. Even rhythm is used in the Schottishce and the Western Waltz.

Finger Pressure: Technique used by the man in directing his partner to move in a forward direction.

Fingertip Pressure: Technique used by the man in directing his partner to move to his right (her left).

Follow: Receiving the lead from the man and responding to pressures designed to cause the lady to move backward, forward, sideward, and/or change directions.

Force Factors: Accented and unaccented beats.

Hand Pressure: Technique used by the man in directing his partner to stay in place.

Heel Pressure: Technique used by the man in directing his partner to move backward.

Hop: An elevation into the air originating on one foot and returning to the same foot.

Inside Foot: The foot that is closest to your partner when the man and lady are facing the same direction.

In Place: A step taken without moving forward, backward, or to the side.

Lead: The way in which the man directs his partner through step patterns and changes of directions.

Left Hand Hold: Man holds the lady's left hand with his left hand.

Left/Right Hand Hold: Man holds the lady's right hand with his left hand.

Line of Dance: The direction (counterclockwise) that dancers move around a dance floor.

Measure: A group of beats enclosed by vertical bars on a musical staff; may be recognized by listening for the accent repeated at regular intervals.

Meter: Expressed as a fraction with the denominator indicating the kind of note and the numerator indicating how many notes are in one measure.

Outside Foot: The foot that is away from your partner when the man and lady are facing the same direction.

Palm Pressure: Technique used by the man in directing his partner to move to his left (lady's right) or to move from an open position to a closed position.

Pivot: Turning on the ball of the foot.

Pressure: Technique used by the man in directing his partner.

Promenade: Term used in some areas instead of "conversation."

Quick: Rhythmic cue used to cue the fast step in uneven rhythm.

Right Hand Hold: Man holds lady's right hand with his right hand.

Right/Left Hand Hold: Man holds lady's left hand with his right hand.

Rhythm: A pattern of movement or sound made by combining force factors and time factors.

Slow: Rhythmic cue used to cue the step in uneven rhythm that is the equivalent of two or more quick steps.

Shuffle Step: A shuffle step is a small progressive movement executed with the balls of the feet remaining in contact with the floor. The shuffle step is prevalent in country-western dances where steps are smaller than regular ballroom dance steps.

Step: Transference of weight from one foot to the other.

Style: The individual characteristics of movement which influence how a dance is performed.

Tap: Step with ball of the foot without taking the weight.

Tempo: The rate of speed at which musical accompaniment is played.

Time Factors: Various notes and divisions of beats.

Touch: Designated foot steps without taking the weight.

Turns: A full turn clockwise or counterclockwise which may be executed in place. A half turn is usually used to change directions, i.e., to change from a forward moving pattern to a backward moving pattern. Any portion of a turn may be executed at the discretion of the man.

Underarm Turns: Inside and ouside turns refer to the lady's underarm turns in closed position. Inside denotes a turn counterclockwise and outside denotes a clockwise turn.

Underlying Beat: The steady, even pulsation heard under the melody of the music.

Uneven Rhythm: Steps that are executed in a combination of slow and quick beats. Dances using uneven rhythm are Cotton Eyed Joe, Texas Two-Step, Texas Two-Step Swing, Western Swing, Western Polka, and Ten-Step Polka.

Cotton-Eyed Joe

COTTON-EYED JOE

Cotton-Eyed Joe is an authentic slavery song that tells about a Black slave who has a tantalizing, intriguing, and devilish character. The dance has been referred to as a "Heel and Toe Polker with fringes added." The tune of the Cotton-Eyed Joe is from an Irish folk song that was originally performed with clogging steps. The Irish immigrants who settled in the South combined the Irish tune and clog steps with the Black footwork and gave birth to the Cotton-Eyed Joe. Its most popular form, especially in Texas, is in groups of straight lines with arms around each other's waists facing down the line of dance. There are also many couple variations that are fun to dance when the dance floor provides enough space in which to maneuver.

Cotton-Eyed Joe

1. Basic Step (Man's and Lady's footwork)

2. Roll Her Out, Roll Her In —Lady Twirls

3. Roll Her Out, She Stays Out —Continuous Lasso

4. Roll Her Out, He Rolls In —Weave the Basket

5. Turn In Place —Single Hand Lasso

Rhythmical Analysis

COTTON-EYED JOE----Time Signature 2/4

Step Pattern

Man and Lady:	Kick in,	Kick out,		Step back,	Step back,	Step back,
Count: Notation:	1	2		1	&	2
Rhythmical Cue:	Slow	Slow		Quick	Quick	Slow

Repeat the sequence above three times.

Man and Lady:	Step forward,	Step together,	Step forward,	Step forward,	Step together,	Step forward
Count: Notation:	1	&	2	1	&	2
Rhythmical Cue	Quick	Quick	Slow	Quick	Quick	Slow

Repeat the sequence above (beginning with step, together, step) three times.

Cotton-Eyed Joe

Basic Step
Man's and Lady's Footwork

Step	Description	Timing	Rhythmic Cue	Lead

Position: Sweetheart Position or Line (side by side)

Note: Sweetheart Position is used in the Lead Column. A "Line" consists of three or more dancers with arms behind the backs of adjacent dancers.

Part I: Kicks—Progressing backwards

Step	Description	Timing	Rhythmic Cue	Lead
1	Kick R foot in, crossing left leg.	1	Slow	L and R hand holds
2	Kick R foot directly forward.	2	Slow	"
3	Step R foot directly backward (small step).	1	Quick	"
4	Step L foot directly backward (small step).	&	Quick	"
5	Step R foot directly backward (small step).	2	Slow	"
6	Kick L foot in, crossing right leg.	1	Slow	"
7	Kick L foot directly forward.	2	Slow	"
8	Step L foot directly backward (small step).	1	Quick	"
9	Step R foot directly backward (small step).	&	Quick	"
10	Step L foot directly backward (small step).	2	Slow	"

Repeat Part I (steps 1-10)

Part II: Eight Triple Steps—Progressing forward

Step	Description	Timing	Rhythmic Cue	Lead
1	Step R foot directly forward.	1	Quick	L and R hand holds
2	Step L foot directly forward bringing feet together. (3rd position - R foot forward).	&	Quick	"
3	Step R foot directly forward.	2	Slow	"
4	Step L foot directly forward passing right foot.	1	Quick	"
5	Step R foot directly forward bringing feet together. (3rd position - L foot forward).	&	Quick	"
6	Step L foot directly forward.	2	Slow	"

Repeat Part II (steps 1-6) three times.

Sweetheart Position

Cotton-eyed Joe Line

COTTON-EYED JOE

Roll Her Out, Roll Her In
Lady Twirls
Man's Footwork

Step	Description	Timing	Rhythmic Cue	Lead
	Position: Sweetheart Position			
	Part I: Kicks—Roll Her Out, Roll Her In			
1	Kick R foot in, crossing left leg.	1	Slow	L and R hand holds
2	Kick R foot directly forward.	2	Slow	L and R hand holds
3	Release L hand hold and step R foot directly backward (small step) as you begin to lead lady to turn clockwise to face you.	1	Quick	R Forearm pressure
4	Step L foot directly backward (small step) as you continue to lead lady clockwise to face you.	&	Quick	R hand pulls and lowers
5	Step R foot directly backward (small step) completing lead and lowering right hand hold to waist level.	2	Slow	R hand lowers
6	Kick L foot in, crossing right leg.	1	Slow	R hand hold
7	Kick L foot directly forward.	2	Slow	R hand hold
8	Step L foot directly forward (small step) as you begin to lead lady to turn counterclockwise returning to Sweetheart Position.	1	Quick	R hand pulls in
9	Step R foot directly forward bringing feet together (3rd position - L foot forward) as you continue leading lady back into Sweetheart Position.	&	Quick	R hand pulls in
10	Step L foot directly forward (small step) completing movement into Sweetheart Position.	2	Slow	Double hand hold
	Repeat Part I (steps 1-10)			
	Part II: Eight Triple Steps —Lady Twirls			
1-3	Execute a Step-Together-Step (1st triple step beginning with the right foot) progressing directly forward down the line of dance. Release the left hand hold raising the right hand hold to twirl the lady 1/2 turn clockwise.	1&2	Q,Q,S	R hand encircling
4-6	Execute a Step-Together-Step (2nd triple step beginning with the left foot) directly forward. Continue to twirl the lady another 1/2 turn clockwise under your right hand hold. The lady will complete a full turn during steps 1-6.	1&2	Q,Q,S	R hand encircling

COTTON-EYED JOE

Roll Her Out, Roll Her In
Lady Twirls
Lady's Footwork

Step	Description	Timing	Rhythmic Cue
	Position: Sweetheart Position		
	Part I: Kicks—Roll Her Out, Roll Her In		
1	Kick R foot in, crossing left leg.	1	Slow
2	Kick R foot directly forward.	2	Slow
3	Step R foot forward (toe outward) as man releases your left hand hold and begins to turn you clockwise to face him.	1	Quick
4	Step L foot around R foot continuing to turn 1/2 turn clockwise to face your partner.	&	Quick
5	Step R foot beside L foot completing 1/2 turn to face your partner as you lower right hand hold to waist level.	2	Slow
6	Kick L foot in, crossing right leg.	1	Slow
7	Kick L foot directly forward.	2	Slow
8	Step L foot forward (toe outward) beginning to turn counterclockwise to return to Sweetheart Position.	1	Quick
9	Step R foot around L foot continuing counter clockwise turn.	&	Quick
10	Step L foot beside R foot completing 1/2 turn counterclockwise returning to Sweetheart Position. Retake your left hand hold to complete movement.	2	Slow
	Repeat Part I (steps 1-10)		
	Part II: Eight Triple Steps—Lady Twirls		
1-3	Execute a Step-Together-Step (1st triple step beginning with the right foot) as the man leads you into 1/2 turn clockwise under his right hand hold. Release the left hand hold keeping the left hand at waist level.	1&2	Q,Q,S
4-6	Execute a Step-Together-Step (2nd triple step beginning with the left foot) as the man leads you into another 1/2 turn clockwise to complete a full turn. Movement should progress down the line of dance as you twirl under his right hand hold.	1&2	Q,Q,S

Roll Her Out, Roll Her In
Lady Twirls
Man's Footwork, *cont'd*

7-12 Repeat steps 1-6 executing the third and fourth triple
steps as you lead the lady into another full turn clock- 1&2 Q,Q,S
wise.   1&2 Q,Q,S   R hand encircling

13-18 Repeat steps 1-6 executing the fifth and sixth triple
steps as you lead the lady into another full turn clock- 1&2 Q,Q,S
wise.   1&2 Q,Q,S   R hand encircling

19-24 Repeat steps 1-6 executing the seventh and eighth
triple steps as you lead the lady into another full turn
clockwise. Upon completing the last triple step return
to Sweetheart Position by lowering the right hand
hold around the lady's shoulder and retaking the left 1&2 Q,Q,S
hand hold in front at waist level.   1&2 Q,Q,S   R hand encircles and lowers

Sweetheart Position

Step 5

Step 10

Roll Her Out, Roll Her In
Lady Twirls
Lady's Footwork, *cont'd*

7-12 Repeat steps 1-6 executing the third and fourth triple
steps as the man leads you into another full turn clock-
wise under his right hand hold, continuing to progress   1&2   Q,Q,S
down the line of dance.   1&2   Q,Q,S

13-18 Repeat steps 1-6 executing the fifth and sixth triple
steps as the man leads you into another full turn
clockwise under his right hand hold. Continue to   1&2   Q,Q,S
progress down the line of dance.   1&2   Q,Q,S

19-24 Repeat steps 1-6 executing the seventh and eighth
triple steps as the man leads you into another full turn
clockwise. Upon completion of the last triple step
return to Sweetheart Position as the right hand hold
lowers around your shoulders. Retake the left hand   1&2   Q,Q,S
hold in front at waist level.   1&2   Q,Q,S

1st Triple Step

2nd Triple Step

8th Triple Step

COTTON-EYED JOE

Roll Her Out, She Stays Out
Continuous Lasso
Man's Footwork

Step	Description	Timing	Rhythmic Cue	Lead
	Position: Sweetheart Position			
	Part I: Kicks—Roll Her Out, She Stays Out			
1	Kick R foot in, crossing left leg.	1	Slow	L and R hand holds
2	Kick R foot directly forward.	2	Slow	L and R hand holds
3	Release L hand hold and step R foot directly backward (small step) as you begin to lead the lady to turn clockwise to face you.	1	Quick	R Forearm pressure
4	Step L foot directly backward (small step) as you continue to lead the lady clockwise to face you.	&	Quick	R hand pulls and lowers
5	Step R foot directly backward (small step) completing the lead and lowering the right hand hold to waist level.	2	Slow	R hand lowers
6	Kick L foot in, crossing right leg.	1	Slow	R hand hold
7	Kick L foot directly forward.	2	Slow	R hand hold
8	Step L foot directly backward (small step) leading the lady to progress toward you.	1	Quick	R hand pulls
9	Step R foot directly backward (small step) continuing to lead the lady to progress toward you.	&	Quick	R hand pulls
10	Step L foot directly backward (small step) continuing to lead the lady to progress toward you.	2	Slow	R hand pulls
11	Kick R foot in, crossing left leg.	1	Slow	R hand hold
12	Kick R foot directly forward.	2	Slow	R hand hold
13	Step R foot directly backward (small step) leading the lady to progress toward you.	1	Quick	R hand pulls
14	Step L foot directly backward (small step) continuing to lead the lady to progress toward you.	&	Quick	R hand pulls
15	Step R foot directly backward (small step) continuing to lead the lady to progress toward you.	2	Slow	R hand pulls

COTTON-EYED JOE

Roll Her Out, She Stays Out
Continuous Lasso
Lady's Footwork

Step	Description	Timing	Rhythmic Cue
	Position: Sweetheart Position		
	Part I: Kicks—Roll Her Out, She Stays Out		
1	Kick R foot in, crossing left leg.	1	Slow
2	Kick R foot directly forward.	2	Slow
3	Release L hand hold and step R foot directly forward (toe outward) beginning to turn clockwise to face your partner.	1	Quick
4	Step L foot around R foot continuing clockwise turn to face partner for a "Roll Her Out" movement.	&	Quick
5	Step R foot beside L foot completing 1/2 turn clockwise to face your partner. Lower the right hand hold in front at waist level placing the left hand on your left hip.	2	Slow
6	Kick L foot in, crossing right leg.	1	Slow
7	Kick L foot directly forward	2	Slow
8	Step L foot directly forward toward your partner (small step) as he progresses backward executing a "She Stays Out" movement.	1	Quick
9	Step R foot directly forward progressing toward your partner (small step).	&	Quick
10	Step L foot directly forward progressing toward your partner (small step) retaining right hand hold.	2	Slow
11	Kick R foot in, crossing left leg.	1	Slow
12	Kick R foot directly forward.	2	Slow
13	Step R foot directly forward (small step) continuing to progress toward your partner.	1	Quick
14	Step L foot directly forward (small step) continuing to progress toward your partner executing the "She Stays Out" movement.	&	Quick
15	Step R foot directly forward (small step) continuing to progress toward your partner retaining a right handhold.	2	Slow

Roll Her Out, She Stays Out
Continuous Lasso
Man's Footwork, *cont'd*

16	Kick L foot in, crossing right leg.	1	Slow	R hand holds
17	Kick L foot directly forward.	2	Slow	R hand holds
18	Step L foot directly forward (small step) as you begin to lead the lady to turn counterclockwise to return to Sweetheart Position.	1	Quick	R hand pulls in and upward
19	Step R foot directly forward bringing feet together (3rd position-L foot forward) as you continue to lead the lady back into Sweetheart Position.	&	Quick	R hand pulls in and upward
20	Step L foot directly forward (small step) completing the movement into Sweetheart Position as you retake the left hand hold.	2	Slow	Double hand hold

Part II: Eight Triple Steps —Continuous Lasso

1-3	Execute a step-together-step (1st triple step beginning with the right foot) progressing directly forward down the line of dance. Keeping the left hand hold at waist level raise the right hand hold upward to lead the lady in a counterclockwise circle around you.	1&2	Q,Q,S	R hand raises
4-6	Execute a step-together step (2nd triple step beginning with the left foot) progressing directly forward down the line of dance. Keeping the left hand hold at waist level raise the right hand hold upward to lead the lady in a counterclockwise circle around you.	1&2	Q,Q,S	R hand hold encircles
7-9	Execute a step-together-step (3rd triple step beginning with the right foot) directly forward continuing to move the lady counterclockwise for a Continuous Lasso movement. The third triple step should move the lady past your left side. Your right hand hold encircles her head and begins to encircle your head. The left hand hold is still at waist level preparing to move upward to your left shoulder.	1&2	Q,Q,S	R hand hold encircles
10-12	Execute a step-together-step (4th triple step beginning with the left foot) directly forward continuing to move the lady around you counterclockwise. The right hand hold will encircle your head leading the lady to progress behind you. Raise the left hand hold up beginning to place it on your left shoulder.	1&2	Q,Q,S	R hand hold encircles L hand hold raises
13-15	Execute a step-together-step (5th triple step beginning with the right foot) directly forward continuing to move the lady behind you and to your right side. Place left hand hold on your left shoulder with the lady's left arm wrapped around you. Lead the lady to your right side by extending your right hand hold to the right at waist level. (See 3rd position of the Lasso, page 33.)	1&2	Q,Q,S	R hand hold extends L hand hold raises

Roll Her Out, She Stays Out
Continuous Lasso
Lady's Footwork, *cont'd*

16	Kick L foot in, crossing right leg.	1	Slow
17	Kick L foot directly forward.	2	Slow
18	Step L foot forward (toe outward) beginning to turn counterclockwise to return to Sweetheart Position.	1	Quick
19	Step R foot around L foot continuing counterclockwise turn.	&	Quick
20	Step L foot beside R foot completing 1/2 turn counter clockwise returning to Sweetheart Position. Retake your left hand hold to complete the movement.	2	Slow

Part II: Eight Triple Steps—Continuous Lasso

1-3	Execute a step-together-step (1st triple step beginning with the right foot) beginning to circle counterclockwise in front of your partner. The man will raise the right hand hold above your head, keeping the left hand hold at waist level to initiate the lead for the Continuous Lasso.	1&2	Q,Q,S
4-6	Execute a step-together-step (2nd triple step beginning with the left foot) continuing to circle counterclockwise around your partner. The second triple step should move you in front of him from his right side to his left side.	1&2	Q,Q,S
7-9	Execute a step-together-step (3rd triple step beginning with the right foot) as the man continues to lead you through the Continuous Lasso. The third triple step will lead you past his left side as the right hand hold encircles your head. The left hand hold remains at waist level.	1&2	Q,Q,S
10-12	Execute a step-together-step (4th triple step beginning with the left foot) continuing to circle counterclockwise around your partner. The right hand hold will encircle the man's head leading you behind him with the left hand hold resting on his left shoulder.	1&2	Q,Q,S
13-15	Execute a step-together-step (5th triple step beginning with the right foot) circling behind the man from his left side to his right side. Your left arm will wrap around his shoulder with the right hand hold extended to the right at waist level. (See 3rd position of the Lasso, page 33.)	1&2	Q,Q,S

Roll Her Out, She Stays Out
Continuous Lasso
Man's Footwork, *cont'd*

16-18 Execute a step-together-step (6th triple step beginning with the left foot) directly forward with your partner on your right side. Keep the right hand hold ex-
tended to the right as you raise the left hand hold   R hand hold extends
up and over your head to chest level in front of you. 1&2 Q,Q,S L hand hold up and over

19-21 Execute a step-together-step (7th triple step beginning with the right foot) directly forward to twirl the
lady counterclockwise returning her to Sweetheart
Position (movement will take her from position #3
into position #1 of the Lasso). Raise the left hand
hold up and over the lady's head and lower it to waist
level. The right hand hold will pull at waist level to   R hand hold pulls
turn the lady counterclockwise.   1&2 Q,Q,S   L hand hold encircles

22-24 Execute a step-together-step (8th triple step beginning with the left foot) directly forward with the lady
on your right side in Sweetheart Position. The eighth
triple step will complete the Continuous Lasso.   1&2 Q,Q,S   L and R hand holds

Sweetheart Position

Steps 5, 10, and 15

Step 20

Roll Her Out, She Stays Out
Continuous Lasso
Lady's Footwork, *cont'd*

16-18 Execute a step-together-step (6th triple step beginning with the left foot) directly forward at the man's
right side as he lifts your left hand hold up and over
his head to chest level. The right hand hold will
remain extended to the right.　　　　　1&2　　Q,Q,S

19-21 Execute a step-together-step (7th triple step beginning with the right foot) as the man leads you to twirl
counterclockwise at his right side. The left hand hold
will encircle your head and lower to waist level as the
right hand hold pulls to turn you into Lasso
Position #1.　　　　　1&2　　Q,Q,S

22-24 Execute a step-together-step (8th triple step beginning with the left foot) directly forward with the man on
your left side in Sweetheart Position to complete the
Continuous Lasso.　　　　　1&2　　Q,Q,S

2nd Triple Step

4th Triple Step

5th Triple Step

6th Triple Step

7th Triple Step

8th Triple Step

COTTON-EYED JOE

Roll Her Out, He Rolls In
Weave the Basket
Man's Footwork

Step	Description	Timing	Rhythmic Cue	Lead
	Position: Sweetheart Position			
	Part I: Kicks—She Rolls Out, He Rolls In			
1	Kick R foot in, crossing left leg.	1	Slow	L and R hand holds
2	Kick R foot directly forward.	2	Slow	L and R hand holds
3	Release L hand hold and step R foot directly backward (small step) as you begin to lead the lady to turn clockwise to face you.	1	Quick	R Forearm pressure
4	Step L foot directly backward (small step) as you continue to lead the lady clockwise to face you.	&	Quick	R hand pulls and lowers
5	Step R foot directly backward (small step) completing the lead and lowering the right hand hold to waist level.	2	Slow	R hand lowers
6	Kick L foot in, crossing right leg.	1	Slow	R hand hold
7	Kick L foot directly forward.	2	Slow	R hand hold
8	Step L foot forward (toe outward) beginning to turn counterclockwise to the Lady's right side. Lift the right hand hold so that the Lady's right arm will wrap around your shoulder.	1	Quick	R hand pulls and lifts
9	Step R foot around L foot continuing to turn 1/2 turn counterclockwise. The lady's right arm will wrap around your shoulder as you roll into her right side. The left hand is at waist level.	&	Quick	R hand lifts
10	Step L foot beside R foot completing 1/2 turn counterclockwise to the lady's right side. Take the left hand hold at waist level. Right hand hold is at your right shoulder with the lady's right arm wrapped around you.	2	Slow	Take L hand hold
11	Kick R foot in, crossing left leg.	1	Slow	R and L hand holds
12	Kick R foot directly forward.	2	Slow	R and L hand holds
13	Release L hand hold and step R foot forward (toe outward) beginning to turn 1/2 turn clockwise to face your partner.	1	Quick	R hand hold
14	Step L foot around R foot continuing clockwise turn as the right hand hold begins to lower.	&	Quick	R hand lowers

COTTON-EYED JOE

Roll Her Out, He Rolls In
Weave the Basket
Lady's Footwork

Step	Description	Timing	Rhythmic Cue
	Position: Sweetheart Position		
	Part I: Kicks—She Rolls Out, He Rolls In		
1	Kick R foot in, crossing left leg.	1	Slow
2	Kick R foot directly forward.	2	Slow
3	Step R foot forward (toe outward) as the man releases your left hand hold beginning to turn you clockwise to face him.	1	Quick
4	Step L foot around R foot continuing to turn 1/2 turn clockwise to face your partner.	&	Quick
5	Step R foot beside L foot completing 1/2 turn to face your partner as you lower the right hand hold to waist level.	2	Slow
6	Kick L foot in, crossing right leg.	1	Slow
7	Kick L foot directly forward.	2	Slow
8	Step L foot in place as the man begins a counter-clockwise turn toward your right side. Begin to lift the right hand hold so that your right arm will wrap around his shoulder.	1	Quick
9	Step R foot in place as the man continues to roll in to your right side.	&	Quick
10	Step L foot in place as the man completes the turn to your right side. Your right hand hold is wrapped around his shoulder as you retake the left hand hold in front at waist level.	2	Slow
11	Kick R foot in, crossing left leg.	1	Slow
12	Kick R foot directly forward.	2	Slow
13	Step R foot in place as the man begins a clockwise turn moving back to his original position to face you.	1	Quick
14	Step L foot in place as the man continues a clockwise turn to face you. The right hand hold will begin to lower to waist level.	&	Quick

Roll Her Out, He Rolls In
Weave the Basket
Man's Footwork, *cont'd*

15	Step R foot beside L foot completing 1/2 turn clockwise to face your partner. Lower the right hand hold to waist level with the left hand on your left hip.	2	Slow	R hand lowers
16	Kick L foot in, crossing right leg.	1	Slow	R hand lowers
17	Kick L foot directly forward.	2	Slow	R hand hold
18	Step L foot directly forward (small step) as you begin to lead the lady to turn counterclockwise into Sweetheart Position.	1	Quick	R hand pulls in
19	Step R foot directly foward bringing feet together (3rd position-L foot forward) as you continue leading the lady back into Sweetheart Position.	&	Quick	R hand pulls in and upward
20	Step L foot directly forward (small step) completing the movement into Sweetheart Position.	2	Slow	Retake L hand hold

Sweetheart Position   Steps 5 and 15   Step 10

Part II: Eight Triple Steps—Weave the Basket

1-3	Execute a step-together-step (1st triple step beginning with the right foot) directly forward as you begin to lead the lady in front of you from your right side to your left side. Lift the left hand hold as you lead the lady to your left progressing down the line of dance.	1&2	Q,Q,S	L hand hold pulls
4-6	Execute a step-together-step (2nd triple step beginning with the left foot) directly forward continuing to lead the lady from your right side to your left side. The second triple step will lead her in front of you as you begin to take a Reverse Sweetheart Position.	1&2	Q,Q,S	L hand pulls and lifts
7-9	Execute a step-together-step (3rd triple step beginning with the right foot) directly forward completing the lead to take the lady from your right side to your left side ending in Reverse Sweetheart Position. The left hand hold is wrapped around her shoulder with the right hand hold in front at waist level.	1&2	Q,Q,S	R hand hold lowers / L hand hold lifts

Roll Her Out, He Rolls In
Weave the Basket
Lady's Footwork, *cont'd*

15	Step R foot in place as the man completes a clockwise turn to face you with the right hand hold at waist level.	2	Slow
16	Kick L foot in, crossing right leg.	1	Slow
17	Kick L foot directly forward.	2	Slow
18	Step L foot forward (toe outward) beginning to turn counterclockwise to return to Sweetheart Position.	1	Quick
19	Step R foot around L foot continuing 1/2 turn counterclockwise.	&	Quick
20	Step L foot beside R foot completing 1/2 turn counterclockwise returning to Sweetheart Position. Retake your left hand hold to complete the movement.	2	Slow

Part II: Eight Triple Steps—Weave the Basket

1-3	Execute a step-together-step (1st triple step beginning with the right foot) forward as the man begins to lead you from his right side to his left side. Face down the line of dance throughout the entire movement.	1&2	Q,Q,S
4-6	Execute a step-together-step (2nd triple step beginning with the left foot) forward passing in front of the man moving from Sweetheart Position into Reverse Sweetheart Position. The left hand hold will lift to shoulder level.	1&2	Q,Q,S
7-9	Execute a step-together-step (3rd triple step beginning with the right foot) forward completing the movement into Reverse Sweetheart Position on the man's left side. His left arm is wrapped around your shoulder with the right hand hold in front at waist level.	1&2	Q,Q,S

**Roll Her Out, He Rolls In
Weave the Basket
Man's Footwork,** *cont'd*

10-12 Execute a step-together-step (4th triple step beginning with the left foot) directly forward lifting your left
hand hold up and over the lady's head to lower it to
waist level. In the fourth triple step you will pass the
lady as she begins to move behind you.   1&2   Q,Q,S   L hand hold lifts upward

13-15 Execute a step-together-step (5th triple step beginning with the right foot) directly forward releasing the
right hand hold and extending it to the right. The left   R hand releases
hand hold moves behind your back to waist level   and extends
leading the lady from your left side to your right side.   L hand moves
Both the man and lady face down the line of dance. 1&2 Q,Q,S   behind back

16-18 Execute a step-together-step (6th triple step beginning with the left foot) directly forward leading the
lady to your right side and taking her right hand in
front at waist level. The left hand hold is behind your
back at waist level.   1&2   Q,Q,S   R hand takes her R hand

19-21 Execute a step-together-step (7th triple step beginning with the right foot) directly forward with the lady
at your right side. Lift the right hand hold up and over
the lady's head placing it around her shoulder. The
left hand hold is behind your back.   1&2   Q,Q,S   R hand hold lifts upward

22-24 Execute a step-together-step (8th triple step beginning with the left foot) directly forward as you release
the left hand hold behind your back and retake it in
front at waist level. Both progress down the line of
dance as you return to Sweetheart Position.   1&2   Q,Q,S   L hand releases and retakes

Bootnote: As the lady progresses counterclockwise around the man they face directly forward moving
down the line of dance.

1st Triple Step   2nd Triple Step   3rd Triple Step

Roll Her Out, He Rolls In
Weave the Basket
Lady's Footwork, *cont'd*

10-12 Execute a step-together-step (4th triple step beginning with the left foot) in place as the man passes you while lifting the left hand hold up and over your head and lowering it to waist level. Retain the right hand hold at waist level.   1&2   Q,Q,S

13-15 Execute a step-together-step (5th triple step beginning with the right foot) directly forward releasing the right hand hold as you begin to move behind the man from his left side to his right side. The left hand hold will move behind your back as you both continue to progress forward down the line of dance.   1&2   Q,Q,S

16-18 Execute a step-together-step (6th triple step beginning with the left foot) forward as you complete the movement from his left side to his right side. Retake your right hand hold extended to the man's right at waist level. Retain the left hand hold behind the man's back.   1&2   Q,Q,S

19-21 Execute a step-together-step (7th triple step beginning with the right foot) directly forward as the man lifts the right hand hold up and over your head and lowers it around your shoulder. Retain the left hand hold behind the man's back.   1&2   Q,Q,S

22-24 Execute a step-together-step (8th triple step beginning with the left foot) directly forward as the man releases your left hand hold behind his back and retakes it in front at waist level. The eighth triple step returns you to Sweetheart Position and completes Weave the Basket.   1&2   Q,Q,S

Bootnote: As the lady progresses counterclockwise around the man they face directly forward moving down the line of dance.

4th Triple Step   6th Triple Step   7th Triple Step

COTTON-EYED JOE

Turn in Place
Single Hand Lasso
Man's Footwork

Step	Description	Timing	Rhythmic Cue	Lead
	Position: Sweetheart Position			
	Part I: Kicks—Turn in Place			
1	Kick R foot in, crossing left leg.	1	Slow	L and R hand holds
2	Kick R foot directly forward.	2	Slow	L and R hand holds
3	Beginning to turn 1/2 turn clockwise in place, step on the R foot. Lead will begin to take the lady from Sweetheart Position into Reverse Sweetheart Position to end backing the line of dance. The left hand hold will begin to lift upward.	1	Quick	Upward
4	Continuing to turn 1/2 turn clockwise step L foot beside R foot. The left land hold will move up to wrap around the lady's shoulder in Reverse Sweetheart Position as the right hand hold begins to lower to waist level.	&	Quick	Upward
5	Completing 1/2 turn clockwise, step R foot to the right (small step). Movement should end in Reverse Sweetheart Position backing the line of dance. The left hand hold is wrapped around the lady's shoulder with the right hand hold in front at waist level.	2	Slow	R and L hand holds
6	Kick L foot in, crossing right leg.	1	Slow	R and L hand holds
7	Kick L foot directly forward.	2	Slow	R and L hand holds
8	Beginning to turn 1/2 turn counterclockwise in place, step on the L foot. Lead will begin to take the lady from Reverse Sweetheart Position back into Sweetheart Position to end facing the line of dance. The right hand hold will begin to lift upward.	1	Quick	Upward
9	Continuing to turn 1/2 turn counterclockwise in place, step R foot beside L foot. Continue to lift the right hand hold to shoulder level as you begin to lower the left hand hold to waist level.	&	Quick	Upward
10	Completing 1/2 turn counterclockwise in place, step L foot to the left (small step). The movement should return you to Sweetheart Position.	2	Slow	L hand hold lowers
	Repeat Part I (steps 1-10)			

COTTON-EYED JOE

Turn in Place
Single Hand Lasso
Lady's Footwork

Step	Description	Timing	Rhythmic Cue
	Position: Sweetheart Position		
	Part I: Kicks—Turn in Place		
1	Kick R foot in, crossing left leg.	1	Slow
2	Kick R foot directly forward.	2	Slow
3	Beginning to turn 1/2 turn in place, step on the R foot. The lead will begin to take you from Sweetheart Position into Reverse Sweetheart Position to end backing the line of dance.	1	Quick
4	Continuing to turn 1/2 turn clockwise, step L foot beside R foot as the man leads you into Reverse Sweetheart Position.	&	Quick
5	Completing 1/2 turn clockwise step R foot to the right (small step) to end in Reverse Sweetheart Position backing the line of dance.	2	Slow
6	Kick L foot in, crossing right leg.	1	Slow
7	Kick L foot directly forward.	2	Slow
8	Beginning to turn 1/2 turn counterclockwise in place, step on the L foot. The lead will begin to take you from Reverse Sweetheart Position back into Sweetheart Postion.	1	Quick
9	Continuing to turn 1/2 turn counterclockwise in place, step R foot beside L foot.	&	Quick
10	Completing 1/2 turn counterclockwise, step L foot to the left (small step). Movement ends in Sweetheart Position facing down the line of dance.	2	Slow

Repeat Part I (steps 1-10)

Turn in Place
Single Hand Lasso
Man's Footwork, *cont'd*

Part II: Progressing Forward—Single Hand Lasso

1-3	Execute a step-together-step (1st triple step beginning with the right foot) directly forward as you release your right hand hold leading the lady with the left hand hold to circle counterclockwise around you.	1&2	Q,Q,S	R hand hold releases L hand hold pulls

1-3   Execute a step-together-step (1st triple step beginning with the right foot) directly forward as you release your right hand hold leading the lady with the left hand hold to circle counterclockwise around you.   1&2   Q,Q,S   R hand hold releases / L hand hold pulls

4-6   Execute a step-together-step (2nd triple step beginning with the left foot) directly forward continuing to lead the lady in front of you with the left hand hold at waist level. Keep the right hand hold extended to the right with palm facing down.   1&2   Q,Q,S   L hand hold pulls

7-9   Execute a step-together-step (3rd triple step beginning with the right foot) directly forward continuing to lead the lady counterclockwise around you. Keep the R hand extended to the right with the left hand hold lowered below waist level.   1&2   Q,Q,S   L hand hold lowers

10-12   Execute a step-together-step (4th triple step beginning with the left foot) directly forward as your left hand hold moves up behind your back. The fourth triple step will begin leading the lady from your left side behind you to your right side. Keep the right hand extended to the right with the palm facing down.   1&2   Q,Q,S   L hand hold lifts behind back

13-15   Execute a step-together-step (5th triple step beginning with the right foot) directly forward leading the lady to your right side. Keeping the right arm extended to the right, turn the palm upward. The left arm is behind your back at waist level.   1&2   Q,Q,S   L hand hold behind back

16-18   Execute a step-together-step (6th triple step beginning with the left foot) directly forward. The lady will take your right hand with her right hand. Retain the left hand hold behind your back at waist level.   1&2   Q,Q,S

19-21   Execute a step-together-step (7th triple step beginning with the right foot) directly forward as you release the left hand hold behind your back. The right hand hold is extended to the right in front of the lady at waist level. Pull with the right hand hold to lead the lady to turn a full turn, in place, counterclockwise to end in Sweetheart Position.   1&2   Q,Q,S   R hand hold turns lady / L hand hold releases

22-24   Execute a step-together-step (8th triple step beginning with the left foot) directly forward as you retake the left hand hold in front at waist level to complete the Single Hand Lasso.   1&2   Q,Q,S   Retake L hand hold

Turn in Place
Single Hand Lasso
Lady's Footwork, *cont'd*

Part II: Progressing forward—Single Hand Lasso

1-3	Execute a step-together-step (1st triple step beginning with the right foot) beginning to progress counter clockwise around your partner. The right hand hold releases as the left hand hold initiates the lead.	1&2	Q,Q,S
4-6	Execute a step-together-step (2nd triple step beginning with the left foot) continuing to move around the man. The right arm extends to the right at waist level.	1&2	Q,Q,S
7-9	Execute a step-together-step (3rd triple step beginning with the right foot) to move past the left side of your partner.	1&2	Q,Q,S
10-12	Execute a step-together-step (4th triple step beginning with the left foot) as you move behind your partner's back.	1&2	Q,Q,S
13-15	Execute a step-together-step (5th triple step beginning with the right foot) as you move to the right of your partner. The left hand hold is behind the man's back with the right arm extended to the right.	1&2	Q,Q,S
16-18	Execute a step-together-step (6th triple step beginning with the left foot) as you take his right hand with your right hand. The left hand hold remains behind the man's back at waist level.	1&2	Q,Q,S
19-21	Execute a step-together-step (7th triple step beginning with the right foot) releasing the left hand hold and turning a full turn, in place, counterclockwise to end in Sweetheart Position.	1&2	Q,Q,S
22-24	Execute a step-together-step (8th triple step beginning with the left foot) directly forward as you retake the left hand hold in front at waist level to complete the Single Hand Lasso.	1&2	Q,Q,S

FAVORITE COTTON-EYED JOE SELECTIONS

"Cotton-Eyed Joe" by Frenchie Burke

"Cotton-Eyed Joe" by Johnny Bush

"Cotton-Eyed Joe" by Al Dean and the All Stars

"Cotton-Eyed Joe" by Johnny Gimble

"Cotton-Eyed Joe" by Adolph Hofner

"Cotton-Eyed Joe" by Isaac Peyton Sweat

44

Turn in Place — Single Hand Lasso
Part I

Sweetheart Position

Steps 5 and 15

Steps 10 and 20

Turn in Place —Single Hand Lasso
Part II

3rd Triple Step

4th Triple Step

6th Triple Step

7th Triple Step

8th Triple Step

Schottische

SCHOTTISCHE

The Schottische is a Texas dance hall favorite that is an original folk dance belonging to the people of central Europe. German immigrants who settled in the hill country of Texas introduced the Schottische where it blossomed and spread into numerous variations. Most western bands play the Schottische immediately following the Cotton-Eyed Joe, since both are line dances and the combination makes a pleasing medley.

Like the Cotton-Eyed Joe, once the basic footwork for the line dance is mastered, numerous variations may be danced with a partner. Most of the couple variations require more floor space than the line dance as the dancers are using more progressive movements. The original Schottische consisted of a step-close-step-hop in 2/4 time. Now played in 4/4 time, it has evolved into a smooth pattern consisting of three steps and a hop. The Schottische in ballroom dance consisted of step-step-step-lift with smooth execution. In country-western dance the couple variations consist of three steps, or runs, and a hop and the line variation has a side, cross in back, side, kick pattern.

Schottische

1. Basic Step
2. Progressive Basic
3. Cross Kick
4. High Kick
5. Swivels
6. Lasso

7. Transition Basic (from R foot lead to L foot lead)
8. Progressive Hops
9. Turning Hops
10. Separation into Progressive Hops
11. Separation into Turning Hops

Rhythmical Analysis

SCHOTTISCHE----Time signature 4/4

Step Pattern

Man and Lady:	Step,	Step,	Step,	Kick,	Step,	Step,	Step,	Kick
Count: Notation:	1	2	3	4	1	2	3	4
Rhythmical Cue:	Slow	Slow	Slow	Slow	Slow	Slow	Slow	Slow

Man and Lady:	Step,	Kick,	Step,	Kick,	Step,	Kick,	Step,	Kick
Count: Notation:	1	2	3	4	1	2	3	4
Rhythmical Cue:	Slow	Slow	Slow	Slow	Slow	Slow	Slow	Slow

To complete a basic step in the Schottische one will use four measures of music in 4/4 time.

Schottische

Basic Step
Man's and Lady's Footwork

Step	Description	Timing	Rhythmic Cue	Lead

Position: Sweetheart Position or Line (side by side)

Note: Sweetheart Position is used in the Lead Column. A "Line" consists of three or more dancers with arms behind the backs of adjacent dancers.

Part I: Side Movement

Step	Description	Timing	Rhythmic Cue	Lead
1	Step R foot diagonally to the right.	1	Slow	L and R hand holds
2	Step L foot to the right crossing behind R foot (flex knees slightly).	2	Slow	"
3	Step R foot directly to the right.	3	Slow	"
4	Kick L foot forward.	4	Slow	"
5	Step L foot diagonally to the left.	1	Slow	"
6	Step R foot to the left crossing behind L foot (flex knees slightly).	2	Slow	"
7	Step L foot directly to the left.	3	Slow	"
8	Kick R foot forward.	4	Slow	"

Part II: Step 'N' Kick

Step	Description	Timing	Rhythmic Cue	Lead
1	Step R foot in place.	1	Slow	L and R hand holds
2	Kick L foot directly forward.	2	Slow	"
3	Step L foot in place.	3	Slow	"
4	Kick R foot directly forward.	4	Slow	"
5	Step R foot in place.	1	Slow	"
6	Kick L foot directly forward.	2	Slow	"
7	Step L foot in place.	3	Slow	"
8	Kick R foot directly forward.	4	Slow	"

Bootnote: The kick is approximately ankle height (2-4 inches off of the floor).

Schottische

Basic Step
Part I

Sweetheart Position

Schottische Line

Step 1

Step 2

Step 3

Step 4

Step 5

Step 6

Step 7

Step 8

SCHOTTISCHE

Progressive Basic
Man's and Lady's Footwork

Step	Description	Timing	Rhythmic Cue	Lead
	Position: Sweetheart Position or Line (side by side)			

Part I: Side Movement

Step	Description	Timing	Rhythmic Cue	Lead
1	Step R foot diagonally to the right.	1	Slow	L and R hand holds
2	Step L foot to the right crossing behind R foot (flex knees slightly).	2	Slow	"
3	Step R foot directly to the right.	3	Slow	"
4	Kick L foot forward.	4	Slow	"
5	Step L foot diagonally to the left.	1	Slow	"
6	Step R foot to the left crossing behind the L foot (flex knees slightly).	2	Slow	"
7	Step L foot directly to the left.	3	Slow	"
8	Kick R foot forward.	4	Slow	"

Part II: Step 'N' Kick

Step	Description	Timing	Rhythmic Cue	Lead
1	Step R foot directly forward.	1	Slow	L and R hand holds
2	Kick L foot directly forward.	2	Slow	"
3	Step L foot directly forward.	3	Slow	"
4	Kick R foot directly forward.	4	Slow	"
5	Step R foot directly forward.	1	Slow	"
6	Kick L foot directly forward.	2	Slow	"
7	Step L foot directly forward.	3	Slow	"
8	Kick R foot directly forward.	4	Slow	"

Part II

| Steps 1 and 5 | Steps 2 and 6 | Steps 3 and 7 | Steps 4 and 8 |

SCHOTTISCHE

Cross Kick
Man's and Lady's Footwork

Step	Description	Timing	Rhythmic Cue	Lead
	Position: Sweetheart Position or Line (side by side)			
	Part I: Side Movement			
1	Step R foot diagonally to the right.	1	Slow	L and R hand holds
2	Step L foot to the right crossing behind R foot (flex knees slightly).	2	Slow	"
3	Step R foot directly to the right.	3	Slow	"
4	Kick L foot forward.	4	Slow	"
5	Step L foot diagonally to the left.	1	Slow	"
6	Step R foot to the left crossing behind R foot (flex knees slightly).	2	Slow	"
7	Step L foot directly to the left.	3	Slow	"
8	Kick R foot forward.	4	Slow"	
	Part II: Step 'N' Kick and Cross Kick			
1	Step R foot directly forward.	1	Slow	L and R hand holds
2	Kick L foot directly forward.	2	Slow	"
3	Step L foot directly forward.	3	Slow	"
4	Kick R foot directly forward.	4	Slow	"
5	Cross R foot in front of left leg.	1	Slow	"
6	Kick R foot directly forward.	2	Slow	"
7	Kick R foot directly backward, bending knee.	3	Slow	"
8	Kick R foot directly forward.	4	Slow	"

Part II

| Step 4 | Step 5 | Step 6 | Step 7 | Step 8 |

SCHOTTISCHE

High Kick
Man's and Lady's Footwork

Step	Description	Timing	Rhythmic Cue	Lead
	Position: Sweetheart Position or Line (side by side)			

Part I: Side Movement

Step	Description	Timing	Rhythmic Cue	Lead
1	Step R foot diagonally to the right.	1	Slow	L and R hand holds
2	Step L foot to the right crossing behind R foot (flex knee slightly).	2	Slow	"
3	Step R foot directly to the right.	3	Slow	"
4	Kick L foot forward.	4	Slow	"
5	Step L foot diagonally to the left.	1	Slow	"
6	Step R foot to the left crossing behind L foot (flex knee slightly).	2	Slow	"
7	Step L foot directly to the left.	3	Slow	"
8	Kick R foot forward.	4	Slow	"

Part II: Step 'N' Kick and High Kick Variations

Step	Description	Timing	Rhythmic Cue	Lead
1	Step R foot directly forward.	1	Slow	L and R hand holds
2	Kick L foot directly forward.	2	Slow	"
3	Step L foot directly forward.	3	Slow	"
4	Kick R foot directly forward.	4	Slow	"
5	Step R foot in place kicking L foot directly forward.	1	Slow	"
6	Step L foot in place kicking R foot directly forward.	2	Slow	"
7	Step R foot in place kicking L foot directly forward.	3	Slow	"
8	Step L foot in place kicking R foot directly forward.	4	Slow	"

Part II

| Step 4 | Step 5 | Step 6 | Step 7 | Step 8 |

SCHOTTISCHE

Swivels
Man's and Lady's Footwork

Step	Description	Timing	Rhythmic Cue	Lead
	Position: Sweetheart Position or Line (side by side)			

Part I: Side Movement

Step	Description	Timing	Rhythmic Cue	Lead
1	Step R foot diagonally to the right.	1	Slow	L and R hand holds
2	Step L foot to the right crossing behind R foot (flex knees slightly).	2	Slow	"
3	Step R foot directly to the right.	3	Slow	"
4	Kick L foot forward.	4	Slow	"
5	Step L foot diagonally to the left.	1	Slow	"
6	Step R foot to the left crossing behind L foot	2	Slow	"
7	Step L foot directly to the left.	3	Slow	"
8	Kick R foot forward.	4	Slow	"

Part II: Step 'N' Kick and Swivel Variation

Step	Description	Timing	Rhythmic Cue	Lead
1	Step R foot directly forward.	1	Slow	L and R hand holds
2	Kick L foot directly forward.	2	Slow	"
3	Step L foot directly forward.	3	Slow	"
4	Kick R foot directly forward.	4	Slow	"
5	Step R foot in place bringing feet together and swiveling to face diagonally left (1/8 turn).	1	Slow	"
6	Swivel to face diagonally right (1/4 turn).	2	Slow	"
7	Swivel to face diagonally left (1/4 turn).	3	Slow	"
8	Swivel to face directly forward (1/8 turn).	4	Slow	"

Bootnote: Swivel movements are executed with the weight on the balls of the feet, knees slightly flexed, changing the body direction from left to right or right to left. Keep feet close together.

Part II

| Step 4 | Step 5 | Step 6 | Step 7 | Step 8 |

SCHOTTISCHE

Lasso
Man's and Lady's Footwork

Step   **Description**

Postion: Lasso Position #1 (Sweetheart Position)
into Lasso Position #2 into Lasso Position #3.

Note: The Lasso combines the Progressive Basic, Cross Kick,
High Kick, and Swivel Variations.

1-16   Execute Progressive Basic, Part I and Part II, in Lasso Position #1.

17-32   Execute Cross Kick Variation in Lasso Position #1.

33-48   Execute Progressive Basic, Part I, in Lasso Position #1. Execute
Progressive Basic, Part II, moving from Lasso Position #1 to Lasso
Position #2. The L hand hold remains at waist level as the man's R
hand hold leads the lady in front of him from his right side to his left
side.

49-64   Execute High Kick Variation in Lasso Position #2.

65-80   Execute Progressive Basic, Part I, in Lasso Position #2. Execute
Progressive Basic, Part II, moving from Lasso Position #2 to Lasso
Position #3. The L hand hold is placed on the man's left shoudler.
The R hand hold extends to the right at waist level leading the lady
to move behind him from the man's left side to his right side.

81-96   Execute Swivels Variation in Lasso Position #3.

97-112 Execute Progressive Basic, Part I, in Lasso Position #3. Execute
Progressive Basic, Part II, with the man turning the lady one full
turn (in place) counterclockwise under his L hand hold to return
her to Lasso Position #1.

Lasso Position #1   Lasso Position #2   Lasso Position #3

SCHOTTISCHE

Transition Basic
Man's Footwork

Step	Description	Timing	Rhythmic Cue	Lead
	Position: Sweetheart Position into Conversation Position			

Part I: Side Movement

Step	Description	Timing	Rhythmic Cue	Lead
1	Step R foot diagonally to the right.	1	Slow	L and R hand holds
2	Step L foot to the right crossing behind R foot (flex knees slightly).	2	Slow	" " "
3	Step R foot directly to the right.	3	Slow	" " "
4	Kick L foot forward.	4	Slow	" " "
5	Step L foot diagonally to the left.	1	Slow	" " "
6	Step R foot to the left crossing behind L foot (flex knees slightly).	2	Slow	" " "
7	Step L foot directly to the left.	3	Slow	" " "
8	Kick R foot forward.	4	Slow	" " "

Part II: Step 'N' Kick

Note: Man will change from a right foot lead to a left foot lead on Steps 7 and 8.

Step	Description	Timing	Rhythmic Cue	Lead
1	Step R foot directly forward beginning to raise the L hand hold over your head. Release the R hand hold as you begin to move from Sweetheart Position into Conversation Position.	1	Slow	L and R hand movements
2	Kick L foot forward continuing to move the L hand hold over your head. Right hand is placed on the lady's left shoulder blade.	2	Slow	L and R hand movements
3	Step L foot directly forward continuing the movement into Conversation Position.	3	Slow	L and R hand movements
4	Kick R foot forward lowering and releasing the L hand hold behind your head.	4	Slow	L and R hand movements
5	Step R foot directly forward continuing the movement into Conversation Position.	1	Slow	L and R hand movements
6	Kick L foot forward taking the lady's right hand with your left hand completing the movement into Conversation Position.	2	Slow	L and R hand movements
7	Touch left foot to the floor. *Do not change weight* (Transition).	3	Slow	L and R hand movements
8	Kick L foot forward completing the Transition Basic from the man's right foot lead to his left foot lead.	4	Slow	L and R hand movements

SCHOTTISCHE

Transition Basic
Lady's Footwork

Step	Description	Timing	Rhythmic Cue
	Position: Sweetheart Position into Conversation Position		

Part I: Side Movement

Step	Description	Timing	Rhythmic Cue
1	Step R foot diagonally to the right.	1	Slow
2	Step L foot to the right crossing behind R foot (flex knees slightly).	2	"
3	Step R foot directly to the right.	3	"
4	Kick L foot forward.	4	"
5	Step L foot diagonally to the left.	1	"
6	Step R foot to the left crossing behind L foot (flex knees slightly).	2	"
7	Step L foot directly to the left.	3	"
8	Kick R foot forward	4	"

Part II: Step 'N' Kick

Step	Description	Timing	Rhythmic Cue
1	Step R foot directly forward as the man begins to raise the left hand hold over his head. He will release the right hand hold as you begin to move from Sweetheart Position into Conversation Position.	1	Slow
2	Kick L foot forward as the man places his right hand on your left shoulder blade.	2	"
3	Step L foot directly forward continuing the movement into Conversation Position.	3	"
4	Kick R foot forward as your left hand is lowered behind the man's head and placed on his left shoulder.	4	"
5	Step R foot directly forward continuing the movement into Conversation Position.	1	"
6	Kick L foot forward as the man takes your right hand with his left hand completing the movement into Conversation Position.	2	"
7	Step L foot directly forward as the man executes the transition movement.	3	"
8	Kick R foot forward completing the Transition Basic.	4	"

Schottische

Transition Basic
Part II

Sweetheart Position   Step 2   Step 4

Schottische

Transition Basic
Part II

Step 6   Step 7   Step 8

SCHOTTISCHE

Progressive Hops
Man's Footwork

Step	Description	Timing	Rhythmic Cue	Lead
	Position: Conversation Position			
	Part I: Forward Movement			
1	Step L foot directly forward.	1	Slow	Right hand pressure
2	Step R foot directly forward passing L foot.	2	"	"
3	Step L foot directly forward passing R foot.	3	"	"
4	Hop on L foot lifting right knee slightly.	4	"	"
5	Step R foot directly forward.	1	"	"
6	Step L foot directly forward passing R foot.	2	"	"
7	Step R foot directly forward passing L foot.	3	"	"
8	Hop on R foot lifting left knee slightly.	4	"	"
	Part II: Step 'N' Hop			
1	Step L foot directly forward.	1	Slow	Right hand pressure
2	Hop on L foot lifting right knee slightly.	2	"	"
3	Step R foot directly forward.	3	"	"
4	Hop on R foot lifting left knee slightly.	4	"	"
5	Step L foot directly forward.	1	"	"
6	Hop on L foot lifting right knee slightly.	2	"	"
7	Step R foot directly forward.	3	"	"
8	Hop on R foot lifting left knee slightly.	4	"	"

Conversation
Position

Part I: Step 4
Part II: Steps 2 and 6

Part I: Step 8
Part II: Steps 4 and 8

SCHOTTISCHE

Progressive Hops
Lady's Footwork

Step	Description	Timing	Rhythmic Cue
	Position: Conversation Position		

Part I: Forward Movement

Step	Description	Timing	Rhythmic Cue
1	Step R foot directly forward.	1	Slow
2	Step L foot directly forward passing R foot.	2	"
3	Step R foot directly forward passing L foot.	3	"
4	Hop on R foot lifting left knee slightly.	4	"
5	Step L foot directly forward.	1	"
6	Step R foot directly forward passing L foot.	2	"
7	Step L foot directly forward passing R foot.	3	"
8	Hop on L foot lifting right knee slightly.	4	"

Part II: Step 'N' Hop

Step	Description	Timing	Rhythmic Cue
1	Step R foot directly forward.	1	Slow
2	Hop on R foot lifting left knee slightly.	2	"
3	Step L foot directly forward.	3	"
4	Hop on L foot lifting right knee slightly.	4	"
5	Step R foot directly forward.	1	"
6	Hop on R foot lifting left knee slightly.	2	"
7	Step L foot directly forward.	3	"
8	Hop on L foot lifting right knee slightly.	4	"

SCHOTTISCHE

Turning Hops
Man's Footwork

Step	Description	Timing	Rhythmic Cue	Lead
	Position: Conversation Position into Closed Dance Position.			
	Part I: Forward Movement			
1	Step L foot directly forward.	1	Slow	R hand pressure
2	Step R foot directly forward passing L foot.	2	Slow	"
3	Step L foot directly forward passing R foot.	3	Slow	"
4	Hop on L foot lifting right knee slightly.	4	Slow	"
5	Step R foot directly forward.	1	Slow	"
6	Step L foot directly forward passing R foot.	2	Slow	"
7	Step on R foot beginning 1/2 turn (pivot) clockwise to face your partner in Closed Dance Position.	3	Slow	R and L hand pressure
8	Hop on R foot completing 1/2 turn clockwise lifting left knee (turned out) in Closed Dance Position.	4	Slow	

Conversation Position

Part I: Step 4

Part I: Step 8

SCHOTTISCHE

Turning Hops
Lady's Footwork

Step	Description	Timing	Rhythmic Cue
	Position: Conversation into Closed Dance Position		
	Part I: Forward Movement		
1	Step R foot directly forward.	1	Slow
2	Step L foot directly forward passing R foot.	2	Slow
3	Step R foot directly forward passing L foot.	3	Slow
4	Hop on R foot lifting left knee slightly.	4	Slow
5	Step L foot directly forward.	1	Slow
6	Step R foot directly forward passing L foot.	2	Slow
7	Step L foot directly forward as man begins 1/2 turn (pivot) clockwise to face you in Closed Dance Position.	3	Slow
8	Hop on L foot in place, lifting right knee as man completes 1/2 turn clockwise into a Closed Dance Position.	4	Slow

Turning Hops
Man's Footwork, *cont'd*

Part II: Turning Hops

1	Step L foot backward (down your line of dance) beginning 1/2 turn (pivot) clockwise with your partner in Closed Dance Position.	1	Slow	Right hand pulls with finger tip pressure
2	Hop on L foot completing 1/2 turn clockwise in Closed Dance Position lifting right knee.	2	Slow	"
3	Step R foot forward (down your line of dance) beginning 1/2 turn (pivot) clockwise with your partner in Closed Dance Position.	3	Slow	"
4	Hop on R foot completing 1/2 turn clockwise in Closed Dance Position lifting right knee.	4	Slow	"
5	Step L foot backward (down your line of dance) beginning 1/2 turn (pivot) clockwise with your partner in Closed Dance Position.	1	Slow	"
6	Hop on L foot completing 1/2 turn clockwise in Closed Dance Position lifting right knee.	2	Slow	"
7	Step R foot directly forward leading lady from closed position into Conversation Position facing down your line of dance.	3	Slow	"
8	Hop on R foot completing lead into Conversation Position.	4	Slow	"

Part II:
Step 2

Part II:
Step 4

Part II:
Step 6

Part II:
Step 8

Turning Hops
Lady's Footwork, *cont'd*

Part II: Turning Hops

1	Step R foot directly forward (down your line of dance) beginning 1/2 turn (pivot) clockwise with your partner in Closed Dance Position.	1	Slow
2	Hop on R foot completing 1/2 turn clockwise in Closed Dance Position lifting right knee.	2	Slow
3	Step L foot backward (down your line of dance) 1/2 turn (pivot) clockwise with your partner in Closed Dance Position.	3	Slow
4	Hop on L foot completing 1/2 turn clockwise in Closed Dance Position lifting right knee.	4	Slow
5	Step R foot directly forward (down your line of dance) beginning 1/2 turn (pivot) clockwise with your partner in Closed Dance Position.	1	Slow
6	Hop on R foot completing 1/2 turn clockwise in Closed Dance Position lifting right knee.	2	Slow
7	Step L foot backward (down your line of dance) beginning 1/2 turn (pivot) clockwise as the man leads you into Conversation Position.	3	Slow
8	Hop on L foot lifting right knee in Conversation Position.	4	Slow

SCHOTTISCHE

Separation into Progressive Hops
Man's Footwork

Step	Description	Timing	Rhythmic Cue	Lead
	Position: Conversation Position into Separation			
	Part I: Separation Movement			
1	Step L foot diagonally to the left away from your partner releasing left hand hold into Separation Movement.	1	Slow	R hand pressure (push)
2	Cross R foot behind L foot moving away from your partner.	2	Slow	R hand movement
3	Step L foot diagonally to the left continuing to move away from your partner taking the lady's left hand with your right hand.	3	Slow	R hand movement
4	Hop on L foot lifting right knee.	4	Slow	R hand movement
5	Step R foot diagonally to the right toward your partner releasing the lady's left hand and beginning to return to Conversation Position.	1	Slow	R hand hold (pull)
6	Cross L foot behind R foot moving toward your partner.	2	Slow	R hand movement
7	Step R foot diagonally to the right continuing to move toward your partner returning to Conversation Position.	3	Slow	R hand movement
8	Hop on R foot lifting right knee in Conversation Position.	4	Slow	R hand movement
	Part II: Progressive Hops			
1	Step L foot directly forward.	1	Slow	R hand pressure
2	Hop on L foot lifting right knee slightly.	2	Slow	"
3	Step R foot directly forward.	3	Slow	"
4	Hop on R foot lifting left knee slightly.	4	Slow	"
5	Step L foot directly forward.	1	Slow	"
6	Hop on L foot lifting right knee slightly.	2	Slow	"
7	Step R foot directly forward.	3	Slow	"
8	Hop on R foot lifting left knee slightly.	4	Slow	"

SCHOTTISCHE

Separation into Progressive Hops
Lady's Footwork

Step	Description	Timing	Rhythmic Cue
	Position: Conversation Position into Separation		
	Part I: Separation Movement		
1	Step R foot diagonally to the right away from your partner releasing left hand hold into Separation Movement.	1	Slow
2	Cross L foot behind right foot moving away from your partner.	2	Slow
3	Step R foot diagonally to the right continuing to move away from your partner as the man takes your left hand with his right hand for Separation Movement.	3	Slow
4	Hop on R foot lifting left knee.	4	Slow
5	Step L foot diagonally to the left toward your partner releasing the man's right hand and beginning to return to Conversation Position.	1	Slow
6	Cross R foot behind L foot moving toward your partner.	2	Slow
7	Step L foot diagonally to the left continuing to move toward your partner returning to Conversation Position.	3	Slow
8	Hop on L foot lifting right knee in Conversation Position.	4	Slow
	Part II: Progressive Hops		
1	Step R foot directly forward.	1	Slow
2	Hop on R foot lifting left knee slightly.	2	Slow
3	Step L foot directly forward.	3	Slow
4	Hop on L foot lifting right knee slightly.	4	Slow
5	Step R foot directly forward.	1	Slow
6	Hop on R foot lifting left knee slightly.	2	Slow
7	Step L foot directly forward.	3	Slow
8	Hop on L foot lifting right knee slightly.	4	Slow

Separation into Progressive Hops
Man's Footwork

Conversation Position

Part I: Step 1

Part I: Step 2

Part I: Step 5

Part I: Step 6

Part I: Step 7

Separation into Progressive Hops
Man's Footwork

Part I: Step 3

Part I: Step 4

Part I: Step 8

Part II:
Steps 2 and 6

Part II:
Steps 4 and 8

SCHOTTISCHE

Separation into Turning Hops
Man's Footwork

Step	Description	Timing	Rhythmic Cue	Lead
	Position: Conversation Position into Separation into Closed Dance Position.			

Part I: Separation Movement

Step	Description	Timing	Rhythmic Cue	Lead
1	Step L foot diagonally to the left away from your partner releasing L hand hold into Separation Movement.	1	Slow	R hand pressure (push)
2	Cross R foot behind L foot moving away from your partner.	2	Slow	R hand movement
3	Step L foot diagonally to the left continuing to move away from your partner taking the lady's left hand with your right hand.	3	Slow	R hand movement
4	Hop on L foot lifting right knee.	4	Slow	R hand movement
5	Step R foot diagonally to the right toward your partner releasing the lady's left hand and beginning to return to Conversation Position.	1	Slow	R hand hold (pull)
6	Cross L foot behind R foot moving toward your partner.	2	Slow	R hand movement
7	Step on R foot beginning 1/2 turn (pivot) clockwise to face your partner in Closed Dance Position.	3	Slow	R hand movement
8	Hop on R foot completing 1/2 turn clockwise lifting left knee (turned out) in Closed Dance Position.	4	Slow	R hand movement

Part II: Turning Hops

Step	Description	Timing	Rhythmic Cue	Lead
1	Step L foot backward (down your line of dance) beginning 1/2 turn (pivot) clockwise with your partner in Closed Dance Position.	1	Slow	R hand pulls with fingertip pressure
2	Hop on L foot completing 1/2 turn clockwise in Closed Dance Position lifting right knee.	2	Slow	R hand pulls with fingertip pressure
3	Step R foot forward (down your line of dance) beginning 1/2 turn (pivot) clockwise with your partner in Closed Dance Position.	3	Slow	R hand pulls with fingertip pressure
4	Hop on R foot completing 1/2 turn clockwise in Closed Dance Position lifting right knee.	4	Slow	R hand pulls with fingertip pressure

SCHOTTISCHE

Separation into Turning Hops
Lady's Footwork

Step	Description	Timing	Rhythmic Cue
	Position: Conversation Position into Separation into Closed Dance Position.		
	Part I: Separation Movement		
1	Step R foot diagonally to the right away from your partner releasing the L hand hold into Separation Movement.	1	Slow
2	Cross L foot behind right foot moving away from your partner.	2	Slow
3	Step R foot diagonally to the right continuing to move away from your partner as the man takes your left hand with his right hand for Separation Movement.	3	Slow
4	Hop on R foot lifting left knee.	4	Slow
5	Step L foot diagonally to the left toward your partner releasing the man's right hand and beginning to return to Conversation Position.	1	Slow
6	Cross R foot behind L foot moving toward your partner.	2	Slow
7	Step L foot diagonally to the left as the man begins 1/2 turn clockwise to face you returning to Closed Dance Position.	3	Slow
8	Hop on L foot in place lifting right knee as man completes 1/2 turn clockwise in Closed Dance Position.	4	Slow
	Part II: Turning Hops		
1	Step R foot directly forward (down your line of dance) beginning 1/2 turn (pivot) clockwise with your partner in Closed Dance Position.	1	Slow
2	Hop on R foot completing 1/2 turn clockwise with your partner in Closed Dance Position.	2	Slow
3	Step L foot backward (down your line of dance) beginning 1/2 turn (pivot) clockwise with your partner in Closed Dance Position.	3	Slow
4	Hop on L foot completing 1/2 turn clockwise in Closed Dance Position lifting right knee.	4	Slow

Separation into Turning Hops
Man's Footwork, *cont'd*

5	Step L foot backward (down your line of dance) beginning 1/2 turn (pivot) clockwise with your partner in Closed Dance Position.	1	Slow	R hand pulls with fingertip pressure
6	Hop on L foot completing 1/2 turn clockwise in Closed Dance Position lifting right knee.	2	Slow	R hand pulls with fingertip pressure
7	Step R foot directly forward leading the lady from closed position into Conversation Position facing down your line of dance.	3	Slow	R hand pulls with fingertip pressure
8	Hop on R foot completing the lead into Conversation Position.	4	Slow	R hand pulls with fingertip pressure

Conversation
Position

Part I:
Step 1

Part I:
Step 4

Part I:
Step 7

Part I:
Step 8

Separation into Turning Hops
Lady's Footwork, *cont'd*

5	Step R foot directly forward (down your line of dance) beginning 1/2 turn (pivot) clockwise with your partner in Closed Dance Position.	1	Slow
6	Hop on R foot completing 1/2 turn clockwise in Closed Dance Position, lifting right knee.	2	Slow
7	Step L foot backward (down your line of dance) beginning 1/2 turn (pivot) clockwise as man leads you into Conversation Position.	3	Slow
8	Hop on L foot lifting right knee and completing 1/2 turn in Conversation Position.	4	Slow

Part I:
Step 5

Part I:
Step 6

Part II:
Step 2

Part II:
Step 4

Part II:
Step 6

Part II:
Step 8

FAVORITE SCHOTTISCHE SELECTIONS

"Frenchie's Schottische" by Frenchie Burke

" All Star Schottische" by Al Dean and The All Stars

"Sweetheart Schottische" by Al Dean and The All Stars

"Schottische" by Isaac Peyton Sweat

"Schottische" by Johnny Bush

"Texas Schottische" by Johnny Gimble

"Dude Ranch Schottische" by Adolph Hofner

Western Two-Step

WESTERN TWO-STEP

The Western Two-Step was inspired by the tempo and rhythm pattern of Ballroom Fox Trot, a dance created in 1914 by Harry Fox, star of the Ziegfield Follies. The Western Two-Step, like many dances, has different names in different parts of the country. Some of these names include the Slow Two-Step, Walking Two-Step, Cowboy Two-Step, Shuffle Two-Step, and the Kicker Two-Step. The name "Two-Step" should not be confused with the traditional folk dance Two-Step footwork which in this book is described as Western Polka (step-close-step). The names may vary but the basic footwork of the Western Two-Step remains the same.

Included in this book is the Western Two-Step, danced to slow tempo music, and the Texas Two-Step, danced to fast tempo music. Another variation, the Country Two-Step, is derived from variations of the Western Two-Step and has a Polka flavor. It may be danced in 2/4 or 4/4 time with the foot work consisting of two triple steps followed by two shuffle steps. The rhythm pattern is the same as Western Swing (1 & 2, 3 & 4, 5, 6). The Country Two-Step may be danced by superimposing the rhythm pattern and weight shift of the Western Swing over the footwork of the Western Two-Step.

The slower Western Two-Step is more popular in Country and Western dance halls where live bands play and the faster Texas Two-Step is more popular in Country and Western night clubs where records are used.

Western Two-Step

1. Basic Step Forward

2. Basic Step Turning Right

3. Basic Step Backward

4. Basic Step Turning Left

5. Conversation

6. Continuous Conversation

7. Underarm Turn

8. Double Underarm Turn

9. Sidewinder

10. Progressive Basic Forward

Rhythmical Analysis

WESTERN TWO-STEP----Time signature 4/4

Step pattern

Man:	Step side,	Touch together,	Step side,	Touch together	Step forward,	Step forward
Lady:	Step side,	Touch together,	Step side,	Touch together	Step backward,	Step backward,
Count: Notation	1 —	2 —	3 —	4 —	1 —	2 —
Rhythmical Cue:	Quick [Slow	Quick	Quick] [	Quick Slow	Quick]	Quick

To complete a basic step in Western Two-Step one will use 1-1/2 measures of music in 4/4 time.

Western Two-Step

Basic Step Forward
Man's Footwork

Step	Description	Timing	Rhythmic Cue	Lead
	Position: Closed Dance Position			
1	Step L foot directly to the left.	1	Quick	R Palm pressure
2	Step R foot directly to the left bringing feet together. Do not change weight.	2	Quick	Hold in place
3	Step R foot directly to the right.	3	Quick	R Finger pressure
4	Step L foot directly to the right bringing feet together. Do not change weight.	4	Quick	Hold in place
5	Step L foot directly forward.	1	Quick	R Heel pressure
6	Step R foot directly forward, passing L foot.	2	Quick	R Heel pressure

Closed
Dance Position

Step 1   Step 2   Step 3

Western Two-Step

Basic Step Forward
Lady's Footwork

Step	Description	Timing	Rhythmic Cue
	Position: Closed Dance Position		
1	Step R foot directly to the right.	1	Quick
2	Step L foot directly to the right bringing feet together. Do not change weight.	2	Quick
3	Step L foot directly to the left.	3	Quick
4	Step R foot directly to the left bringing feet together. Do not change weight.	4	Quick
5	Step R foot directly backward.	1	Quick
6	Step L foot directly backward, passing R foot.	2	Quick

Step 4

Step 5

Step 6

Western Two-Step

Basic Step Turning Right (Clockwise)
Man's Footwork

Step	Description	Timing	Rhythmic Cue	Lead
	Position: Closed Dance Position			
1	Step L foot directly to the left.	1	Quick	R Palm pressure
2	Step R foot directly to the left bringing feet together. Do not change weight.	2	Quick	Hold in place
3	Step R foot directly to the right.	3	Quick	R Finger pressure
4	Step L foot directly to the right bringing feet together. Do not change weight.	4	Quick	Hold in place
5	Step L foot (circling movement) to the left turning right (clockwise) approximately 1/4 turn.	1	Quick	R Hand pressure
6	Step R foot directly to the left bringing feet together continuing to turn right (clockwise).	2	Quick	Hold in place

Closed
Dance Position

Step 1

Step 2

Step 3

Western Two-Step

Basic Step Turning Right (Clockwise)
Lady's Footwork

Step	Description	Timing	Rhythmic Cue
	Position: Closed Dance Position		
1	Step R foot directly to the right.	1	Quick
2	Step L foot directly to the right bringing feet together. Do not change weight.	2	Quick
3	Step L foot directly to the left.	3	Quick
4	Step R foot directly to the left bringing feet together. Do not change weight.	4	Quick
5	Step R foot (small step) to the right turning right (clockwise) approximately 1/4 turn.	1	Quick
6	Step L foot directly to the right bringing feet together, continuing to turn right.	2	Quick

Step 4   Step 5   Step 6

Western Two-Step

Basic Step Backward
Man's Footwork

Step	Description	Timing	Rhythmic Cue	Lead
	Position: Closed Dance Position			
1	Step L foot directly to the left.	1	Quick	R Palm pressure
2	Step R foot directly to the left bringing feet together. Do not change weight.	2	Quick	Hold in place
3	Step R foot directly to the right.	3	Quick	R Finger pressure
4	Step L foot directly to the right bringing feet together. Do not change weight.	4	Quick	Hold in place
5	Step L foot directly backward.	1	Quick	R Finger pressure
6	Step R foot directly backward, passing L foot.	2	Quick	R Finger pressure

Closed Dance
Position

Step 1

Step 2

Step 3

Western Two-Step

Basic Step Backward
Lady's Footwork

Step	Description	Timing	Rhythmic Cue
	Position: Closed Dance Position		
1	Step R foot directly to the right.	1	Quick
2	Step L foot directly to the right bringing feet together. Do not change weight.	2	Quick
3	Step L foot directly to the left.	3	Quick
4	Step R foot directly to the left bringing feet together. Do not change weight.	4	Quick
5	Step R foot directly forward.	1	Quick
6	Step L foot directly forward, passing R foot.	2	Quick

Step 4   Step 5   Step 6

Western Two-Step

Basic Step Turning Left (Counterclockwise)
Man's Footwork

Step	Description	Timing	Rhythmic Cue	Lead
	Position: Closed Dance Position			
1	Step L foot directly to the left.	1	Quick	R Palm pressure
2	Step R foot directly to the left bringing feet together. Do not change weight.	2	Quick	Hold in place
3	Step R foot directly to the right.	3	Quick	R Finger pressure
4	Step L foot directly to the right bringing feet together. Do not change weight.	4	Quick	Hold in place
5	Step L foot (small step) to the left turning left (counterclockwise) approximately 1/4 turn.	1	Quick	R Palm pressure
6	Step R foot directly to the left bringing feet together, continuing to turn left (counterclockwise).	2	Quick	Hold in place

Closed Dance
Position

Step 1

Step 2

Step 3

Western Two-Step

Basic Step Turning Left (Counterclockwise)
Lady's Footwork

Step	Description	Timing	Rhythmic Cue
	Position: Closed Dance Position		
1	Step R foot directly to the right.	1	Quick
2	Step L foot directly to the right bringing feet together. Do not change weight.	2	Quick
3	Step L foot directly to the left.	3	Quick
4	Step R foot directly to the left bringing feet together. Do not change weight.	4	Quick
5	Step R foot (circling movement) to the right turning left (counterclockwise) approximately 1/4 turn.	1	Quick
6	Step L foot directly to the right bringing feet together, continuing to turn left (counterclockwise).	2	Quick

Step 4   Step 5   Step 6

Western Two-Step

Conversation
Man's Footwork

Step	Description	Timing	Rhythmic Cue	Lead
	Position: Closed Dance Position into Conversation			
1	Step L foot directly to the left.	1	Quick	R Palm pressure
2	Step R foot directly to the left bringing feet together. Do not change weight.	2	Quick	Hold in place
3	Step R foot directly to the right.	3	Quick	R Finger pressure
4	Step L foot directly to the right bringing feet together. Do not change weight.	4	Quick	Hold in place
5	Step L foot (conversation position) to the left turning approximately 1/4 turn counterclockwise.	1	Quick	R Palm pressure
6	Step R foot directly forward in conversation position, passing L foot.	2	Quick	R Hand pressure

Note: Return to Closed Position

Closed Dance
Position

Step 1   Step 2   Step 3

Western Two-Step

Conversation
Lady's Footwork

Step	Description	Timing	Rhythmic Cue
	Position: Closed Dance Position into Conversation		
1	Step R foot directly to the right.	1	Quick
2	Step L foot directly to the right bringing feet together. Do not change weight.	2	Quick
3	Step L foot directly to the left.	3	Quick
4	Step R foot directly to the left bringing feet together. Do not change weight.	4	Quick
5	Step R foot (conversation position) to the right turning approximately 1/4 turn clockwise.	1	Quick
6	Step L foot directly forward in conversation position, passing R foot.	2	Quick

Note: Return to Closed Position

Step 4

Step 5

Step 6

Western Two-Step

Continuous Conversation
Man's Footwork

Step	Description	Timing	Rhythmic Cue	Lead
	Position: Conversation			
1	Step L foot directly forward.	1	Quick	R Hand pressure
2	Step R foot directly forward bringing feet together. Do not change weight.	2	Quick	Hold in place
3	Step R foot directly backward.	3	Quick	R Finger pressure
4	Step L foot directly backward bringing feet together. Do not change weight.	4	Quick	Hold in place
5	Step L foot directly forward.	1	Quick	R Hand pressure
6	Step R foot directly forward passing L foot.	2	Quick	R Hand pressure

Note: Repeat variation or return to Closed Dance Position.

Conversation
Position

Step 1   Step 2   Step 3

Western Two-Step

Continuous Conversation
Lady's Footwork

Step	Description	Timing	Rhythmic Cue
	Position: Conversation		
1	Step R foot directly forward.	1	Quick
2	Step L foot directly forward bringing feet together. Do not change weight.	2	Quick
3	Step L foot directly backward.	3	Quick
4	Step R foot directly backward bringing feet together. Do not change weight.	4	Quick
5	Step R foot directly forward.	1	Quick
6	Step L foot directly forward passing R foot.	2	Quick

Note: Repeat variation or return to Closed Dance Position.

Step 4

Step 5

Step 6

Western Two-Step

Underarm Turn
Man's Footwork

Step	Description	Timing	Rhythmic Cue	Lead
	Position: Closed Dance Position			
1	Step L foot directly to the left.	1	Quick	R Palm pressure
2	Step R foot directly to the left bringing feet together. Do not change weight.	2	Quick	Hold in place
3	Step R foot directly to the right.	3	Quick	R Finger pressure
4	Step L foot directly to the right bringing feet together. Do not change weight.	4	Quick	Hold in place
5	Step L foot (small step) directly forward leading the lady into an underarm turn. Your left hand hold will encircle your partner's head as your R Hand Hold leads her to pivot a full turn clockwise.	1	Quick	L Hand Hold lifts and encircles R Hand pressure
6	Step R foot (small step) directly forward completing the Underarm Turn as you return to Closed Dance Position.	2	Quick	L and R Hand movements

Closed Dance
Position

Step 1

Step 2

Step 3

Western Two-Step

Underarm Turn
Lady's Footwork

Step	Description	Timing	Rhythmic Cue
	Position: Closed Dance Position		
1	Step R foot directly to the right.	1	Quick
2	Step L foot directly to the right bringing feet together. Do not change weight.	2	Quick
3	Step L foot directly to the left.	3	Quick
4	Step R foot directly to the left bringing feet together. Do not change weight.	4	Quick
5	Step R foot diagonally to the right under your R Hand Hold pivoting into a full turn clockwise.	1	Quick
6	Step L foot directly backward as you return to Closed Dance Position.	2	Quick

Step 4

Step 5

Step 6

Western Two-Step

Double Underarm Turn
Man's Footwork

Step	Description	Timing	Rhythmic Cue	Lead
	Position: Closed Dance Position			
1	Step L foot directly to the left.	1	Quick	R Palm pressure
2	Step R foot directly to the left bringing feet together. Do not change weight.	2	Quick	Hold in place
3	Step R foot directly to the right.	3	Quick	R Finger pressure
4	Step L foot directly to the right bringing feet together. Do not change weight.	4	Quick	Hold in place
5	Step L foot (small step) directly forward leading the lady into a double underarm turn. Your L Hand Hold will encircle your partner's head as your R Hand Hold leads her to pivot a full turn clockwise.	1	Quick	L Hand Hold lifts and encircles R Hand pressure
6	Step R foot (small step) directly forward completing the lady's first turn clockwise. The L Hand Hold remains raised beginning to encircle the lady's head into the second underarm turn. The R Hand Hold remains at waist level.	2	Quick	L Hand Hold movement
7	Step L foot (small step) directly forward leading the lady into the second underarm turn. Your L Hand Hold will encircle your partner's head as the R Hand Hold remains at waist level.	3	Quick	L Hand Hold encircles
8	Step R foot (small step) directly forward completing the Double Underarm Turn as you return to Closed Dance Position.	4	Quick	L and R Hand movements

| Closed Dance Position | Step 1 | Step 2 | Step 3 | Step 4 |

Western Two-step

Double Underarm Turn
Lady's Footwork

Step	Description	Timing	Rhythmic Cue
	Position: Closed Dance Position		
1	Step R foot directly to the right.	1	Quick
2	Step L foot directly to the right bringing feet together. Do not change weight.	2	Quick
3	Step L foot directly to the left.	3	Quick
4	Step R foot directly to the left bringing feet together. Do not change weight.	4	Quick
5	Step R foot diagonally to the right under your R Hand Hold pivoting into a full turn clockwise.	1	Quick
6	Step L foot directly backward completing the first underarm turn.	2	Quick
7	Step R foot diagonally to the right under your R Hand Hold pivoting into the second full turn clockwise.	3	Quick
8	Step L foot directly backward completing the Double Underarm Turn returning to Closed Dance Position.	4	Quick

Step 5   Step 6   Step 7   Step 8

Western Two-Step

Sidewinder
Man's Footwork

Step	Description	Timing	Rhythmic Cue	Lead
	Position: Closed Dance Position into Sidewinder Position following a Basic Step Backward. The man turns Left (counterclockwise) 1/4 turn away from his partner with her facing his right side. Note: Precede with basic step backward.			
1	Step L foot directly to the left.	1	Quick	R Finger pressure
2	Step R foot directly to the left bringing feet together. Do not change weight.	2	Quick	Hold in place
3	Step R foot directly to the right.	3	Quick	R Palm pressure
4	Step L foot directly to the right bringing feet together. Do not change weight.	4	Quick	Hold in place
5	Step L foot directly to the left.	1	Quick	R Finger pressure
6	Step R foot directly to the left crossing right foot behind left foot.	2	Quick	R Finger pressure

Bootnote: Execute the Sidewinder as many times as you wish before returning to Basic Step Backward.

Closed Dance
Position

Step 1   Step 2   Step 3

Western Two-Step
Sidewinder
Lady's Footwork

Step	Description	Timing	Rhythmic Cue
	Position: Closed Dance Position into Sidewinder Position		
1	Step R foot directly forward.	1	Quick
2	Step L foot directly forward bringing feet together. Do not change weight.	2	Quick
3	Step L foot directly backward.	3	Quick
4	Step R foot directly backward bringing feet together. Do not change weight.	4	Quick
5	Step R foot directly forward.	1	Quick
6	Step L foot directly forward, passing R foot.	2	Quick

Note: May be repeated or return to Closed Dance Position.

| Step 4 | Step 5 | Step 6 |

Western Two-Step

Progressive Step Forward
Man's Footwork

Step	Description	Timing	Rhythmic Cue	Lead
	Position: Closed Dance Position			
1	Step L foot diagonally forward to the left.	1	Quick	R Heel pressure
2	Step R foot diagonally forward to the left bringing feet together. Do not change weight.	2	Quick	Hold in place
3	Step R foot diagonally forward to the right.	3	Quick	R Heel pressure
4	Step L foot diagonally forward to the right bringing feet together. Do not change weight.	4	Quick	Hold in place
5	Step L foot directly forward.	1	Quick	R Heel pressure
6	Step R foot directly forward, passing L foot.	2	Quick	R Heel pressure

Closed Dance
Position

Step 1

Step 2

Step 3

Western Two-Step

Progressive Step Forward
Lady's Footwork

Step	Description	Timing	Rhythmic Cue
	Position: Closed Dance Position		
1	Step R foot diagonally backward to the right.	1	Quick
2	Step L foot diagonally backward to the right bringing feet together. Do not change weight.	2	Quick
3	Step L foot diagonally backward to the left.	3	Quick
4	Step R foot diagonally backward to the left bringing feet together. Do not change weight.	4	Quick
5	Step R foot directly backward.	1	Quick
6	Step L foot directly backward, passing R foot.	2	Quick

Step 4

Step 5

Step 6

Western Two-Step

AMALGAMATIONS

1. Basic Step Forward (three times)
   Basic Step Turning Right (twice, to execute 1/2 turn clockwise)
   Basic Step Backward (three times)
   Basic Step Turning Left (twice, to execute 1/2 turn counterclockwise)

2. Basic Step Forward
   Underarm Turn
   Double Underarm Turn

3. Basic Step Forward
   Conversation Step (twice)
   Continuous Conversation

4. Basic Step Backward (three times)
   Sidewinder (several times)
   Basic Step Backward (three times)

FAVORITE WESTERN TWO-STEP SELECTIONS

"All My Exes Are from Texas" by George Strait

"Amarillo by Morning" by George Strait

"Back on Her Mind Again" by Johnny Rodriguez

"Beautiful You" by The Oak Ridge Boys

"Big City" by Merle Haggard

"Coca Cola Cowboy" by Mel Tillis

"Crazy Arms" by Willie Nelson and Ray Price

"Dancin' Cowboys" by The Bellamy Brothers

"Deep Water" by Asleep at the Wheel or by George Strait

"Faded Love" by Bob Wills & The Texas Playboys

"Fraulien" by Darrell McCall

"Have I Got a Deal for You" by Reba McEntire

"I Fall to Pieces" by Patsy Cline

"I Love You a Thousand Ways" by John Anderson

"I Wonder" by Rosanne Cash

"If I Ever Need a Lady" by Billy Parker

"It Won't Hurt" by Dwight Yoakum

"Looking for Love" by Johnny Lee

"Luckenbach, Texas" by Waylon Jennings

"Maiden's Prayer" by Bob Wills and The Texas Playboys

"My Woman Loves the Devil Out of Me" by Moe Bandy

"Old Flame" by Alabama

"On My Mind Again" by Bubba Littrell

"Sentimental Ol' You" by Charly McClain

"She Thinks I Still Care" by George Jones

"Tequila Express" by Susie Taylor and Mike Wells

"The Kind of Love I Can't Forget" by Asleep at the Wheel

"There's Still Alot of Love in San Antone" by Connie Hanson

"Thirthy-Nine and Holding" by Jerry Lee Lewis

"Undo the Right" by Johnny Bush

Texas
Two-Step

Texas Two-Step

The Texas Two-Step is the western version of the Ballroom Fox Trot, a dance created in 1914 by Harry Fox, star of the Ziegfield Follies. The basic step of the Texas Two-Step closely resembles the basic "magic step" in the Fox Trot. Both dances are danced to 4/4 time and the tempo in both ranges from slow to medium to fast. The tempo of the music dictates the size of the footwork; the faster the music the smaller the step.

The name two-step should not be confused with the traditional folk dance two-step which in this book is described as Western Polka (step-close-step). Like so many dances, the Two-Step and Polka have various names in different parts of the country.

The Texas Two-Step is usually danced to a medium tempo. Some enjoy dancing the Texas Two-Step to a slower tempo using a double time. Those who execute the step patterns in a double tempo move around the floor at a faster pace than those who use the slow tempo.

Dancing the Texas Two-Step becomes much more enjoyable after you master the basic step and variations and begin to create movements of your own.

Texas Two-Step

1. Basic Step Forward
2. Basic Step Turning Right
3. Basic Step Backward
4. Basic Step Turning Left
5. Conversation

6. Continuous Conversation
7. Underarm Turn
8. Sidewinder
9. Diagonal Basic
10. Parallel Basic

Rhythmical Analysis

Texas Two-Step----Time Signature 4/4

Step pattern, Man:	Step forward,	Step forward,	Step forward,	Step together
Lady:	Step backward,	Step backward,	Step backward,	Step together
Count: Notation:	1,2	3,4	1	2
Rhythmical Cue:	Slow	Slow	Quick	Quick

To complete a basic Texas Two-Step one will use 1-1/2 measures of music in 4/4 time.

Texas Two-Step

Basic Step Forward
Man's Footwork

Step	Description	Timing	Rhythmic Cue	Lead
	Position: Closed Dance Position			
1	Step L foot directly forward.	1-2	Slow	R Heel pressure
2	Step R foot directly forward passing L foot.	3-4	Slow	R Heel pressure
3	Step L foot directly forward passing R foot.	1	Quick	R Heel pressure
4	Step R foot directly forward bringing feet together (3rd position, L foot forward).	2	Quick	R Hand pressure

Closed Dance
Position

Step 1

Step 2

Texas Two-Step

Basic Step Forward
Lady's Footwork

Step	Description	Timing	Rhythmic Cue
	Position: Closed Dance Position		
1	Step R foot directly backward.	1-2	Slow
2	Step L foot directly backward passing R foot.	3-4	Slow
3	Step R foot directly backward passing L foot.	1	Quick
4	Step L foot directly backward bringing feet together (3rd position, L foot forward).	2	Quick

Step 3

Step 4

Texas Two-Step

Basic Step Turning Right (Clockwise)
Man's Footwork

Step	Description	Timing	Rhythmic Cue	Lead
	Position: Closed Dance Position *			
1	Step L foot diagonally to the left moving into parallel position (right shoulders adjacent).	1-2	Slow	R Heel pressure
2	Step R foot forward passing L foot (toe outward) in parallel position as you begin clockwise turn.	3-4	Slow	R Hand pressure
3	Step L foot forward passing around right foot as you continue clockwise turn with your partner.	1	Quick	R Finger pressure
4	Step R foot directly to the left bringing feet together to complete clockwise turn ending in Closed Dance Position.	2	Quick	R Hand pressure

* Note: A clockwise turn is more easily executed when preceded by a Basic Step Forward.

Bootnote: Steps 1 and 2 may be executed by stepping directly into your partner rather than around her. (See photos below.)

Closed Dance
Position

Step 1

Step 2

Texas Two-Step

Basic Step Turning Right (Clockwise)
Lady's Footwork

Step	Description	Timing	Rhythmic Cue
	Position: Closed Dance Position		
1	Step R foot directly backward as man steps into parallel position, right shoulders adjacent.	1-2	Slow
2	Step L foot backward passing R foot (toe inward) in parallel position as you begin 1/2 turn clockwise.	3-4	Slow
3	Step R foot backward and around L foot continuing clockwise turn.	1	Quick
4	Step L foot to the right bringing feet together to complete 1/2 turn clockwise ending in Closed Dance Position.	2	Quick

 Bootnote: Steps 1 and 2 may be executed by your partner stepping directly into you rather than around you. (See photos below.)

Step 3   Step 4

Texas Two-Step

Basic Step Backward
Man's Footwork

Step	Description	Timing	Rhythmic Cue	Lead
	Position: Closed Dance Position			
1	Step L foot directly backward.	1-2	Slow	R Finger pressure
2	Step R foot directly backward passing L foot.	3-4	Slow	R Finger pressure
3	Step L foot directly backward passing R foot.	1	Quick	R Finger pressure
4	Step R foot directly backward bringing feet together (3rd position, R foot forward).	2	Quick	R Finger pressure

Closed Dance
Position

Step 1

Step 2

Texas Two-Step

Basic Step Backward
Lady's Footwork

Step	Description	Timing	Rhythmic Cue
	Position: Closed Dance Position		
1	Step R foot directly forward.	1-2	Slow
2	Step L foot directly forward passing R foot.	3-4	Slow
3	Step R foot directly forward passing L foot.	1	Quick
4	Step L foot directly forward bringing feet together (3rd position, R foot forward).	2	Quick

Step 3   Step 4

Texas Two-Step

Basic Step Turning Left (Counterclockwise)
Man's Footwork

Step	Description	Timing	Rhythmic Cue	Lead
	Position: Closed Dance Position *			
1	Step L foot directly backward beginning to lead your partner into parallel position, left shoulders adjacent.	1-2	Slow	R Finger pressure
2	Step R foot backward (toe turned inward) passing left foot beginning 1/2 turn counterclockwise in parallel position.	3-4	Slow	R Hand pressure
3	Step L foot backward and around R foot continuing counterclockwise turn.	1	Quick	R Hand pressure
4	Step R foot to the left bringing feet together to complete 1/2 turn counterclockwise ending in Closed Dance Position.	2	Quick	R Hand pressure

*Note: A counterclockwise turn is more easily executed when preceded by a Basic Step Backward.

Bootnote: Steps 1 and 2 may be executed by your partner stepping directly into you rather than around you. (See photos below.)

Closed Dance Position   Step 1   Step 2

Texas Two-Step

Basic Step Turning Left (Counterclockwise)
Lady's Footwork

Step	Description	Timing	Rhythmic Cue
	Position: Closed Dance Position		
1	Step R foot directly forward as the man begins to lead you into parallel position, left shoulders adjacent.	1-2	Slow
2	Step L foot forward (toe turned outward) passing R foot beginning 1/2 turn counterclockwise in parallel position.	3-4	Slow
3	Step R foot forward and around L foot continuing counterclockwise turn.	1	Quick
4	Step L foot to the right bringing feet together to complete 1/2 turn counterclockwise ending in Closed Dance Position.	2	Quick

 Bootnote: Steps 1 and 2 may be executed by your stepping directly into your partner rather than around him. (See photos below.)

Step 3

Step 4

Texas Two-Step

Conversation Step
Man's Footwork

Step	Description	Timing	Rhythmic Cue	Lead
	Position: Closed Dance Position			
1	Step L foot directly to the left turning 1/4 turn into conversation position.	1-2	Slow	R Palm pressure
2	Step R foot directly forward in conversation position, (toe turned outward) passing the left foot.	3-4	Slow	R Hand pressure
3	Step L foot directly forward passing the right foot, turning back into Closed Dance Position.	1	Quick	R Finger pressure
4	Step R foot directly to the left bringing feet together.	2	Quick	R Palm pressure

Closed Dance
Position

Step 1

Step 2

Texas Two-Step

Conversation Step
Lady's Footwork

Step	Description	Timing	Rhythmic Cue
	Position: Closed Dance Position		
1	Step R foot directly to the right turning 1/4 turn into conversation position.	1-2	Slow
2	Step L foot directly forward in conversation position, (toe turned outward) passing the right foot.	3-4	Slow
3	Step R foot directly forward passing the left foot, turning back into Closed Dance Position.	1	Quick
4	Step L foot directly to the right bringing feet together.	2	Quick

Step 3   Step 4

Texas Two-Step

Continuous Conversation
Man's Footwork

Step	Description	Timing	Rhythmic Cue	Lead
	Position: Closed Dance Position			
1	Step L foot directly to the left turning 1/4 turn into Conversation Position.	1-2	Slow	R Palm pressure
2	Step R foot directly forward in Conversation Position, passing the left foot.	3-4	Slow	R Hand pressure
3	Step L foot directly forward passing right foot.	1	Quick	R Hand pressure
4	Step R foot directly forward bringing feet together (3rd position, L foot forward).	2	Quick	R Hand pressure

MAY BE REPEATED AT MAN'S DISCRETION

Return to Closed Position by substituting the following for Steps 3 and 4 above:

Step	Description	Timing	Rhythmic Cue	Lead
3	Step L foot directly forward passing the right foot, turning back into Closed Dance Position.	1	Quick	R FInger pressure
4	Step R foot directly to the left bringing feet together.	2	Quick	R Palm pressure

Closed Dance
Position

Step 1

Step 2

Texas Two-Step

Continuous Conversation
Lady's Footwork

Step	Description	Timing	Rhythmic Cue
	Position: Closed Dance Position		
1	Step R foot directly to the right turning 1/4 turn into Conversation Position.	1-2	Slow
2	Step L foot directly forward in Conversation Position, passing the right foot.	3-4	Slow
3	Step R foot directly forward passing L foot.	1	Quick
4	Step L foot directly forward bringing feet together (3rd position, R foot forward).	2	Quick

MAY BE REPEATED AT MAN'S DISCRETION

Return to Closed Position by substituting the following for Steps 3 and 4 above:

Step	Description	Timing	Rhythmic Cue
3	Step R foot directly forward passing the left foot, turning back into Closed Dance Position.	1	Quick
4	Step L foot directly to the right bringning feet together.	2	Quick

Step 3

Step 4

Texas Two-Step

Underarm Turn
Man's Footwork

Step	Description	Timing	Rhythmic Cue	Lead
	Position: Closed Dance Position			
1	Step L foot directly forward.	1-2	Slow	R Heel pressure
2	Step R foot directly forward passing L foot.	3-4	Slow	R Heel pressure
3	Step L foot directly forward passing R foot leading the lady into an Underarm Turn clockwise under your L hand hold.	1	Quick	R Hand pressure L Hand hold raises and encircles
4	Step R foot directly forward bringing feet together (3rd position, L foot forward) returning to Closed Dance Position.	2	Quick	L Hand hold lowers

Bootnote: The Underarm Turn may be executed on Steps 1 and 2 (slow, slow) rather than Steps 3 and 4 (quick, quick).

Closed Dance
Position

Step 1

Step 2

Texas Two-Step

Underarm Turn
Lady's Footwork

Step	Description	Timing	Rhythmic Cue
	Position: Closed Dance Position		
1	Step R foot directly backward.	1-2	Slow
2	Step L foot directly backward passing R foot.	3-4	Slow
3	Step R foot diagonally to the right under your R hand hold pivoting into a full turn clockwise.	1	Quick
4	Step L foot directly backward returning to Closed Dance Position.	2	Quick

Step 3

Step 4

Texas Two-Step

Sidewinder
Man's Footwork

Step	Description	Timing	Rhythmic Cue	Lead
	Position: Closed Dance Position into Side-winder Position. *			
1	Step L foot directly to the left into sidewinder position.	1-2	Slow	R Hand pressure
2	Step R foot to the left crossing behind the left foot.	3-4	Slow	R Hand pressure
3	Step L foot directly to the left.	1	Quick	R Hand pressure
4	Step R foot to the left bringing feet together.	2	Quick	R Hand pressure

* Note: Following a Basic Step Backwards the man turns 1/4 turn left (counterclockwise) away from his partner with her facing his right side in Sidewinder Position.

 Bootnote: The lady will be progressing towards the man (on his right side) as the man progresses sideways down his line of dance. This step pattern substitutes for the Basic Step Backwards so the man can see behind him. Execute the Sidewinder as many times as you wish before returning to the Basic Step Backward.

Closed Dance
Position

Step 1

Step 2

Texas Two-Step

Sidewinder
Lady's Footwork

Step	Description	Timing	Rhythmic Cue
	Position: Closed Dance Position into Sidewinder Position. *		
1	Step R foot directly forward progressing toward the man.	1-2	Slow
2	Step L foot directly forward passing R foot.	3-4	Slow
3	Step R foot directly forward passing L foot.	1	Quick
4	Step L foot forward bringing feet together (3rd position, R foot forward).	2	Quick

* Note: Following a Basic Step Backwards the man turns 1/4 turn left (counterclockwise) away from his partner with the lady facing his right side in Sidewinder Position.

Bootnote: The lady will be progressing toward the man (on his right side) as the man progresses sideways down his line of dance. This step pattern substitutes for the Basic Step Backward so the man can see behind him. Execute the Sidewinder as many times as you wish before returning to the Basic Step Backward.

Step 3   Step 4

Texas Two-Step

Diagonal Basic, Forward & Backward
Man's Footwork

Step	Description	Timing	Rhythmic Cue	Lead
	Position: Closed Dance Position *			
1	Step L foot directly forward.	1-2	Slow	R Heel pressure
2	Step R foot (toe outward) diagonally forward between partner's feet beginning to turn 3/8 turn to the right (clockwise).	3-4	Slow	R Heel pressure
3	Step L foot to the side to complete 3/8 turn.	1	Quick	R Palm pressure
4	Step R foot to the left bringing feet together and completing a Diagonal Basic Step Forward.	2	Quick	R Palm pressure
5	Step L foot directly backward.	3-4	Slow	R Hand pressure
6	Step R foot (toe inward) diagonally backward beginning to turn 3/8 turn to the left (counter-clockwise).	1-2	Slow	R Hand pressure
7	Step L foot (small step) to the side to complete 3/8 turn.	3	Quick	R Hand pressure
8	Step R foot to the left bringing feet together and completing a Diagonal Basic Step Backward.	4	Quick	R Hand pressure

* Note: Remain in Closed Position as you move down the line of dance executing the Diagonal Basic Step Forward and the Diagonal Basic Step Backward.

Bootnote: You may repeat the sequence or return to the Basic Step Forward.

| Closed Dance Position | Step 1 | Step 2 | Step 3 | Step 4 |

Texas Two-Step

Diagonal Basic, Forward & Backward
Lady's Footwork

Step	Description	Timing	Rhythmic Cue
	Position: Closed Dance Position *		
1	Step R foot directly backward.	1-2	Slow
2	Step L foot diagonally backward (toe inward) beginning to turn 3/8 turn to the right (clockwise).	3-4	Slow
3	Step R foot to the side (small step) to complete 3/8 turn.	1	Quick
4	Step L foot to the right bringing feet together and completing a Diagonal Basic Step Forward.	2	Quick
5	Step R foot directly forward.	3-4	Slow
6	Step L foot diagonally forward (toe outward) beginning to turn 3/8 turn to the left (counterclockwise).	1-2	Slow
7	Step R foot to the side to complete 3/8 turn.	3	Quick
8	Step L foot to the right bringing feet together.	4	Quick

* Note: Remain in Closed Position as you move down the line of dance executing the Diagonal Basic Step Forward and the Diagonal Basic Step Backward.

Bootnote: You may repeat the sequence or return to the Basic Step Forward.

| Step 5 | Step 6 | Step 7 | Step 8 |

Texas Two-Step

Parallel Basic, Forward & Backward
Man's Footwork

Step	Description	Timing	Rhythmic Cue	Lead
	Position: Closed Dance Position *			
1	Step L foot forward diagonally to the left moving into parallel position with right shoulders adjacent.	1-2	Slow	R Heel pressure
2	Step R foot forward (toe outward) beginning to turn 3/8 turn to the right (clockwise) in parallel position.	3-4	Slow	R Hand pressure
3	Step L foot to the side to complete 3/8 turn to face partner.	1	Quick	R Palm pressure
4	Step R foot to the left bringing feet together and completing a Parallel Basic Step Forward.	2	Quick	R Palm pressure
5	Step L foot to the left (toe inward) moving into parallel position with left shoulders adjacent. Continue to progress down the line of dance.	3-4	Slow	R Hand pressure
6	Step R foot backward in parallel position beginning to turn 3/8 turn to the left (counterclockwise).	1-2	Slow	R Hand pressure
7	Step L foot (small step) to the side to complete 3/8 turn to face your partner.	3	Quick	R Hand pressure
8	Step R foot to the left bringing feet together and completing a Parallel Basic Step Backward.	4	Quick	R Hand pressure

* Note: Remain in Closed Position as you move down the line of dance executing the Parallel Basic Step Forward and the Parallel Basic Step Backward.

Bootnote: You may repeat the sequence or return to the Basic Step Forward.

| Closed Dance Position | Step 1 | Step 2 | Step 3 | Step 4 |

Texas Two-Step

Parallel Basic, Forward & Backward
Lady's Footwork

Step	Description	Timing	Rhythmic Cue
	Position: Closed Dance Position *		
1	Step R foot directly backward.	1-2	Slow
2	Step L foot directly backward.	3-4	Slow
3	Step R foot to the side (small step) to execute 3/8 turn to face partner.	1	Quick
4	Step L foot to the right bringing feet together and completing a Parallel Basic Step Forward.	2	Quick
5	Step R foot to the right moving into Parallel Position, left shoulders adjacent.	3-4	Slow
6	Step L foot forward in Parallel Position (toe outward) beginning to turn 3/8 turn to the left (counterclockwise).	1-2	Slow
7	Step R foot to the side to complete 3/8 turn to face your partner.	3	Quick
8	Step L foot to the right bringing feet together and completing a Parallel Basic Step Backward.	4	Quick

* Note: Remain in Closed Dance Position as you move down the line of dance executing the Parallel Basic step Forward and the Parallel Basic Step Backward.

Bootnote: You may repeat the sequence or return to the Basic Step Forward.

| Step 5 | Step 6 | Step 7 | Step 8 |

Texas Two-Step

Amalgamations

1. Basic Step Forward (three times)
Basic Step Turning Right (to execute 1/2 turn clockwise)
Basic Step Backward (three times)
Basic Step Turning Left (to execute 1/2 turn counter-clockwise)

2. Basic Step Backward (three times)
Sidewinder (several times)
Basic Step Backward

3. Basic Step Forward
Conversation Step (twice)
Continuous Conversation

4. Basic Step Forward
Underarm Turn
Basic Step Forward
Basic Step Parallel, forward and backward (three times)

FAVORITE TEXAS TWO-STEP SELECTIONS

"Bad Love" (medium) by Pake McEntire

"Ballroom Roses" (medium) by Mel McDaniel

"Cherokee Fiddle" (medium) by Johnny Lee

"Cow Town" (medium) by George Strait

"Diggin' Up Bones" (medium) by Randy Travis

"Fool Hearted Memory" (medium) by George Strait

"Girls, Women, and Ladies" (medium slow) by Ed Bruce

"Hangin' Around" (medium) by The Whites

"Heartbroke" (medium fast) by The Whites

"Here I Am Drunk Again" (medium) by Moe Bandy

"Honky Tonkin'" (medium fast) by Hank Williams, Jr.

"I'm Countryfied" (medium) by Mel McDaniel

"I'm Gonna Hire a Wino to Decorate My Home" (medium) by David Frizzell

"I'm Only in It For the Love" (medium fast) by John Conlee

"Let's Chase Each Other Around the Room" (medium) by Merle Haggard

"Long Haired Country Boy" (medium) by Charley Daniel's Band

"Louisiana Saturday Night" (medium) by Mel McDaniel

"Ocean Front Property" (medium) by George Strait

"Pure Love" (medium) by Ronnie Milsap

"Right or Wrong" (medium fast) by George Strait

"San Antonio Medley" (medium fast) by Darrell McCall and Curtis Potter

"San Antonio Rose" (medium fast) by Bob Wills and the Texas Playboys

"Step That Step" (medium) by Sawyer Brown

"Since I Found You" (medium) by Sweethearts of the Rodeo

"Somebody's Knocking" (medium fast) by Terri Gibbs

"Stay a Little Longer" (medium fast) by Mel Tillis

"Texas Proud" (medium slow) by Curtis Potter

"The Lady Takes the Cowboy Everytime" (medium) by Larry Gatlin and the Gatlin Brothers

"When You Need Someone to Hold" (medium) by Susie Taylor and Mike Wells.

Texas Two-Step Swing

Texas Two-Step Swing

The Texas Two-Step Swing consist of "break-a-way" movements and variations retaining the Texas Two-Step tempo and footwork of slow, slow, quick, quick. Underarm turn movements found in Western Swing and Western Polka such as the Whip, Sweetheart, Wringer, and Pretzel are also done in the Texas Two-Step Swing. Like Western Swing and Western Polka, the variations become more difficult to execute as the tempo gets faster. The Texas Two-Step is designed to progress around the dance floor. The Texas Two-Step Swing variations may progress or be executed in place. Combining the two dances as one through amalgamating the step patterns creates a more exciting dance. Because the Texas Two-Step is progressive, the dancers should take into consideration when executing Texas Two-Step Swing variations that are stationary they may be "halting traffic" unless they have ample room in which to execute their moves.

Texas Two-Step Swing is strongly influenced by the movements in Single-Time Swing (Jitterbug), which shares the same rhythmic cue of slow, slow, quick, quick.

Texas Two-Step Swing

1. Separation Basic
2. Whip (Alternate Underarms)
3. String-A-Long
4. Side Pass
5. Underarm Turn Right
6. Sweetheart
7. Wringer
8. Sweetheart to Wringer
9. Back to Back Turns
10. Pretzel
11. Lariat to Double Wringer
12. Advanced Two-Step Turns

Rhythmical Analysis

Texas Two-Step Swing----Time Signature 4/4

Step Pattern, Man:	Step Forward,	Step Forward,	Step Forward,	Step Together
Lady:	Step Backward,	Step Backward,	Step Backward,	Step Together
Count: Notation:	1,2	3,4	1	2
Rhythmical Cue:	Slow	Slow	Quick	Quick

To complete a basic Texas Two-Step Swing one will use 1-1/2 measures of music in 4/4 time.

Texas Two-Step Swing

Separation Basic
Man's Footwork

Step	Description	Timing	Rhythmic Cue	Lead
	Position: Closed Dance Position into Open Position with double hand hold. *			
1	Step L foot directly forward releasing Closed Position. Retain single hand hold (your left, her right).	1-2	Slow	L Hand hold
2	Step R foot directly forward passing L foot.	3-4	Slow	L Hand pressure
3	Step L foot to the left and slightly backward (small step) taking a double hand hold.	1	Quick	L Hand push
4	Step R foot to the left bringing feet together ending in Open Position with a double hand hold.	2	Quick	L and R Hand holds

* Note: The Separation Basic refers to the footwork and can be executed from Closed Dance Position into Open Dance Position with double hand hold or it may be executed in Open Dance Position with a double hand hold. The purpose of the Separation Basic is to create distance between partners which helps in executing designated variations.

Closed Dance
Position

Step 1

Step 2

Texas Two-Step Swing

Separation Basic
Lady's Footwork

Step	Description	Timing	Rhythmic Cue
	Position: Closed Dance Position into Open Position with double hand hold. *		
1	Step R foot directly backward releasing Closed Dance Position. Retain single hand hold (his left, your right).	1-2	Slow
2	Step L foot directly backward passing R foot.	3-4	Slow
3	Step R foot to the right and slightly backward taking a double hand hold.	1	Quick
4	Step L foot to the right bringing feet together ending in Open Position with a double hand hold.	2	Quick

* Note: The Separation Basic refers to the footwork and can be executed from Closed Dance Position into Open Dance Position with double hand hold or it may be executed in Open Dance Position with a double hand hold. The purpose of the Separation Basic is to create distance between partners which helps in executing designated variations.

Step 3   Step 4

Texas Two-Step Swing

Whip (Alternate Underarms)
Man's Footwork

Step	Description	Timing	Rhythmic Cue	Lead
	Position: Open Position with double hand hold *			
1	Step L foot diagonally to the left as you raise your R hand hold leading the lady to your right side.	1-2	Slow	L Hand hold pulls R Hand hold raises and encircles.
2	Step R foot forward pivoting 1/2 turn left (counter-clockwise) to face your partner. Encircle your head with your R hand hold releasing the L hand hold.	3-4	Slow	L Hand hold pulls and releases R Hand hold encircles.
3	Step L foot to the left and slightly backward. Re-take double hand hold at waist level.	1	Quick	Retake L Hand hold R Hand hold lowers
4	Step R foot to the left bringing feet together.	2	Quick	L and R Hand holds
5	Step L foot diagonally to the left as you raise your L hand hold leading the lady to your right side.	3-4	Slow	R Hand hold pulls L Hand hold raises and encircles
6	Step R foot forward pivoting 1/2 turn right (clock-wise) to face your partner. Encircle her head with your L hand hold as you release the R hand hold.	1-2	Slow	R Hand hold pulls and releases L Hand hold encircles
7	Step L foot to the left and slightly backward. Re-take double hand hold at waist level.	3	Quick	Retake R Hand hold L Hand hold lowers
8	Step R foot to the left bringing feet together.	4	Quick	L and R Hand holds

* Note: Precede with a Separation Basic.

Bootnote 1 : Small steps should be executed to attain proper distance from your partner. Too much or too little distance will cause movements to be awkward.

Bootnote 2 : The Whip may be repeated at your discretion. When you wish to return to the Basic Step Forward steps 7 and 8 should move forward instead of backward.

Texas Two-Step Swing

Whip (Alternate Underarms)
Lady's Footwork

Step	Description	Timing	Rhythmic Cue
	Position: Open Position with double hand hold *		
1	Step R foot diagonally to the left as the man raises your L hand hold.	1-2	Slow
2	Step L foot forward pivoting 1/2 turn right (clockwise) to face your partner as he encircles his head with your L hand hold. He then releases your R hand hold.	3-4	Slow
3	Step R foot to the right and slightly backward (small step) as he retakes your R hand hold.	1	Quick
4	Step L foot to the right bringing feet together.	2	Quick
5	Step R foot diagonally to the left as the man raises your R hand hold.	3-4	Slow
6	Step L foot forward pivoting 1/2 turn left (counterclockwise) to face your partner as he encircles your head with your R hand hold. He then releases your L hand hold.	1-2	Slow
7	Step R foot to the right and slightly backward (small step) as he retakes your L hand hold.	3	Quick
8	Step L foot to the right bringing feet together.	4	Quick

* Note: Precede with a Separation Basic.

Bootnote: Small steps should be executed to attain proper distance from your partner. Too much or too little distance will cause movements to be awkward.

Whip (Alternate Underarms)

Open Position with
Double Hand Hold

Step 1

Step 2

Step 5

Step 6

Whip (Alternate Underarms)

Step 3

Step 4

Step 7

Step 8

Texas Two-Step Swing

String-A-Long
Man's Footwork

Step	Description	Timing	Rhythmic Cue	Lead
	Position: Open Position with double hand hold *			
1	Step L foot diagonally to the left as you raise your L hand hold leading the lady to your right side.	1-2	Slow	R Hand hold pulls L Hand hold raises and encircles
2	Step R foot forward pivoting 1/2 turn left (counter clockwise) to face your partner as your L hand hold encircles your head. Release the R hand hold.	3-4	Slow	R Hand hold pulls and releases L Hand hold encircles and lowers
3	Step L foot to the left and slightly backward. Retake double hand hold at waist level.	1	Quick	Retake R Hand hold L Hand hold lowers
4	Step R foot to the left bringing feet together.	2	Quick	L and R Hand holds
5	Step L foot diagonally to the left as you raise your R hand hold leading the lady to your right side.	3-4	Slow	L Hand hold pulls R Hand hold raises and encircles
6	Step R foot forward pivoting 1/2 turn right (clockwise) to face your partner as your R hand hold encircles the lady's head. Release the L Hand hold.	1-2	Slow	L Hand hold pulls and releases R Hand hold encircles and lowers
7	Step L foot to the left and slightly backward. Retake double hand hold at waist level.	3	Quick	Retake L Hand hold R Hand hold lowers
8	Step R foot to the left bringing feet together.	4	Quick	L and R Hand holds.

* Note: Precede with a Separation Basic.

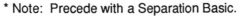

Bootnote 1: Small steps should be executed to attain proper distance from your partner. Too much or too little distance will cause movements to be awkward.

Bootnote 2: The String-A-Long may be repeated at your discretion. When you wish to return to the Basic Step Forward steps 7 and 8 should move forward instead of backward.

Texas Two-Step Swing

String-A-Long
Lady's Footwork

Step	Description	Timing	Rhythmic Cue
	Position: Open Position with double hand hold *		
1	Step R foot diagonally to the left as your partner raises your R hand hold.	1-2	Slow
2	Step L foot forward pivoting 1/2 turn right (clockwise) to face your partner as your R hand hold encircles his head. Release the L hand hold.	3-4	Slow
3	Step R foot to the right and slightly backward (small step). Retake your L hand hold.	1	Quick
4	Step L foot to the right bringing feet together.	2	Quick
5	Step R foot diagonally to the left as your partner raises your L hand hold.	3-4	Slow
6	Step L foot forward pivoting 1/2 turn left (counterclockwise) to face your partner as your L hand hold encircles your head. Release the R hand hold.	1-2	Slow
7	Step R foot to the right and slightly backward (small step). Retake your R hand hold.	3	Quick
8	Step L foot to the right bringing feet together.	4	Quick

* Note: Precede with a Separation Basic

Bootnote: Small steps should be executed to attain proper distance from your partner. Too much or too little distance will cause movements to be awkward.

String-a-Long

Open Position with
Double Hand Hold

Step 1

Step 2

Step 5

Step 6

String-a-Long

Step 3

Step 4

Step 7

Step 8

Texas Two-Step Swing

Side Pass/Neck Pass
Man's Footwork

Step	Description	Timing	Rhythmic Cue	Lead
	Position: Open Position with single hand hold (his left, her right)			
1	Step L foot diagonally to the left placing your L hand hold near your right side (waist level). Keep right arm above left arm.	1-2	Slow	L Hand hold pulls
2	Step R foot forward pivoting 1/2 turn left (counterclockwise) to face your partner as you release the L hand hold at waist level.	3-4	Slow	L Hand hold releases
3	Step L foot to the left and slightly backward. Retake the L hand hold at waist level.	1	Quick	Retake L Hand hold
4	Step R foot to the left bringing feet together.	2	Quick	L Hand hold

Neck Pass - To execute a Neck Pass, substitute the following for Step #1:

Step	Description	Timing	Rhythmic Cue	Lead
1	Step R foot diagonally to the left as the man places his L hand hold above his right shoulder at neck level. Keep right arm at waist level.	1-2	Slow	L Hand hold pulls and raises

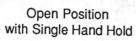

Bootnote: The Side Pass/Neck Pass is usually followed by an Underarm Turn Right.

Open Position
with Single Hand Hold

Step 1

Step 2

Texas Two-Step Swing

Side Pass/Neck Pass
Lady's Footwork

Step	Description	Timing	Rhythmic Cue
	Position: Open Position with single hand hold (his left, her right)		
1	Step R foot diagonally to the left as the man places your R hand hold near his right side (waist level).	1-2	Slow
2	Step L foot forward pivoting 1/2 turn right (clockwise) to face your partner as he releases your R hand hold.	3-4	Slow
3	Step R foot to the right and slightly backward (small step) as he retakes your R hand hold.	1	Quick
4	Step L foot to the right bringing feet together.	2	Quick

Neck Pass - To execute a Neck pass, substitute the following for Step #1:

Step	Description	Timing	Rhythmic Cue
1	Step R foot diagonally to the left as the man places your R hand hold above his right shoulder at neck level.	1-2	Slow

Bootnote: The Side Pass/Neck Pass is usually followed by an Underarm Turn Right.

Step 3   Step 4

Texas Two-Step Swing

Underarm Turn Right
Man's Footwork

Step	Description	Timing	Rhythmic Cue	Lead
	Position: Open Position with single hand hold (his left, her right)			
1	Step L foot diagonally to the left as you raise your L hand hold leading the lady to your right side.	1-2	Slow	L Hand hold pulls and raises
2	Step R foot forward pivoting 1/2 turn right (clockwise) to face your partner as you encircle her head with your L hand hold.	3-4	Slow	L Hand hold encircles and lowers
3	Step L foot to the left and slightly backward as you lower your L hand hold to waist level.	1	Quick	L Hand hold lowers
4	Step R foot to the left bringing feet together.	2	Quick	L Hand hold

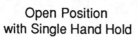 *Bootnote:* Repeat Side Pass/Neck Pass - Underarm Turn Right sequence or return to the Basic Step Forward.

Open Position
with Single Hand Hold

Step 1

Step 2

Texas Two-Step Swing

Underarm Turn Right
Lady's Footwork

Step	Description	Timing	Rhythmic Cue
	Position: Open Position with single hand hold (his left, her right)		
1	Step R foot diagonally to the left as the man raises your R hand hold leading you to his right side.	1-2	Slow
2	Step L foot forward pivoting 1/2 turn left (counter-clockwise) to face your partner as he encircles your head with your R hand hold.	3-4	Slow
3	Step R foot to the right and slightly backward (small step) as he lowers your R hand hold to waist level.	1	Quick
4	Step L foot to the right bringing feet together.	2	Quick

Bootnote: Repeat Side Pass/Neck Pass - Underarm Turn Right sequence or return to the Basic Step Forward.

Step 3   Step 4

Texas Two-Step Swing

Sweetheart
Man's Footwork

Step	Description	Timing	Rhythmic Cue	Lead
	Position: Open Position with double hand hold into Sweetheart Wrap Position. *			
1	Step L foot diagonally to the left beginning to move clockwise around your partner. The L hand hold begins to encircle the lady's head as the R hand hold remains at waist level.	1-2	Slow	R Hand hold pulls L Hand hold pulls and raises
2	Step R foot diagonally to the right, passing L foot, continuing to move around your partner.	3-4	Slow	L Hand hold encircles and lowers
3	Step L foot diagonally to the left, passing R foot, as you move around your partner into Sweetheart Wrap Position. L hand hold lowers to waist level.	1	Quick	L Hand hold lowers
4	Step R foot to the left bringing feet together with the lady on your right side.	2	Quick	R and L Hand holds
5	Step L foot diagonally to the right beginning to circle clockwise with your partner in Sweetheart Wrap Position. Lead the lady to circle backward with your R hand hold as you circle forward.	3-4	Slow	R Hand hold pulls
6	Step R foot diagonally to the right continuing clockwise circle.	1-2	Slow	R Hand hold pulls
7	Step L foot diagonally to the right completing approximately 1/2 circle clockwise.	3	Quick	R Hand hold pulls
8	Step R foot forward bringing feet together.	4	Quick	R Hand hold pulls
9	Step L foot diagonally to the right beginning to lead the lady out of Sweetheart Wrap Position. The R hand hold pulls at waist level as the L hand hold begins to encircle the lady's head to turn her clockwise.	1-2	Slow	R Hand hold pulls L Hand hold raises and encircles
10	Step R foot diagonally to the right as you complete movement out of Sweetheart Wrap Position.	3-4	Slow	L Hand hold encircles and lowers

Texas Two-Step Swing

Sweetheart
Lady's Footwork

Step	Description	Timing	Rhythmic Cue
	Position: Open Position with double hand hold into Sweetheart Wrap Position. *		
1	Step R foot directly forward as the man moves to your right side and begins to encircle your head with the R hand hold.	1-2	Slow
2	Step L foot directly forward passing R foot as the man continues to move around you clockwise.	3-4	Slow
3	Step R foot forward (small step) passing L foot as the man completes the movement into Sweetheart Wrap Position.	1	Quick
4	Step L foot forward bringing feet together.	2	Quick
5	Step R foot diagonally to the left (backward) beginning to circle clockwise with your partner in Sweetheart Wrap Position.	3-4	Slow
6	Step L foot diagonally to the left (backward) continuing clockwise circle.	1-2	Slow
7	Step R foot diagonally to the left completing approximately 1/2 circle clockwise.	3	Quick
8	Step L foot diagonally to the left (backward) bringing feet together.	4	Quick
9	Step R foot diagonally to the right as the man begins to lead you out of Sweetheart Wrap Position. The L hand hold pulls at waist level as the R hand hold encircles your head to turn you clockwise.	1-2	Slow
10	Step L foot diagonally to the right passing right foot as you complete the turn out of Sweetheart Wrap Position.	3-4	Slow

Texas Two-Step Swing

Sweetheart
Man's Footwork, cont'd

11	Step L foot to the left and slightly backward as you lower double hand hold to waist level.	1	Quick	R and L Hand holds
12	Step R foot to the left bringing feet together.	2	Quick	R and L Hand holds

* Note: Retain a double hand hold throughout entire Sweetheart.

Bootnote 1: Steps 1-4 take your partner into Sweetheart Wrap Position. Steps 5-8 circle clockwise in Sweetheart Wrap Position. Steps 9-12 take your partner out of Sweetheart Wrap Position into Open Dance Position with a double hand hold.

Bootnote 2: To continue Sweetheart movement repeat steps 5-8 as many times as you wish before taking your partner back to Open Dance Position with a double hand hold.

Open Position
with Double Hand Hold

Step 1

Step 3

Texas Two-Step Swing

Sweetheart
Lady's Footwork, cont'd

11	Step R foot backward as you lower double hand hold to waist level.	1	Quick
12	Step L foot backward bringing feet together.	2	Quick

* Note: Retain a double hand hold throughout entire Sweetheart.

Bootnote 1: Steps 1-4 take you into Sweetheart Wrap Position. Steps 5-8 circle clockwise in Sweetheart Wrap Position. Steps 9-12 take you out of Sweetheart Wrap Position into Open Dance Position with a double hand hold.

Bootnote 2: To continue Sweetheart movement repeat steps 5-8 as many times as you wish before returning to Open Dance Position with a double hand hold.

Steps 5-8   Step 9   Step 12

Texas Two-Step Swing

Wringer
Man's Footwork

Step	Description	Timing	Rhythmic Cue	Lead
	Position: Open Position with double hand hold *			
1	Step L foot in place as the L hand hold begins to encircle the lady's head to turn her 3/4 turn clockwise. The R hand hold remains at waist level.	1-2	Slow	L Hand hold encircles
2	Step R foot in place completing a clockwise turn of your partner. The L hand hold continues to encircle as the R hand hold is placed behind the lady's back.	3-4	Slow	L Hand hold encircles
3	Step L foot to the left (small step) making 1/4 turn counterclockwise. Lower the L hand hold to chest level with the R hand hold placed behind the lady's back.	1	Quick	L Hand hold lowers
4	Step R foot beside the L foot bringing feet together completing the movement into Wringer Position.	2	Quick	L Hand hold lowers
5	Step L foot diagonally to the right beginning to circle clockwise with your partner in Wringer Position. With the R hand hold on the lady's back lead her to circle forward as you circle forward.	3-4	Slow	R Hand pressure
6	Step R foot diagonally to the right continuing to lead the lady in a clockwise circle.	1-2	Slow	R Hand pressure
7	Step L foot diagonally to the right completing approximately 1/2 circle clockwise.	3	Quick	R Hand pressure
8	Step R foot forward bringing feet together.	4	Quick	R Hand pressure
9	Step L foot diagonally to the right beginning to lead the lady out of Wringer Position. The R hand hold pulls as the L hand hold begins to encircle the lady to turn her counterclockwise.	1-2	Slow	R Hand hold pulls L Hand hold encircles
10	Step R foot to the left and slightly backward as you lower double hand hold to waist level.	3-4	Slow	L Hand hold encircles

Texas Two-Step Swing

Wringer
Lady's Footwork

Step	Description	Timing	Rhythmic Cue
	Position: Open Position with double hand hold *		
1	Step R foot diagonally to the right (small step) beginning 3/4 turn clockwise into Wringer Position. Your R hand hold encircles your head as your L hand hold remains at waist level.	1-2	Slow
2	Step L foot around R foot completing clockwise turn as your R hand hold continues to encircle your head.	3-4	Slow
3	Step R foot forward (small step) into Wringer Position. Lower R hand hold to chest level as L hand hold is placed behind your back.	1	Quick
4	Step L foot forward bringing feet together completing the movement into Wringer Position.	2	Quick
5	Step R foot diagonally to the right beginning to circle clockwise with your partner in Wringer Position.	3-4	Slow
6	Step L foot diagonally to the right continuing clockwise circle.	1-2	Slow
7	Step R foot diagonally to the right completing approximately 1/2 circle clockwise.	3	Quick
8	Step L foot forward bringing feet together.	4	Quick
9	Step R foot diagonally to the left around left foot pivoting to face your partner. Your R hand hold will encircle your head turning you counterclockwise.	1-2	Slow
10	Step L foot diagonally to the left completing the movement out of Wringer Position.	3-4	Slow

Texas Two-Step Swing

Wringer
Man's Footwork, cont'd

11	Step L foot to the left and slightly backward as you lower double hand hold to waist level.	1	Quick	L Hand hold encircles
12	Step R foot to the left bringing feet together completing the Wringer.	2	Quick	L and R hand holds

* Note: Retain a double hand hold throughout entire Wringer.

Bootnote 1: Steps 1-4 take your partner into Wringer Position. Steps 5-8 circle clockwise in Wringer Position. Steps 9-12 take your partner out of Wringer into Open Position with a double hand hold.

Bootnote 2: To continue Wringer movement repeat steps 5-8 as many times as you wish before taking your partner back to Open Position. Wringer should end with man facing down his line of dance.

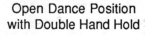

Open Dance Position with Double Hand Hold

Step 1

Step 2

Step 4

Texas Two-Step Swing

Wringer
Lady's Footwork, cont'd

11	Step R foot to the right and slightly backward to face your partner as you lower double hand hold to waist level.	1	Quick
12	Step L foot to the right bringing feet together completing the Wringer.	2	Quick

* Note: Retain a double hand hold throughout entire Wringer.

Bootnote 1: Steps 1-4 take you into Wringer Position. Steps 5-8 circle clockwise in Wringer Position. Steps 9-12 take you out of Wringer Position into Open Dance Position with a double hand hold.

Bootnote 2: To continue Wringer movement repeat steps 5-8 as many times as you wish before returning to Open Dance Position with a double hand hold.

Steps 5-8   Step 9   Step 12

Texas Two-Step Swing

Sweetheart into Wringer
Man's Footwork

Step	Description	Timing	Rhythmic Cue	Lead
	Position: Open Position with double hand hold into Sweetheart Wrap Position into Wringer Position. *			
1	Step L foot diagonally to the left beginning to move clockwise around your partner. Raise the L hand hold beginning to encircle the lady's head. Keep the R hand hold at waist level.	1-2	Slow	R Hand hold pulls L Hand hold lifts and encircles
2	Step R foot diagonally to the left, passing L foot, as you progress around your partner into Sweetheart Wrap Position. Lower the L hand hold to waist level.	3-4	Slow	L Hand hold encircles and lowers
3	Step L foot diagonally to the left, passing R foot, as you progress around your partner into Sweetheart Wrap Position. Lower the L hand hold to waist level.	1	Quick	L Hand hold lowers
4	Step R foot to the left bringing feet together with the lady on your right side.	2	Quick	R and L Hand holds
5	Step L foot diagonally to the right beginning to circle clockwise with your partner in Sweetheart Wrap Position. Lead the lady to circle backward with the R hand hold as you circle forward.	3-4	Slow	R Hand hold pulls
6	Step R foot diagonally to the right continuing clockwise circle.	1-2	Slow	R Hand hold pulls
7	Step L foot diagonally to the right completing approximately 1/2 circle clockwise.	3	Quick	R Hand hold pulls
8	Step R foot forward bringing feet together.	4	Quick	R Hand hold pulls
9	Step L foot in place as the L hand hold begins to lead the lady from Sweetheart Wrap Position into Wringer Position. The L hand hold begins to encircle the lady's head to turn her 1-1/2 turns in place clockwise.	1-2	Slow	R Hand hold pulls L Hand hold raises and encircles
10	Step R foot in place continuing to encircle the lady's head with your L hand hold. The R hand hold remains at waist level.	3-4	Slow	L Hand hold encircles

Texas Two-Step Swing

Sweetheart into Wringer
Lady's Footwork

Step	Description	Timing	Rhythmic Cue
	Position: Open Position with double hand hold into Sweetheart Wrap Position into Wringer Position. *		
1	Step R foot directly forward as the man steps to your right side and begins to encircle your head with your R hand hold.	1-2	Slow
2	Step L foot directly forward passing R foot as the man continues to circle around you clockwise.	3-4	Slow
3	Step R foot forward (small step) passing L foot as the man completes the movement into Sweetheart Wrap Position.	1	Quick
4	Step L foot forward bringing feet together.	2	Quick
5	Step R foot diagonally to the left (backward) beginning to circle clockwise with your partner in Sweetheart Wrap Position.	3-4	Slow
6	Step L foot diagonally to the left (backward) continuing clockwise circle.	1-2	Slow
7	Step R foot diagonally to the left completing approximately 1/2 circle clockwise.	3	Quick
8	Step L foot diagonally to the left (backward) bringing feet together.	4	Quick
9	Step R foot diagonally to the right as the man begins to lead you from Sweetheart Wrap Position. Lead consists of your R hand hold beginning to encircle your head to turn you in place 1-1/2 turns clockwise.	1-2	Slow
10	Step L foot around the right foot completing clockwise turn out of Sweetheart Wrap Position and beginning clockwise turn into Wringer Position. The R hand hold continues to encircle your head as the L hand hold remains at waist level.	3-4	Slow

Texas Two-Step Swing

Sweetheart into Wringer
Man's Footwork, cont'd

11	Step L foot in place continuing to encircle the lady's head as you complete clockwise turn. The R hand hold is placed behind the lady's back at waist level.	1	Quick	L Hand hold encircles
12	Step R foot in place bringing feet together as you lower L hand hold to chest level completing the lead into Wringer Position. The R hand hold is behind the lady's back.	2	Quick	L Hand hold lowers
13	Step L foot diagonally to the right beginning to circle clockwise with your partner in Wringer Position.	3-4	Slow	R Hand pressure
14	Step R foot diagonally to the right continuing to lead the lady into clockwise circle.	1-2	Slow	R Hand pressure
15	Step L foot diagonally to the right completing approximately 1/2 circle clockwise.	3	Quick	R Hand pressure
16	Step R foot forward bringing feet together.	4	Quick	R Hand pressure
17	Step L foot diagonally to the right beginning to lead the lady out of Wringer Position. The R hand hold pulls as the L hand hold begins to turn the lady counterclockwise.	1-2	Slow	R Hand hold pulls L Hand hold encircles
18	Step R foot diagonally to the right as you continue to lead the lady out of Wringer Position.	3-4	Slow	L Hand hold encircles and lowers
19	Step L foot to the left and slightly backward as you lower double hand hold to waist level.	1	Quick	L Hand hold lowers
20	Step R foot to the left bringing feet together completing the Wringer.	2	Quick	R and L Hand holds

*Note: Retain a double hand hold throughout the entire Sweetheart to Wringer.

Bootnote 1: Steps 1-4 take your partner into Sweetheart Wrap Position. Steps 5-8 circle clockwise in Sweetheart Wrap Position. Steps 9-12 take your partner from Sweetheart Wrap Position into Wringer Position (footwork is executed in place with the lady remaining on the man's right side). Steps 13-16 circle clockwise in Wringer Position. Steps 17-20 take your partner out of Wringer Position into Open Position.

Bootnote 2: The circle clockwise in Sweetheart Wrap Position and in Wringer Position may be repeated as many times as you wish before taking partner back to Open Position. Sweetheart into Wringer should end with the man facing down his line of dance.

Texas Two-Step Swing

Sweetheart into Wringer
Lady's Footwork, cont'd

11	Step R foot diagonally to the right as the man continues to encircle your head completing 1-1/2 turns into Wringer Position. The R hand hold is placed behind your back at waist level.	1	Quick
12	Step L foot forward bringing feet together as the man lowers your R hand hold to chest level. The L hand hold is behind your back at waist level.	2	Quick
13	Step R foot diagonally to the right beginning to circle clockwise with your partner in Wringer Position.	3-4	Slow
14	Step L foot diagonally to the right continuing clockwise circle.	1-2	Slow
15	Step R foot diagonally to the right completing approximately 1/2 circle clockwise.	3	Quick
16	Step L foot forward bringing feet together.	4	Quick
17	Step R foot diagonally to the left around left foot pivoting to face your partner. Your R hand hold will encircle your head to turn you counter-clockwise.	1-2	Slow
18	Step L foot diagonally to the left completing movement out of Wringer Position.	3-4	Slow
19	Step R foot to the right and slightly backward as you lower double hand hold to waist level.	1	Quick
20	Step L foot to the right bringing feet together completing the Wringer.	2	Quick

* Note: Retain a double hand hold throughout the entire Sweetheart to Wringer.

Bootnote 1: Steps 1-4 take you into Sweetheart Wrap Position. Steps 5-8 circle clockwise in Sweetheart Wrap Position. Steps 9-12 take you from Sweetheart Wrap Position into Wringer Position (footwork is executed in place with the lady remaining on the man's right side). Steps 13-16 circle clockwise in Wringer Position. Steps 17-20 take you out of Wringer Position into Open Position.

Bootnote 2: The circle clockwise in Sweetheart Wrap Position and in Wringer Position may be repeated as many times as you wish before returning to Open Position. Sweetheart into Wringer should end with the man facing down his line of dance.

150

Sweetheart Into Wringer

Open Dance Position

Step 1

Step 3

Steps 5-8

Step 11

Step 12

Sweetheart Into Wringer

Step 9

Step 10

Steps 13-16

Step 18

Step 20

Texas Two-Step Swing

Back to Back Turns
Man's Footwork

Step	Description	Timing	Rhythmic Cue	Lead
	Position: Conversation Position *			
1	Step L foot directly forward in Conversation Position.	1-2	Slow	R Palm pressure
2	Step R foot directly forward passing L foot.	3-4	Slow	R Palm pressure
3	Step L foot directly forward passing R foot.	1	Quick	R Palm pressure
4	Step R foot forward bringing feet together.	2	Quick	R Palm pressure
5	Step L foot directly forward pivoting 1/2 turn clockwise. Release R hand from the lady's shoulder blade as the L hand hold lowers below waist level leading the lady to pivot 1/2 turn counterclockwise. Partners now face opposite line of dance with his left shoulder adjacent to her right shoulder.	3-4	Slow	R Hand releases L Hand hold lowers
6	Step R foot directly backward progressing down the line of dance with partner on your left side. Raise and extend the L hand hold outward at chest level.	1-2	Slow	L Hand hold raises and extends
7	Step L foot directly backward, passing R foot, continuing to progress down the line of dance.	3	Quick	L Hand hold extended
8	Step R foot directly backward bringing feet together.	4	Quick	L Hand hold extended
9	Step L foot down the line of dance turning 1/2 turn counterclockwise pivoting another 1/2 turn to face opposite the line of dance. L hand hold leads lady (firmly) to begin 1-1/2 turn clockwise. Release L hand hold following lead.	1-2	Slow	L Hand hold toss
10	Step R foot directly backward pivoting 1/2 turn counterclockwise to face down the line of dance completing 1-1/2 turns.	3-4	Slow	
11	Step L foot directly forward progressing down the line of dance with your partner on your right. Take a R hand hold (her left) with hand hold extended forward at chest level.	1	Quick	R Hand hold
12	Step R foot forward bringing feet together.	2	Quick	R Hand hold
13	Step L foot directly forward down the line of dance with the lady on your right. Retain the R hand hold extended at chest level.	3-4	Slow	R Hand hold

Texas Two-Step Swing

Back to Back Turns
Lady's Footwork

Step	Description	Timing	Rhythmic Cue
	Position: Conversation Position *		
1	Step R foot directly forward in Conversation Position.	1-2	Slow
2	Step L foot directly forward passing R foot.	3-4	Slow
3	Step R foot directly forward passing L foot.	1	Quick
4	Step L foot forward bringing feet together.	2	Quick
5	Step R foot directly forward as the man leads you to pivot 1/2 turn counterclockwise out of Conversation Position. The R hand hold lowers below waist level as you turn to face opposite line of dance with your right shoulder adjacent to your partner's left shoulder.	3-4	Slow
6	Step L foot directly backward progressing down the line of dance with your partner on your right side. Raise and extend the R hand hold to chest level.	1-2	Slow
7	Step R foot directly backward passing the L foot continuing to progress down the line of dance.	3	Quick
8	Step L foot directly backward bringing feet together.	4	Quick
9	Step R foot down the line of dance turning 1/2 turn clockwise pivoting another 1/2 turn to face opposite the line of dance. Hand hold (his left, your right) leads you to begin 1-1/2 turns clockwise. Release hand hold following lead.	1-2	Slow
10	Step L foot directly backward pivoting 1/2 turn clockwise to face down the line of dance completing 1-1/2 turns.	3-4	Slow
11	Step R foot directly forward progressing down the line of dance. With your partner on your left take extended hand hold (his right, your left).	1	Quick
12	Step L foot forward bringing feet together.	2	Quick
13	Step R foot directly forward down the line of dance with the man on your left. Retain the L hand hold extended at chest level.	3-4	Slow

Texas Two-Step Swing

Back to Back Turns
Man's Footwork, cont'd

14	Step R foot directly forward passing L foot.	1-2	Slow	R Hand hold
15	Step L foot directly forward passing R foot.	3	Quick	R Hand hold
16	Step R foot forward bringing feet together.	4	Quick	R Hand hold
17	Step L foot directly forward pivoting a full turn clockwise to face down the line of dance. The R hand hold leads the lady (firmly) to turn a full turn counterclockwise. Release the R hand hold following the lead.	1-2	Slow	R Hand hold toss
18	Step R foot forward down the line of dance.	3-4	Slow	
19	Step L foot directly forward, passing right foot, returning to Conversation Position.	1	Quick	R Palm pressure
20	Step R foot forward bringing feet together completing Back to Back Turns.	2	Quick	R Palm pressure

* Note: Back to Back turns progress down the line of dance with the lady on the outside and the man on the inside.

Bootnote 1: Keep arms at chest level during pivot turns. Turns are executed towards your partner.

Bootnote 2: Steps 1-4 comprise a Basic Step progressing forward in Conversation Position. Steps 5-8 execute a 1/2 turn clockwise to progress backward down your line of dance. Steps 9-12 execute 1-1/2 turns counterclockwise to end facing down your line of dance. Steps 13-16 comprise a Basic Step progressing forward with the lady on your right. Steps 17-20 execute a full turn clockwise to end facing down your line of dance in Conversation Position.

Texas Two-Step Swing

Back to Back Turns
Lady's Footwork, cont'd

14	Step L foot directly forward passing R foot.	1-2	Slow
15	Step R foot directly forward passing L foot.	3	Quick
16	Step L foot forward bringing feet together.	4	Quick
17	Step R foot forward pivoting a full turn counter-clockwise to face down the line of dance. Hand hold (his right, your left) leads you to execute a full turn. Release the hand hold following lead.	1-2	Slow
18	Step L foot forward down the line of dance.	3-4	Slow
19	Step R foot directly forward passing L foot returning to Conversation Position.	1	Quick
20	Step L foot forward bringing feet together completing Back to Back Turns.	2	Quick

* Note: Back to Back turns progress down the line of dance with the lady on the outside and the man on the inside.

Bootnote 1: Keep arms at chest level during pivot turns. Turns are executed towards your partner.

Bootnote 2: Steps 1-4 comprise a Basic Step progressing forward in Conversation Position. Steps 5-8 execute a 1/2 turn counterclockwise to progress backward down your line of dance. Steps 9-12 execute 1-1/2 turns counterclockwise to end facing down your line of dance. Steps 13-16 comprise a Basic Step progressing forward with the man on your left. Steps 17-20 execute a full turn counterclockwise to end facing down your line of dance in Conversation Position.

Back to Back Turns

Conversation
Position

Step 1

Step 5

Step 11

Step 12

Step 15

Back to Back Turns

Step 6

Step 9

Step 10

Step 17

Step 18

Step 20

Texas Two-Step Swing

Pretzel
Man's Footwork

Step	Description	Timing	Rhythmic Cue	Lead
	Position: Open Position with double hand hold *			
1	Step L foot diagonally to the left turning counter-clockwise beginning to raise your L hand hold to encircle your head. The R hand hold is placed behind your back. (Lady will execute steps 1-4 in place).	1-2	Slow	L Hand hold encircles R Hand hold placed
2	Step R foot around L foot continuing counter-clockwise turn to face your partner. The L hand hold encircles your head and begins to lower to waist level. The R hand hold is placed behind your back at waist level.	3-4	Slow	R Hand hold placed L Hand hold encircles and lowers
3	Step L foot to the left completing a full turn counterclockwise to face your partner. Extend the L hand hold to the left at waist level. The R hand hold is wrapped behind your back.	1	Quick	L Hand hold extends
4	Step R foot beside L foot.	2	Quick	
5	Step L foot diagonally to the right (turning clockwise). Raise the L hand hold to encircle the lady's head and then lower it near waist level. Keep the R hand hold near waist level ending in a Back to Back Position.	3-4	Slow	L Hand hold encircles and lowers
6	Step R foot diagonally to the right continuing clockwise turn to face your partner. The R hand hold encircles the lady's head turning her 1/2 turn clockwise, and begins to lower to waist level. The L hand hold is placed behind your back at waist level.	1-2	Slow	L Hand hold placed R Hand hold encircles and lowe
7	Step L foot to the left completing a full turn clockwise to face your partner. Extend the R hand hold to the right at waist level. The L hand hold is wrapped behind your back.	3	Quick	R Hand hold lowers
8	Step R foot beside L foot.	4	Quick	
9	Step L foot diagonally to the left turning counter-clockwise raising your R hand hold to encircle your head. The L hand hold remains at waist level.	1-2	Slow	R Hand hold encircles
10	Step R foot around L foot continuing counter-clockwise turn to face your partner. Lower your R hand hold to waist level beside L hand hold.	3-4	Slow	R Hand hold lowers

Texas Two-Step Swing

Pretzel
Lady's Footwork

Step	Description	Timing	Rhythmic Cue
	Position: Open Position with double hand hold *		
1	Step R foot in place as the man begins to turn counterclockwise under his L hand hold. Your R hand hold begins to encircle the man's head as your L hand hold is placed behind his back.	1-2	Slow
2	Step L foot in place as the man continues counterclockwise turn. The R hand hold encircles the man's head and begins to lower to waist level. The L hand hold is placed behind his back at waist level.	3-4	Slow
3	Step R foot in place as your partner completes a counterclockwise turn to face you. Extend the R hand hold to the right at waist level with the L hand hold behind your partners back.	1	Quick
4	Step L foot beside R foot.	2	Quick
5	Step R foot diagonally to the right (turning clockwise). Raise R hand hold to encircle your head and then lower it near waist level. Keep the L hand hold near waist level ending in a Back to Back Position.	3-4	Slow
6	Step L foot diagonally to the right around R foot completing a clockwise turn to face your partner. The L hand hold encircles your head and begins to lower to waist level. The R hand hold remains at waist level.	1-2	Slow
7	Step R foot to the right completing a full turn clockwise to face your partner. Extend the L hand hold to the left at waist level. The R hand hold is place behind your partner's back.	3	Quick
8	Step L foot beside R foot.	4	Quick
9	Step R foot in place as the L hand hold encircles the man's head. The R hand hold remains at waist level.	1-2	Slow
10	Step L foot in place. The L hand hold lowers beside the R hand hold as your partner turns to face you.	3-4	Slow

Texas Two-Step Swing

Pretzel
Man's Footwork, cont'd

11	Step L foot forward (small step) leading the lady into Sweetheart Wrap Position. The L hand hold encircles the lady's head, lowering to waist level, as you lead her into 1/2 turn counterclockwise to your right side. The R hand hold remains at waist level.	

	1	Quick	L Hand hold encircles and lowers
12	Step R foot beside L foot.		
	2	Quick	L Hand hold lowers
13	Step L foot in place leading the lady out of Sweetheart Wrap Position. The L hand hold encircles the lady's head, turning her 1/2 turn clockwise to face you. The R hand hold remains at waist level.		
	3-4	Slow	L Hand hold encircles
14	Step R foot in place as you lower the L hand hold to waist level.		
	1-2	Slow	L Hand hold lowers
15	Step L foot to the left and slightly forward.	3	Quick	Double hand hold pressure
16	Step R foot to the left bringing feet together to complete the Pretzel.	4	Quick	Double hand hold pressure

* Note: Retain a double hand hold throughout entire Pretzel.

Open Position with
Double Hand Hold

Step 1

Step 2

Step 8

Step 9

Step 10

Texas Two-Step Swing

Pretzel
Lady's Footwork, cont'd

11	Step R foot diagonally to the left pivoting 1/2 turn counterclockwise into Sweetheart Wrap Position. The R hand hold encircles your head, lowering to waist level. The L hand hold remains at waist level.	1	Quick
12	Step L foot beside R foot.	2	Quick
13	Step R foot diagonally to the right out of Sweetheart Wrap Position as you pivot 1/2 turn clockwise to face your partner. The R hand hold encircles your head as the L hand hold remains at waist level.	3-4	Slow
14	Step L foot beside right foot as the R hand hold lowers to waist level.	1-2	Slow
15	Step R foot to the right and slightly backward.	3	Quick
16	Step L foot to the right bringing feet together to complete the Pretzel.	4	Quick

* Note: Retain a double hand hold throughout entire Pretzel.

Step 4

Step 5

Step 7

Step 11

Step 12

Step 16

Texas Two-Step Swing

Lariat into Double Wringer
Man's Footwork

Step	Description	Timing	Rhythmic Cue	Lead
	Position: Open Position with double hand hold *			
1	Step L foot forward (small step) as you begin to lead the lady past your right side to move clockwise around you.	1-2	Slow	Double hand hold pulls and raises
2	Step R foot forward (small step) as you continue the lead for the Lariat movement beginning to encircle your head with double hand hold. The lady will progress clockwise around you.	3-4	Slow	Double hand hold encircles
3	Step L foot forward (small step) continuing Lariat movement.	1	Quick	Double hand hold encircles
4	Step R foot forward bringing feet together. Lead has positioned your partner directly behind you.	2	Quick	Double hand hold encircles
5	Step L foot backward (small step) as you continue to lead the lady clockwise around you passing your left side.	3-4	Slow	Double hand hold encircles
6	Step R foot backward (small step) as you continue Lariat movement.	1-2	Slow	Double hand hold encircles
7	Step L foot backward (small step).	3	Quick	Double hand hold encircles
8	Step R foot backward bringing feet together as you complete Lariat movement facing your partner in Open Position. Lower double hand hold to chest level.	4	Quick	Double hand hold lowers slightly
9	Step L foot in place beginning to circle the lady's head with double hand hold to turn her clockwise.	1-2	Slow	Double hand hold encircles
10	Step R foot in place completing clockwise turn of partner and beginning clockwise turn into Wringer Position. The L hand hold continues to encircle the lady's head as the R hand hold lowers to waist level.	3-4	Slow	L Hand hold encircles R Hand hold lowers
11	Step L foot to the L (small step) making 1/4 turn counterclockwise. Lower L hand hold to chest level with the R hand hold placed behind the lady's back in Wringer Position.	1	Quick	L Hand hold lowers R Hand hold placed
12	Step R foot next to L foot bringing feet together completing movement into Wringer Position.	2	Quick	L Hand hold extends

Texas Two-Step Swing

Lariat into Double Wringer
Lady's Footwork

Step	Description	Timing	Rhythmic Cue
	Position: Open Position with double hand hold *		
1	Step R foot diagonally to the left as the man begins to lead you to his right to move clockwise around him. Lead consists of a double hand hold encircling the man's head.	1-2	Slow
2	Step L foot diagonally to the left as you continue Lariat movement.	3-4	Slow
3	Step R foot forward continuing to circle your partner clockwise.	1	Quick
4	Step L foot forward bringing feet together. Lead has positioned you directly behind your partner.	2	Quick
5	Step R foot diagonally to the right as the man continues to lead you clockwise past his left side.	3-4	Slow
6	Step L foot diagonally to the right as you continue Lariat movement.	1-2	Slow
7	Step R foot diagonally to the right continuing to circle your partner clockwise.	3	Quick
8	Step L foot to the right bringing feet together as you complete Lariat movement facing your partner in Open Position.	4	Quick
9	Step R foot diagonally to the right as the man begins to turn you clockwise. Double hand hold encircles your head.	1-2	Slow
10	Step L foot around R foot as you complete a full turn and begin clockwise turn into Wringer. Your R hand hold encircles your head.	3-4	Slow
11	Step R foot diagonally to the right continuing clockwise turn into Wringer Position. Your L hand hold is placed behind your back at waist level.	1	Quick
12	Step L foot beside R foot completing the movement into Wringer Position. Your L hand hold is placed behind your back at waist level.	2	Quick

Texas Two-Step Swing

Lariat into Double Wringer
Man's Footwork, cont'd

13	Step L foot diagonally to the right beginning to circle clockwise with your partner in Wringer Position. With the R hand hold on the lady's back lead her to circle forward as you circle forward.	3-4	Slow	R Hand pressure
14	Step R foot diagonally to the right continuing to lead the lady into a clockwise circle.	1-2	Slow	R Hand pressure
15	Step L foot diagonally to the right completing approximately 1/2 circle clockwise.	3	Quick	R Hand pressure
16	Step R foot forward bringing feet together.	4	Quick	R Hand pressure
17	Step L foot diagonally to the right beginning to move clockwise around your partner leading the lady out of Wringer Position into Reverse Wringer Position. The L hand hold encircles the lady's head to turn her counterclockwise in place as the R hand hold remains at waist level.	1-2	Slow	L Hand hold encircles
18	Step R foot diagonally to the right continuing to circle clockwise around your partner. The L hand hold begins to lower to waist level as the R hand hold begins to encircle the lady's head counterclockwise leading her into Reverse Wringer Position.	3-4	Slow	L Hand hold lowers R Hand hold encircles
19	Step L foot diagonally to the left pivoting 1/2 turn into Reverse Wringer Position. Lower the R hand hold to chest level and place the L hand hold behind the lady's back at waist level.	1	Quick	R Hand hold lowers L Hand hold placed
20	Step R foot to the left bringing feet together completing movement into Reverse Wringer Position. Partner is on your left facing the opposite direction.	2	Quick	
21	Step L foot diagonally ro the left beginning to circle counterclockwise with your partner in Reverse Wringer Position. With the L hand hold on the lady's back lead her to circle forward as you circle forward.	3-4	Slow	L Hand hold pressure
22	Step R foot diagonally to the left continuing counterclockwise circle.	1-2	Slow	L Hand hold pressure
23	Step L foot diagonally to the left completing approximately 1/2 circle counterclockwise.	3	Quick	L Hand hold pressure
24	Step R foot forward bringing feet together.	4	Quick	L Hand hold pressure

Texas Two-Step Swing

Lariat into Double Wringer
Lady's Footwork, cont'd

13	Step R foot diagonally to the right beginning to circle clockwise with your partner in Wringer Position.	3-4	Slow
14	Step L foot diagonally to the right continuing clockwise circle.	1-2	Slow
15	Step R foot diagonally to the right completing approximately 1/2 circle clockwise.	3	Quick
16	Step L foot forward bringing feet together.	4	Quick
17	Step R foot diagonally to the left as the man begins to lead you to turn counterclockwise out of Wringer into Reverse Wringer. Your movement is executed in place as the man travels clockwise around you. The R hand hold encircles your head as the L hand hold remains at waist level.	1-2	Slow
18	Step L foot backward around R foot as you complete counterclockwise turn out of Wringer and begin to turn into Reverse Wringer. The R hand hold is lowered to waist level as the L hand hold begins to encircle your head counterclockwise.	3-4	Slow
19	Step R foot diagonally to the left pivoting to turn counterclockwise into Reverse Wringer Position. The R hand hold is lowered to chest level and the L hand hold is placed behind your back at waist level.	1	Quick
20	Step L foot to the right bringing feet together completing movement into Reverse Wringer Position. Partner is on your left facing opposite direction.	2	Quick
21	Step R foot diagonally to the left beginning to circle counterclockwise with your partner in Reverse Wringer Position. The man will lead you to circle forward as he circles forward.	3-4	Slow
22	Step L foot diagonally to the left continuing counterclockwise circle.	1-2	Slow
23	Step R foot diagonally to the left completing approximately 1/2 circle counterclockwise.	3	Quick
24	Step L foot forward bringing feet together.	4	Quick

Texas Two-Step Swing

Lariat into Double Wringer
Man's Footwork, cont'd

25	Step L foot diagonally to the left continuing to circle counterclockwise with your partner in Reverse Wringer Position. With the L hand hold on the lady's back lead her to circle forward as you circle forward.	1-2	Slow	L Hand hold pressure
26	Step R foot diagonally to the left continuing counterclockwise circle.	3-4	Slow	L Hand hold pressure
27	Step L foot diagonally to the left completing approximately one circle counterclockwise.	1	Quick	L Hand hold pressure
28	Step R foot forward bringing feet together.	2	Quick	L Hand hold pressure
29	Step L foot diagonally to the left (small step) beginning to lead the lady out of Reverse Wringer Position. The L hand hold pulls at waist level as the R hand hold begins to encircle the lady's head turning her clockwise to face you.	3-4	Slow	L Hand hold pulls R Hand hold encircles
30	Step R foot beside L foot continuing to lead the lady out of Reverse Wringer Position.	1-2	Slow	R Hand hold encircles and lowers
31	Step L foot beside R foot and slightly forward as you face your partner. Lower double hand hold to waist level.	3	Quick	R Hand hold lowers
32	Step R foot to the left bringing feet together completing Lariat to Double Wringer.	4	Quick	Double Hand hold

* Note: Retain a double hand hold throughout entire Lariat into Double Wringer.

 Bootnote: Steps 1-8 comprise the Lariat. Steps 9-12 turn your partner in place leading her into Wringer Position. Steps 13-16 circle clockwise in Wringer Position. Steps 17-20 turn your partner in place leading her out of Wringer Position and into Reverse Wringer Position. Steps 21-28 circle counterclockwise in Reverse Wringer Position. Steps 29-32 turn your partner in place leading her out of Reverse Wringer Position into Open Position with a double hand hold.

Texas Two-Step Swing

Lariat into Double Wringer
Lady's Footwork, cont'd

25	Step R foot diagonally to the left continuing to circle counterclockwise with your partner in Reverse Wringer Position. The man will lead you to circle forward as he circles forward.	1-2	Slow
26	Step L foot diagonally to the left continuing counterclockwise circle.	3-4	Slow
27	Step R foot diagonally to the left completing approximately one circle counterclockwise.	1	Quick
28	Step L foot forward bringing feet together.	2	Quick
29	Step R foot diagonally to the right as the man begins to lead you out of Reverse Wringer Position. The R hand hold remains at waist level as the L hand hold begins to encircle your head to turn you clockwise to face your partner.	3-4	Slow
30	Step L foot diagonally to the right around R foot as you continue to turn out of Reverse Wringer Position.	1-2	Slow
31	Step R foot to the right and slightly backward as you face your partner lowering double hand hold to waist level.	3	Quick
32	Step L foot to the right bringing feet together completing Lariat to Double Wringer.	4	Quick

* Note: Retain a double hand hold throughout entire Lariat into Double Wringer.

Bootnote: Steps 1-8 comprise the Lariat. Steps 9-12 turn you in place into Wringer Position. Steps 13-16 circle clockwise in Wringer Position. Steps 17-20 turn you in place leading you out of Wringer Position and into Reverse Wringer Position. Steps 21-28 circle counterclockwise in Reverse Wringer Position. Steps 29-32 turn you in place out of Reverse Wringer Position into Open Position with a double hand hold.

Lariat into Double Wringer

Open Position with
Double Hand Hold

Step 1

Step 5

Step 8

Step 16

Step 17

Step 18

Step 20

Lariat into Double Wringer

Step 9

Step 10

Step 11

Step 12

Step 24

Step 29

Step 30

Step 31

Texas Two-Step Swing

Advanced Two-Step Turns
Man's Footwork

Step	Description	Timing	Rhythmic Cue	Lead
	Position: Closed Dance Position *			
1	Step L foot directly forward.	1-2	Slow	R Heel pressure
2	Step R foot diagonally to the right turning 1/4 turn clockwise. Lead keeps the lady directly in front of you as your R foot steps between her feet.	3-4	Slow	R Finger pressure
3	Step L foot directly to the left positioning your left side to face down the line of dance.	1	Quick	R Hand hold
4	Step R foot to the left bringing feet together.	2	Quick	R Palm pressure
5	Step L foot around your partner and pivot to complete 3/4 turn clockwise with your partner in Closed Position. End facing down the line of dance.	3-4	Slow	R Finger pressure
6	Step R foot diagonally to the right down the line of dance (between partner's feet) and pivot 1/4 turn clockwise with your partner remaining in Closed Position.	1-2	Slow	R Finger pressure
7	Step L foot to the left completing a full turn clockwise and position your left side to face down the line of dance.	3	Quick	R Hand hold
8	Step R foot to the left bringing feet together and completing an Advanced Two-Step Turn.	4	Quick	R Palm pressure

* Note: The line of dance is on your left as you begin each basic step. Advanced Two-Step Turns travel sideways down the line of dance. Steps 1-4 prepare you for the Advanced Turns by positioning you sideways. Momentum helps in maintaining the continuous turns.

Bootnote 1: Steps 5-8 may be repeated as many times as you wish to continue the Advanced Two-Step Turns. To terminate the movement you may end in Conversation Position on steps 7-8 (see video) or in Closed Position facing down the line of dance on steps 7-8.

Bootnote 2: "Spotting" is a technique that helps to maintain balance and insure proper direction. As you progress down the line of dance keep your eyes focused in that direction. As you execute the first step of each Advanced Two-Step Turn (step 5) the head should turn clockwise to face down the line of dance and stay there throughout the entire turn. The head will begin the turn as the body follows.

Texas Two-Step Swing

Advanced Two-Step Turns
Lady's Footwork

Step	Description	Timing	Rhythmic Cue
	Position: Closed Dance Position *		
1	Step R foot directly backward.	1-2	Slow
2	Step L foot backward and diagonally to the left turning 1/4 turn clockwise.	3-4	Slow
3	Step R foot to the right positioning your right side to face down the line of dance.	1	Quick
4	Step L foot to the right bringing feet together.	2	Quick
5	Step R foot diagonally to the right between your partner's feet and pivot to complete 3/4 turn clockwise.	3-4	Slow
6	Step L foot around your partner and pivot 1/4 turn clockwise in Closed Position.	1-2	Slow
7	Step R foot to the right completing a full turn clockwise and position your right side to face down the line of dance.	3	Quick
8	Step L foot to the right bringing feet together and completing an Advanced Two-Step Turn.	4	Quick

* Note: The line of dance is on your right as you begin each basic step. Advanced Two-Step turns travel sideways down the line of dance. Steps 1-4 prepare you for the Advanced Turns by positioning you sideways. Momentum helps in maintaining the continuous turns.

Bootnote 1: Steps 5-8 may be repeated as many times as you wish to continue the Advanced Two-Step Turns. To terminate the movement you may end in Conversation Position in steps 7-8 (see video) or in Closed Position facing down the line of dance on steps 7-8.

Bootnote 2: "Spotting" is a technique that helps to maintain balance and insure proper direction. As you progress down the line of dance keep your eyes focused in that direction. Between steps 6 and 7 the head turns to face down the line of dance. As long as you are in continuous Two-Step Turns this pattern is repeated.

Advanced Two-Step Turns

Closed Dance
Position

Step 1

Step 2

Step 5

Step 6

Advanced Two-Step Turns

Step 3

Step 4

Step 7

Step 8

Texas Two-Step Swing

Amalgamations

1 Separation Basic
   Side Pass
   Underarm Turn Right
   Neck Pass
   Underarm Turn Right

2 Separation Basic
   Whip (twice)
   String-a-Long (twice)

3 Separation Basic
   Sweetheart
   Separation Basic
   Wringer
   Separation Basic
   Sweetheart to Wringer

Favorite Texas Two-Step Selections

"Bad Love" (medium) by Pake McEntire

"Ballroom Roses" (medium) by Mel McDaniel

"Cherokee Fiddle" (medium) by Johnny Lee

"Cow Town" (medium) by George Strait

"Diggin' Up Bones" (medium) by Randy Travis

"Fool Hearted Memory" (medium) by George Strait

"Girls, Women, and Ladies" (medium slow) by Ed Bruce

"Hangin' Around" (medium) by The Whites

"Heartbroke" (medium fast) by Rodney Cromwell

"Here I Am Drunk Again" (medium) by Moe Bandy

"Honky Tonkin'" (medium fast) by Hank Williams, Jr.

"I'm Countryfied" (medium) by Mel McDaniel

"I'm Gonna Hire a Wino to Decorate My Home" (medium) by David Frizzell

"I'm Just An Old Chunk of Coal" (medium) by John Anderson

"I'm Only in It For the Love" (medium fast) by John Conlee

"Let's Chase Each Other Around the Room" (medium) by Merle Haggard

"Long Haired Country Boy" (medium) by The Charley Daniel's Band

"Louisiana Saturday Night" (medium) by Mel McDaniel

"Ocean Front Property" (medium) by George Strait

"Pure Love" (medium) by Ronnie Milsap

"Right or Wrong" (medium fast) by George Strait

"San Antonio Medley" (medium fast) by Bob Wills and the Texas Playboys

"Step That Step" (medium) by Sawyer Brown

"Since I Found You" (medium) by Sweethearts of the Rodeo

"Somebody's Knocking" (medium fast) by Terri Gibbs

"Stay a Little Longer" (medium fast) by Mel Tillis

"Texas Proud" (medium slow) by Curtis Potter

"The Lady Takes the Cowboy Everytime" (medium) by Larry Gatlin and the Gatlin Brothers

"When You Need Someone to Hold" (medium) by Susie Taylor and Mike Wells

Western
Waltz

WESTERN WALTZ

The Waltz was first known as a voluptuous turning dance with an intoxicating rhythm that consisted of gliding, leaping, and stamping. Known as one of the most beautiful dances in the world, its original roots date back to the Middle Ages. The Waltz was flavored by the "Volta" from Italy, the "Volte" from France, the "Walzen" from Germany, and the "Landler" from Austria. A folk dance in 3/4 time, the Landler was a step-close-step pattern bringing the feet together on the second count of music. When the dance moved from rough planks and packed-earth to polished hardwood ballrooms, the styling and the name changed. The Waltz came from the German word "Walzer" meaning "sliding or gliding." Gentlemen selected their partners and danced for the first time in Closed Dance Position, an act considered "indecent and promiscuous." As the Waltz entered the ballrooms of Europe around 1760, it was transformed into a graceful turning flow of movement, with the footwork changing to a step-side-close bringing the feet together on the third count. The reason is believed to be that the European courts encouraged this in order to make the dance too complicated for the peasants.

The Waltz traveled across the Atlantic migrating westward with the American cowboy and has continued to grow in popularity around the world. It has survived the test of time unlike so many fad dances that pass through each generation. Many ethnic groups have adapted their dance to the music of the Waltz, often changing the flavor but never diminishing the excitement.

Western Waltz

1. Basic Box Step
2. Left Box Turn
3. Progressive Box Step
4. Underarm Turn
5. Single Twinkle
6. Triple Twinkle
7. Fall Away Twinkle
8. Spirals
9. Hesitation Left Turns
10. Advanced Left Turns

Rhythmical Analysis

WESTERN WALTZ--Time Signature 3/4

Step Pattern:						
Man:	Forward,	Side,	Together,	Back,	Side,	Together
Lady:	Back,	Side,	Together,	Forward,	Side,	Together
Count:	1	2	3	1	2	3
Notation:						
Rhythmical Cue:	Slow	Slow	Slow	Slow	Slow	Slow

To complete a basic step in Western Waltz, one will use two measures of music in 3/4 time.

Note: Tempo of the music may be slow, medium, or fast.

Western Waltz

Basic Box Step
Man's Footwork

Step	Description	Timing	Rhythmic Cue	Lead
	Position: Closed Dance Position			
1	Step L foot directly forward.	1	Slow	R Heel pressure
2	Step R foot diagonally to the right directly in line with L foot.	2	Slow	R Finger pressure
3	Step L foot to the right bringing feet together.	3	Slow	R Hand pressure
4	Step R foot directly backward.	1	Slow	R Finger pressure
5	Step L foot diagonally to the left directly in line with R foot.	2	Slow	R Palm pressure
6	Step R foot to the left bringing feet together.	3	Slow	R Hand pressure

| Closed Dance Position | Step 1 | Step 2 | Step 3 |

Western Waltz

Basic Box Step
Lady's Footwork

Step	Description	Timing	Rhythmic Cue
	Position: Closed Dance Position		
1	Step R foot directly backward.	1	Slow
2	Step L foot diagonally to the left directly in line with R foot.	2	Slow
3	Step R foot directly to the left bringing feet together.	3	Slow
4	Step L foot directly forward.	1	Slow
5	Step R foot diagonally to the right directly in line with L foot.	2	Slow
6	Step L foot to the right bringing feet together.	3	Slow

Step 4   Step 5   Step 6

Western Waltz

Left Box Turn (counterclockwise)
Man's Footwork

Step	Description	Timing	Rhythmic Cue	Lead
	Position: Closed Dance Position			
1	Step L foot forward turning toe outward (beginning 1/4 turn counterclockwise).	1	Slow	R Palm pressure
2	Step R foot to the side completing 1/4 turn.	2	Slow	R Finger pressure
3	Step L foot to the right bringing feet together.	3	Slow	R Hand pressure
4	Step R foot backward turning toe inward (beginning 1/4 turn counterclockwise).	1	Slow	R Hand pressure
5	Step L foot to the side completing 1/4 turn.	2	Slow	R Palm pressure
6	Step R foot to the left bringing feet together.	3	Slow	R Hand pressure

Closed Dance Position

Step 1

Step 2

Step 3

Western Waltz

Left Box Turn (counterclockwise)
Lady's Footwork

Step	Description	Timing	Rhythmic Cue
	Position: Closed Dance Position		
1	Step R foot backward turning toe inward (beginning 1/4 turn counterclockwise).	1	Slow
2	Step L foot to the side completing 1/4 turn.	2	Slow
3	Step R foot to the left bringing feet together.	3	Slow
4	Step L foot forward turning toe outward (beginning 1/4 turn counterclockwise).	1	Slow
5	Step R foot to the side completing 1/4 turn.	2	Slow
6	Step L foot to the right bringing feet together.	3	Slow

Step 4   Step 5   Step 6

Western Waltz

Progressive Box Step
Man's Footwork

Step	Description	Timing	Rhythmic Cue	Lead
	Position: Closed Dance Position			
1	Step L foot directly foward.	1	Slow	R Heel pressure
2	Step R foot diagonally to the right directly in line with L foot.	2	Slow	R Finger pressure
3	Step L foot to the right bringing feet together.	3	Slow	R Hand pressure
4	Step R foot directly forward.	1	Slow	R Heel pressure
5	Step L foot diagonally to the left directly in line with R foot.	2	Slow	R Palm pressure
6	Step R foot to the left bringing feet together.	3	Slow	R Hand pressure

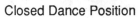

Closed Dance Position Step 1 Step 2 Step 3

Western Waltz

Progressive Box Step
Lady's Footwork

Step	Description	Timing	Rhythmic Cue
	Position: Closed Dance Position		
1	Step R foot directly backward.	1	Slow
2	Step L foot diagonally to the left directly in line with R foot.	2	Slow
3	Step R foot to the left bringing feet together.	3	Slow
4	Step L foot directly backward.	1	Slow
5	Step R foot diagonally to the right directly in line with L foot.	2	Slow
6	Step L foot to the right bringing feet together.	3	Slow

Step 4

Step 5

Step 6

Western Waltz

Underarm Turn
Man's Footwork

Step	Description	Timing	Rhythmic Cue	Lead
	Position: Closed Dance Position into Underarm Turn			
1	Step L foot directly forward.	1	Slow	R Heel pressure
2	Step R foot diagonally to the right directly in line with L foot.	2	Slow	R Finger pressure
3	Step L foot to the right bringing feet together.	3	Slow	R Hand pressure
4	Step R foot directly backward.	1	Slow	R Hand pressure
5	Step L foot diagonally to the left directly in line with R foot, beginning to lead the lady under your L hand hold to turn her clockwise.	2	Slow	L Hand hold raises and encircles
6	Step R foot to the left bringing feet together, continuing to lead the lady under your L hand hold.	3	Slow	L Hand hold encircles
7	Step L foot directly forward, continuing underarm lead.	1	Slow	L Hand hold encircles
8	Step R foot diagonally to the right directly in line with L foot, continuing underarm lead and beginning to lower L hand hold.	2	Slow	L Hand hold encircles
9	Step L foot to the right bringing feet together, beginning to return to Closed Dance Position.	3	Slow	L Hand hold encircles and lowers
10	Step R foot directly backward returning to Closed Dance Position.	1	Slow	L and R Hand movements
11	Step L foot diagonally to the left directly in line with R foot.	2	Slow	R Palm pressure
12	Step R foot to the left bringing feet together.	3	Slow	R Hand pressure

Closed Dance Position

Step 1

Step 2

Step 3

Step 4

Step 5

Western Waltz

Underarm Turn
Lady's Footwork

Step	Description	Timing	Rhythmic Cue
	Position: Closed Dance Position into Underarm Turn		
1	Step R foot directly backward.	1	Slow
2	Step L foot diagonally to the left directly in line with R foot.	2	Slow
3	Step R foot to the left bringing feet together.	3	Slow
4	Step L foot directly forward.	1	Slow
5	Step R foot 1/4 turn to the right beginning to move clockwise under your R hand hold.	2	Slow
6	Step L foot forward continuing to move clockwise under your R hand hold.	3	Slow
7	Step R foot forward continuing to move clockwise under your R hand hold.	1	Slow
8	Step L foot forward continuing to circle clockwise.	2	Slow
9	Step R foot forward beginning to return to Closed Dance Position.	3	Slow
10	Step L foot directly forward returning to Closed Dance Position.	1	Slow
11	Step R foot diagonally to the right directly in line with L foot.	2	Slow
12	Step L foot to the right bringing feet together.	3	Slow

| Step 7 | Step 9 | Step 10 | Step 11 | Step 12 |

Western Waltz

Single Twinkle
Man's Footwork

Step	Description	Timing	Rhythmic Cue	Lead
	Position: Closed Dance Position			
1	Step L foot directly forward.	1	Slow	R Heel pressure
2	Step R foot diagonally to the right (toe inward) directly in line with L foot.	2	Slow	R Finger pressure
3	Step L foot to the right turning approximately 1/4 turn left (counterclockwise) into Conversation Position as you bring your feet together. Lead the lady to turn into Conversation Position as you turn.	3	Slow	R Hand pressure
4	Step R foot directly forward beginning to turn clockwise returning to Closed Dance Position. Lead the lady to turn into Closed Position as you turn.	1	Slow	R Finger pressure
5	Step L foot directly to the left facing your partner in Closed Dance Position.	2	Slow	R Palm pressure
6	Step R foot directly to the left bringing feet together and completing the Single Twinkle.	3	Slow	R Palm pressure

Bootnote: The L hand hold will remain at shoulder level as lead is executed in and out of the Single Twinkle. The lead is executed with the man's right hand.

Closed Dance Position	Step 1	Step 2	Step 3

Western Waltz

Single Twinkle
Lady's Footwork

Step	Description	Timing	Rhythmic Cue
	Position: Closed Dance Position		
1	Step R foot directly backward.	1	Slow
2	Step L foot diagonally to the left (toe inward) directly in line with R foot.	2	Slow
3	Step R foot to the left turning approximately 1/4 turn into Conversation Position as you bring your feet together. Man will lead you to turn right (clockwise) into Conversation Position as he turns left.	3	Slow
4	Step L foot directly forward beginning to turn counterclockwsie returning to Closed Position.	1	Slow
5	Step R foot directly to the right facing your partner in Closed Dance Position.	2	Slow
6	Step L foot directly to the right bringing feet together and completing the Single Twinkle.	3	Slow

Bootnote: R hand hold will remain at shoulder level as lead is executed in and out of the Single Twinkle. Lead is executed from the man's right hand.

| Step 4 | Step 5 | Step 6 |

Western Waltz

Triple Twinkle
Man's Footwork

Step	Description	Timing	Rhythmic Cue	Lead
	Position: Closed Dance Position			
1-3	Steps 1-3 of the Triple Twinkle are the same as Steps 1-3 of the Single Twinkle.			
4	Step R foot directly forward with the lady on your right side. Retain Conversation Position as you lead the lady forward.	1	Slow	R Palm pressure
5	Step L foot directly forward (small step) passing right foot leading the lady forward and into a pivot turning her 1/2 turn counterclockwise. The lady will end in a Parallel Position on your right side. Your right shoulder is adjacent to her right shoulder.	2	Slow	R Hand pressure
6	Step R foot forward bringing feet together ending in Parallel Position with the lady facing the opposite direction on your right side. Retain a Closed Position contact throughout the entire movement.	3	Slow	R Hand pressure
7	Step L foot directly backward with the lady on your right side. Retain Parallel Position as you lead the lady forward.	1	Slow	R Finger pressure
8	Step R foot directly backward (small step) passing left foot leading the lady forward and into a pivot turning her 1/2 turn clockwise. The lady will end in Conversation Position on your right side.	2	Slow	R Palm pressure
9	Step L foot backward bringing feet together ending in Conversation Position. Retain a Closed Position contact throughout the entire movement.	3	Slow	R Hand pressure
10-12	Steps 10-12 of the Triple Twinkle are the same as Steps 4-6 of the Single Twinkle.			

Bootnote: Steps 1-3 lead your partner into Twinkle (Conversation) Position. Steps 4-9 lead your partner through the Triple Twinkle (figure "8" movement). Steps 10-12 lead your partner back into Closed Position.

Western Waltz

Triple Twinkle
Lady's Footwork

Step	Description	Timing	Rhythmic Cue
	Position: Closed Dance Position		
1-3	Steps 1-3 of the Triple Twinkle are the same as steps 1-3 of the Single Twinkle.		
4	Step L foot directly forward in Conversation Position.	1	Slow
5	Step R foot directly forward (small step) passing left foot and pivoting 1/2 turn counterclockwise. You will end in Parallel Position on your partner's right side. Your right shoulder is adjacent to his right shoulder.	2	Slow
6	Step L foot backward bringing feet together ending in Parallel Position facing the opposite direction than your partner. Retain a Closed Position contact throughout the entire movement.	3	Slow
7	Step R foot directly forward in Parallel Position as the man steps backward.	1	Slow
8	Step L foot directly forward (small step) passing right foot and pivoting 1/2 turn clockwise. You will end in Conversation Position on the man's right side.	2	Slow
9	Step R foot backward bringing feet together ending in Conversation Position. Retain a Closed Position contact throughout the entire movement.	3	Slow
10-12	Steps 10-12 of the Triple Twinkle are the same as steps 4-6 of the Single Twinkle.		

Bootnote: Steps 1-3 lead you into Twinkle (Conversation) Position. Steps 4-9 lead you through the Triple Twinkle (figure "8" movement). Steps 10-12 lead you back into Closed Position.

Triple Twinkle

Closed Dance
Position

Step 1

Step 2

Step 3

Step 7

Step 8

Step 9

Triple Twinkle

Step 4

Step 5

Step 6

Step 10

Step 11

Step 12

Western Waltz

Fall-a-Way-Twinkle
Man's Footwork

Step	Description	Timing	Rhythmic Cue	Lead
	Position: Closed Dance Position			
1-3	Steps 1-3 of the Fall-a-Way Twinkle are the same as steps 1-3 of the Single and Triple Twinkles.			
4	Step R foot directly forward with the lady on your right side.	1	Slow	R Hand pressure
5	Step L foot directly forward slightly passing R foot leading the lady to step forward. Remain in Conversation Position as the lady shadows your footwork.	2	Slow	R Hand pressure
6	Step R foot forward bringing feet together with the lady on your right side in Conversation Position.	3	Slow	R Hand pressure
7	Step L foot directly backward leading the lady to step backward into a Fall-a-Way Twinkle.	1	Slow	L and R Hand holds
8	Step R foot directly backward slightly passing L foot. The lady remains on your right side in Conversation Position.	2	Slow	L and R Hand holds
9	Step L foot backward bringing feet together completing the Fall-a-Way Twinkle movement. The lady remains in Conversation Position.	3	Slow	L and R Hand holds
10-12	Steps 10-12 of the Fall-a-Way Twinkle are the same as Steps 10-12 of the Single and Triple Twinkles.			

Bootnote: Steps 1-3 lead your partner into Twinkle (Conversation) Position. Steps 4-9 lead your partner through the Fall-a-Way Twinkle movement. Steps 10-12 lead your partner back into Closed Position.

Western Waltz

Fall-a-Way-Twinkle
Lady's Footwork

Step	Description	Timing	Rhythmic Cue
	Position: Closed Dance Position		
1-3	Steps 1-3 of the Fall-a-Way Twinkle are the same as steps 1-3 of the Single and Triple Twinkles.		
4	Step L foot directly forward in Conversation Position.	1	Slow
5	Step R foot directly forward slightly passing L foot. Remain in Conversation Position as you shadow the man's footwork.	2	Slow
6	Step L foot forward bringing feet together.	3	Slow
7	Step R foot backward in Conversation Position as you begin the Fall-a-Way Twinkle movement.	1	Slow
8	Step L foot backward slightly passing R foot. Remain on the man's right side in Conversation Position.	2	Slow
9	Step R foot backward bringing feet together completing the Fall-a-Way Twinkle movement. Remain in Conversation Position.	3	Slow
10-12	Steps 10-12 of the Fall-a-Way Twinkle are the same as steps 10-12 of the Single and Triple Twinkles.		

Bootnote: Steps 1-3 lead you into Twinkle (Conversation) Position. Steps 4-9 lead you through the Fall-a-Way Twinkle movement. Steps 10-12 lead you back into Closed Position.

Fall-a-way Twinkle

Closed Dance
Position

Step 1

Step 2

Step 3

Step 7

Step 8

Step 9

Fall-a-way Twinkle

Step 4

Step 5

Step 6

Step 10

Step 11

Step 12

Western Waltz

Spirals
Man's Footwork

Step	Description	Timing	Rhythmic Cue	Lead
	Position: Closed Dance Position			
1	Step L foot directly forward.	1	Slow	R Heel pressure
2	Step R foot diagonally forward and to the right directly in line with L foot. As you place weight on the R foot begin to lead the lady into Spiral Position by turning her slightly counterclockwise.	2	Slow	R Hand pressure
3	Step L foot to the right turning approximately 1/8 turn left into Spiral Position as you bring your feet together. As you turn counterclockwise into position lead the lady to face the opposite direction.	3	Slow	R Hand pressure
4	Step R foot forward in parallel movement with the lady on your right side progressing backward.	1	Slow	R Hand pressure
5	Step L foot to the left turning approximately 1/4 turn clockwise into Reverse Spiral Position. Lead the lady to turn clockwise to face the opposite direction.	2	Slow	R Hand pressure
6	Step R foot to the left bringing feet together in Reverse Spiral Position.	3	Slow	R Hand pressure
7	Step L foot forward in parallel movement with the lady on your left side progressing backward.	1	Slow	R Hand pressure
8	Step R foot to the right turning approximately 1/4 turn counterclockwise into Spiral Position. Lead the lady to turn counterclockwise to face the opposite direction.	2	Slow	R Hand pressure
9	Step L foot to the right bringing feet together in Spiral Position.	3	Slow	R Hand pressure
10	Step R foot forward in parallel movement with the lady progressing backward on your right side.	1	Slow	R Hand pressure
11	Step L foot to the left as you lead the lady to face you returning to Closed Dance Position.	2	Slow	R Hand pressure
12	Step R foot to the left bringing feet together completing the Spirals and returning to Closed Position.	3	Slow	R Hand pressure

Bootnote 1: The Spirals may be used like the Progressive Box Step to progress down your line of dance.

Bootnote 2: Steps 1-3 lead your partner into Spiral Position. Steps 4-9 execute a Spiral and a Reverse Spiral. To continue Spiral movement repeat steps 4 thru 9. Steps 10-12 lead your partner out of the Spiral and into Closed Position.

Western Waltz

Spirals
Lady's Footwork

Step	Description	Timing	Rhythmic Cue
	Position: Closed Dance Position		
1	Step R foot directly backward.	1	Slow
2	Step L foot diagonally backward and to the left directly in line with R foot. As you place weight on the L foot your partner begins to lead you into Spiral Position by turning you slightly counterclockwise.	2	Slow
3	Step R foot to the left bringing feet together ending in Spiral Position. Face the opposite direction from the man.	3	Slow
4	Step L foot backward in a parallel movement with the man progressing forward on your right side.	1	Slow
5	Step R foot to the right as the man leads you to turn approximately 1/4 turn clockwise into Reverse Spiral Position.	2	Slow
6	Step L foot to the right bringing feet together to face opposite direction from your partner.	3	Slow
7	Step R foot backward in a parallel movement with the man progressing forward on your left side.	1	Slow
8	Step L foot to the left as the man leads you to turn approximately 1/4 turn counterclockwise into Spiral Position.	2	Slow
9	Step R foot to the left bringing feet together to face opposite direction from your partner.	3	Slow
10	Step L foot backward in a parallel movement with the man progressing forward on your right side.	1	Slow
11	Step R foot to the right as the man leads you to face him returning to Closed Dance Position.	2	Slow
12	Step L foot to the right bringing feet together completing the Spirals and returning to Closed Position.	3	Slow

 Bootnote: Steps 1-3 lead you into Spiral Position. Steps 4-9 execute a Spiral and a Reverse Spiral. To continue Spiral movement repeat steps 4 through 9. Steps 10-12 lead you out of the Spiral and into Closed Dance Position.

Spirals

Closed Dance
Position

Step 1

Step 2

Step 3

Step 7

Step 8

Step 9

Spirals

Step 4

Step 5

Step 6

Step 10

Step 11

Step 12

Western Waltz

Hesitation Left Turns
Man's Footwork

Step	Description	Timing	Rhythmic Cue	Lead
	Position: Closed Dance Position			
1	Step L foot directly forward.	1	Slow	R Heel pressure
2	Step R foot forward bringing feet together. Do not change weight.	2	Slow	R Hand pressure
3	Hold L foot in place for Hesitation movement.	3	Slow	R Hand pressure
4	Step R foot directly backward (toe inward) beginning to turn 1/4 turn counterclockwise.	1	Slow	R Hand pressure
5	Step L foot to the left turning 1/4 turn counterclockwise as you keep your partner directly in front of you.	2	Slow	R Hand pressure
6	Step R foot to the left bringing feet together and completing the Hesitation Left Turn.	3	Slow	R Hand pressure

Bootnote: Steps 1-3 execute the Hesitation movement without changing weight on steps 2 and 3. Steps 4-6 execute the second half of a box step turning left (approximately 1/4 turn).

Closed Dance
Position

Step 1

Step 2 and 3

Western Waltz

Hesitation Left Turns
Lady's Footwork

Step	Description	Timing	Rhythmic Cue
	Position: Closed Dance Position		
1	Step R foot directly backward.	1	Slow
2	Step L foot backward bringing feet together. Do not change weight.	2	Slow
3	Hold R foot in place for Hesitation movement.	3	Slow
4	Step L foot directly forward (toe outward) beginning to turn 1/4 turn counterclockwise.	1	Slow
5	Step R foot to the right turning 1/4 turn counterclockwise in Closed Dance Position.	2	Slow
6	Step L foot to the right bringing feet together and completing the Hesitation Left Turn.	3	Slow

Bootnote: Steps 1-3 execute the Hesitation movement without changing weight on steps 2 and 3. Steps 4-6 execute the second half of a box step turning left (approximately 1/4 turn).

| Step 4 | Step 5 | Step 6 |

Western Waltz

Advanced Left Turns
Man's Footwork

Step	Description	Timing	Rhythmic Cue	Lead
	Position: Closed Dance Position*			
1	Step L foot forward turning toe outward beginning 1/4 turn left (counterclockwise).	1	Slow	R Heel pressure
2	Step R foot to the right completing 1/4 turn (counterclockwise); then pivot on the ball of the R foot an additional 1/8 turn.	2	Slow	R Hand pressure
3	Step L foot backward into a lock step crossing the L foot in front of the R foot. Take the weight on the L foot as you execute the lock step.	3	Slow	R Hand pressure
4	Step R foot backward turning toe inward executing 1/4 turn left (counterclockwise).	1	Slow	R Hand pressure
5	Step L foot to the left executing an additional 1/8 turn left (counterclockwise).	2	Slow	R Hand pressure
6	Step R foot to the left bringing feet together as the lady moves into a lock step.	3	Slow	R Hand pressure

*Note: Remain in Closed Dance Position throughout the entire movement as you progress down your line of dance executing the Advanced Left Turns.

Bootnote 1: Steps 1-3 execute the lock step for the man as he progresses around the lady and down the line of dance. Steps 4-6 execute the second half of the box step as the lady executes the lock step to progress around you.

Bootnote 2: The Advanced Left Turns may be repeated as many times as you wish. Proper alignment is essential in executing the Advanced Left Turns continuously.

| Closed Dance Position | Step 1 | Step 2 | Step 3 |

Western Waltz

Advanced Left Turns
Lady's Footwork

Step	Description	Timing	Rhythmic Cue
	Position: Closed Dance Position*		
1	Step R foot backward turning toe inward executing 1/4 turn left (counterclockwise).	1	Slow
2	Step L foot to the left executing an additional 1/8 turn left (counterclockwise).	2	Slow
3	Step R foot to the left bringing feet together as the man moves into a lock step.	3	Slow
4	Step L foot forward turning toe outward beginning 1/4 turn left (counterclockwise).	1	Slow
5	Step R foot to the right turning 1/4 turn (counter-clockwise); then pivot on the ball of the R foot an additional 1/8 turn.	2	Slow
6	Step L foot backward into a lock step with the L foot crossing in front of the right foot. Change weight to the L foot as you slide L foot into position.	3	Slow

*Note: Remain in Closed Dance Position throughout the entire movement as you progress down your line of dance executing the Advanced Left Turns.

Bootnote: Steps 1-3 execute the first half of a box step as the man executes a lock step to progress around you and down the line of dance. Steps 4-6 execute your lock step to progress around the man and down the line of dance as he executes the second half of his box step.

| Step 4 | Step 5 | Step 6 |

Western Waltz

Amalgamations

1. Basic Box Step
   Left Box Turn (counterclockwise)
   Progressive Box Step

2. Basic Box Step
   Underarm Turn
   Progressive Box Step

3. Single Twinkle (twice)
   Triple Twinkle
   Fall-a-Way Twinkle

4. Progressive Box Step
   Spirals (several)
   Progressive Box Step

5. Progressive Box Step
   Advanced Left Turns (several)
   Progressive Box Step

Favorite Western Waltz Selections

"Almost Persuaded" (slow) by David Houston

"Amanda" (medium fast) by Waylon Jennings

"Backward Turn Backward" (medium) by Bubba Littrell

"Blue Texas Waltz" (slow) by Susie Taylor and Mike Wells

"Could I Have This Dance" (slow) by Anne Murray

"Dancing Your Memory Away" (medium) by Charly McClain

"Four In The Morning" (medium) by Faron Young

"I Wonder Who's Holding Her Tonight" (medium fast) by The Whites

"If You've Got Ten Minutes (Let's Fall in Love)" (medium) by Moe Bandy

"Jole Blon" (medium) by Frenchie Burke

"Last Cheater's Waltz" (slow) by T.G. Sheppard

"Let's Fall to Pieces Together" (medium fast) by George Strait

"Love In the Hot Afternoon" (medium) by Gene Watson

"Lucille" (fast) by Kenny Rogers

"Rose Colored Glasses" (slow) by John Conlee

"Round-Up Saloon" (medium) by Bobby Goldsboro

"Send Me Down to Tuscon" (medium) by Mel Tillis

"South Texas Waltz" (medium) by Al Dean and The All Stars

"Some Days It Rains All Night" (medium slow) by Terri Gibbs

"The Bandera Waltz" (medium) by Slim Whitman

"The Last Cowboy Song" (medium) by Ed Bruce

"The Waltz You Saved For Me" (medium slow) by John Anderson and Emmy Lou Harris

"Waltz Across Texas" (medium) by Ernest Tubb

"Westphalia Waltz" (medium fast) by Adolph Hofner or by Hank Thompson

"Whisper" (medium slow) by Lacy J. Dalton

"Wild and Blue" (medium fast) by John Anderson

"With Pen in Hand" (medium slow) by Bobby Goldsboro

"You Done Me Wrong" (fast) by Mel Tillis

"You Look So Good in Love" (medium fast) by George Strait

Western Swing

206

WESTERN SWING

Swing made its debut at the Savoy Ballroom in New York City in 1927. It was originally known as the Lindy Hop after Charles Lindberg's "Hop" across the Atlantic to Paris. The music of the Fox Trot, the dance craze of the early twenties with a swinging jazz sound, stimulated the dancers to "break-away" from the Fox Trot's closed dance position into the open position of swing. A competitiveness developed among the dancers as an acrobatic style emerged. Couples created their own steps, trying to surpass other couples. The variations of the Lindy were not completely new to the public having been inspired by dances from the "Roaring Twenties" such as the Charleston, Black Bottom, Big Apple, Shimmy, and Texas Tommy. As years passed, the Lindy, with changes in style, became known as Swing, Jitterbug, Shag, Jive, Boogie Woogie, and Rock 'N' Roll. It later influenced such dances as the Hully Gully, Twist, and Disco Hustle variations.

Country and Western music in the honky-tonks ran parallel with the Big Band sound in the ballrooms. Benny Goodman was dubbed the "King of Swing" with Bob Wills being crowned "King of Western Swing." The Ballroom Fox Trot inspired the Western Two-Step and Texas Two-Step; the Lindy Hop influenced the Western Swing; and the Waltz and Polka continued in popularity across the U.S.A. Swing movements strongly overlapped from the polished ballroom floors to the rustic country and western dance halls and into the brightly lit surroundings of Disco and Rock 'N' Roll.

Western Swing

1. Basic Step
2. Basic Step Turning Right (Clockwise)
3. Underarm Turn Left
4. Reverse Underarm Turn
5. Throw Out
6. Sugar Push
7. Underarm Turn Right
8. Side Pass/Neck Pass
9. Layover
10. Layover with Basic Step
11. Sweetheart
12. Sweetheart with Basic Step
13. Wringer
14. Wringer with Basic Step
15. Sweetheart Turns
16. Kick 'N
17. Back to Back
18. Shuttle
19. Thread the Needle
20. Twin Cities
21. Continuous Layover

Rhythmical Analysis

Western Swing----Time Signature 4/4

Step pattern Man and Lady:	Step Side,	Step together,	Step side,	Step Side,	Step together,	Step side,	Rock back,	Step forward,
Count: Notation:	1	&	2	3	&	4	1	2
Rhythmical Cue:	Quick	Quick	Slow	Quick	Quick	Slow	Slow	Slow

To complete a basic step in Western Swing, one will use 1-1/2 measures of music in 4/4 time.

Western Swing

Basic Step (triple time)
Man's Footwork

Step	Description	Timing	Rhythmic Cue	Lead
	Position: Closed Swing Position. Knees are slightly flexed with majority of the weight on the balls of the feet.*			
1	Step L foot directly to the left.	1	Quick	R Palm pressure
2	Step R foot to the left bringing feet together.	&	Quick	R Palm pressure
3	Step L foot directly to the left completing a triple step to your left.	2	Slow	R Palm pressure
4	Step R foot directly to the right.	3	Quick	R Fingertip pressure
5	Step L foot to the right bringing feet together.	&	Quick	R Fingertip pressure
6	Step R foot directly to the right completing a triple step to your right.	4	Slow	R Fingertip pressure
7	Step L foot diagonally back into Fall-a-Way Position (rock step).	1	Slow	R Hand pressure
8	Step R foot forward completing the basic step.	2	Slow	R Hand pressure

*Note: The man's left hand holds the lady's right at waist level with palms facing down. His fingers are under her hand and his thumb is placed on the back of her hand. The man's right hand is placed on the lady's left shoulder blade and her left hand is on his right shoulder. There is additional contact throughout the arms for resistance.

Bootnote I: Steps 7 and 8 comprise the rock step. When dancing in closed position the rock step is executed from a fallaway position. In open position the rock step moves directly away from your partner.

Bootnote II: The swing is danced in a small area as opposed to progressing around the dance floor.

| Closed Swing Position | Step 1 | Step 2 | Step 3 |

Western Swing

Basic Step (triple time)
Lady's Footwork

Step	Description	Timing	Rhythmic Cue
	Position: Closed Swing Position*		
1	Step R foot directly to the right.	1	Quick
2	Step L foot to the right bringing feet together.	&	Quick
3	Step R foot directly to the right completing a triple step to your right.	2	Slow
4	Step L foot directly to the left.	3	Quick
5	Step R foot to the left bringing feet together.	&	Quick
6	Step L foot directly to the left completing a triple step to your left.	4	Slow
7	Step R foot diagonally back into Fall-a-Way Position (rock step).	1	Slow
8	Step L foot forward completing the basic step.	2	Slow

*Note: The man's left hand holds the lady's right at waist level with palms facing down. His fingers are under her hand and his thumb is placed on the back of her hand. The man's right hand is placed on the lady's left shoulder blade and her left hand is on his right shoulder. There is additional contact throughout the arms for resistance.

Bootnote I: Steps 7 and 8 comprise the rock step. When dancing in closed position the rock step is executed from a fallaway position. In open position the rock step moves directly away from your partner.

Bootnote II: The swing is danced in a small area as opposed to progressing around the dance floor.

| Step 4 | Step 5 | Step 6 | Steps 7 and 8 |

Western Swing

Basic Step Turning Right (clockwise)
(Triple Time)
Man's Footwork

Step	Description	Timing	Rhythmic Cue	Lead
	Position: Closed Swing Position*			
1	Step L foot to the left beginning to turn approximately 1/4 turn to the right (clockwise).	1	Quick	R Heel pressure
2	Step R foot to the left bringing feet together continuing clockwise turn.	&	Quick	R Heel pressure
3	Step L foot to the left completing a triple step and approximately 1/4 turn to the right (clockwise).	2	Slow	R Heel pressure
4	Step R foot directly to the right.	3	Quick	R Finger pressure
5	Step L foot to the right bringing feet together.	&	Quick	R Finger pressure
6	Step R foot directly to the right completing a triple step to your right.	4	Slow	R Finger pressure
7	Step L foot diagonally back into Fallaway Position (Rock Step).	1	Slow	R Hand pressure
8	Step R foot forward completing the Basic Step.	2	Slow	R Hand pressure

*Note: Precede with Basic Swing Step.

Bootnote: The amount of turn varies with each couple. A series of this step will complete a full turn.

Basic Swing Step

Step 1

Step 2

Step 3

Western Swing

Basic Step Turning Right (clockwise)
(Triple Time)
Lady's Footwork

Step	Description	Timing	Rhythmic Cue
	Position: Closed Swing Position*		
1	Step R foot to the right into approximately 1/4 turn right as the man begins to turn clockwise around you.	1	Quick
2	Step L foot to the right bringing feet together continuing clockwise turn.	&	Quick
3	Step R foot to the right completing a triple step and approximately 1/4 turn to the right (clockwise).	2	Slow
4	Step L foot directly to the left.	3	Quick
5	Step R foot to the left bringing feet together.	&	Quick
6	Step L foot directly to the left completing a triple step to your left.	4	Slow
7	Step R foot diagonally back into Fallaway Position (Rock Step).	1	Slow
8	Step L foot forward completing the Basic Step.	2	Slow

*Note: Precede with Basic Swing Step.

Bootnote: Basic Step Turning may vary from 1/4 to 1/2 turn.

| Step 4 | Step 5 | Step 6 | Steps 7 and 8 |

Western Swing

Underarm Turn Left (triple time)
Man's Footwork

Step	Description	Timing	Rhythmic Cue	Lead
	Position: Closed Swing Position*			
1	Step L foot directly forward (small step) from Conversation Position beginning to lead the lady under your L hand hold (his left, her right).	1	Quick	R Hand pressure L Hand hold raises
2	Step R foot forward bringing feet together continuing to lead the lady under your L hand hold to turn clockwise.	&	Quick	L Hand hold raises
3	Step L foot directly forward (small step) in Conversation Position completing the movement to lead the lady under your L hand hold.	2	Slow	L Hand hold encircles
4	Step R foot directly to the right (small step) moving parallel with your partner in Open Swing Position.	3	Quick	L Hand hold lowers
5	Step L foot to the right bringing feet together as you lower the L hand hold to waist level.	&	Quick	L Hand hold
6	Step R foot directly to the right (small step) completing a triple step to your right.	4	Slow	L Hand hold
7	Step L foot directly back facing your partner (Rock Step).	1	Slow	L Hand hold pushes
8	Step R foot forward completing an Underarm Turn Left.	2	Slow	L Hand hold pulls

*Note: Underarm Turn Left refers to position in relation to your partner rather than direction. Lady turns to *her right* (clockwise) under *man's left arm* moving to *his left*. The Underarm Turn Left is preceded with a Basic Step in Closed Swing Position.

 Bootnote: Steps 1-3 comprise the Underarm Turn Left movement. Steps 4-6 move parallel with your partner to your right. Steps 7-8 comprise the Rock Step that moves directly away from your partner.

Basic Swing
Step

Steps 1-3

Western Swing

Underarm Turn Left (triple time)
Lady's Footwork

Step	Description	Timing	Rhythmic Cue
	Position: Closed Swing Position*		
1	Step R foot forward from Conversation Position as the man begins to lead you under your R hand hold (her right, his left) to turn clockwise.	1	Quick
2	Step L foot forward bringing feet together continuing clockwise turn.	&	Quick
3	Step R foot diagonally to the right pivoting clockwise to face your partner to complete the movement under your R hand hold.	2	Slow
4	Step L foot directly to the left moving parallel with your partner.	3	Quick
5	Step R foot directly to the left bringing feet together.	&	Quick
6	Step L foot directly to the left (small step) completing a triple step to your left.	4	Slow
7	Step R foot directly back facing your partner (Rock Step).	1	Slow
8	Step L foot forward completing the Underarm Turn Left.	2	Slow

*Note: Underarm Turn Left refers to position in relation to your partner rather than direction. Lady turns to *her right* (clockwise) under *man's left* arm moving to *his left*. The Underarm Turn Left is preceded with a Basic Step in Closed Swing Position.

Bootnote: In Open Swing Position the Rock Step is executed directly away from your partner.

Steps 4-6   Steps 7-8

Western Swing

Reverse Underarm Turn (triple time)
Man's Footwork

Step	Description	Timing	Rhythmic Cue	Lead
	Position: Open Swing Position with single hand hold (his left, her right).*			
1	Step L foot directly forward beginning 1/4 turn clockwise while leading the lady to turn counterclockwise under your L hand hold.	1	Quick	L Hand hold pulls and raises
2	Step R foot to the left bringing feet together continuing to turn the lady counterclockwise.	&	Quick	L Hand hold raises
3	Step L foot directly to the left completing a triple step and the movement of leading the lady under your L hand hold.	2	Slow	L Hand hold encircles
4	Step R foot directly to the right moving parallel with your partner. Lower the L hand hold to waist level.	3	Quick	L Hand hold lowers
5	Step L foot to the right bringing feet together.	&	Quick	L Hand hold lowers
6	Step R foot directly to the right completing a triple step to your right.	4	Slow	L Hand hold
7	Step L foot directly back (Rock Step).	1	Slow	L Hand hold pushes
8	Step R foot forward completing the Reverse Underarm Turn.	2	Slow	L Hand hold pulls

*Note: Precede with Underarm Turn Left.

Bootnote: Steps 1-3 comprise the Reverse Underarm Turn movement. Steps 4-6 move parallel with your partner to your right. Steps 7-8 comprise the Rock Step that moves directly away from your partner.

Open Swing Position   Steps 1-3

Western Swing

Reverse Underarm Turn (triple time)
Lady's Footwork

Step	Description	Timing	Rhythmic Cue
	Position: Open Swing Position with single hand hold (her right, his left).*		
1	Step R foot diagonally to the left beginning to turn counterclockwise under your R hand hold.	1	Quick
2	Step L foot forward bringing feet together continuing counterclockwise turn under your R hand hold.	&	Quick
3	Step R foot diagonally to the left pivoting to turn counterclockwise to face your partner.	2	Slow
4	Step L foot to the left moving parallel with your partner.	3	Quick
5	Step R foot ot the left bringing feet together.	&	Quick
6	Step L foot to the left completing a triple step to your left.	4	Slow
7	Step R foot directly back (Rock Step).	1	Slow
8	Step L foot forward completing the Reverse Underarm Turn.	2	Slow

*Note: Precede with Underarm Turn Left.

Bootnote: In Open Swing Position the Rock Step is executed directly away from your partner.

Steps 4-6   Steps 7 and 8

Western Swing

Throw-Out (triple time)
Man's Footwork

Step	Description	Timing	Rhythmic Cue	Lead
	Position: Conversation Position into Throw-Out*			
1	Step L foot directly forward (small step) beginning to lead the lady into Open Dance Position. Lower the L hand hold to waist level leading the lady forward with the right hand.	1	Quick	R hand pressure L hand hold lowers
2	Step R foot forward bringing feet together continuing to lead the lady forward, passing you, into Open Dance Position.	&	Quick	R hand pressure
3	Step L foot directly forward completing a triple step and leading the lady to turn into Open Swing Position.	2	Slow	L hand hold
4	Step R foot directly to the right moving parallel with your partner with a single hand hold (his left, her right).	3	Quick	L hand hold
5	Step L foot directly to the right bringing feet together.	&	Quick	L hand hold
6	Step R foot directly to the right completing a triple step to your right facing your partner.	4	Slow	L hand hold
7	Step L foot directly back facing your partner. (Rock Step).	1	Slow	L hand hold pushes
8	Step R foot forward completing the Throw-Out.	2	Slow	L hand hold pulls

*Note: Precede with a Basic Step ending in Conversation Position on the Rock Step.

Bootnote: Steps 1-3 comprise the Throw-Out movement. Steps 4-6 move parallel with your partner to your right. Steps 7-8 comprise the Rock Step that moves directly away from your partner.

Basic Swing Step

Steps 1-3

Western Swing

Throw-Out (triple step)
Lady's Footwork

Step	Description	Timing	Rhythmic Cue
	Position: Conversation Position into Throw-Out*		
1	Step R foot directly forward (shuffle step) as the man begins to lead you past him into Open Swing Position.	1	Quick
2	Step L foot directly forward (shuffle step) as you progress past your partner beginning to turn counterclockwise 1/2 turn to face your partner.	&	Quick
3	Step R foot diagonally to the left pivoting to face your partner ending in Open Swing Position with a single hand hold (his left, her right).	2	Slow
4	Step L foot directly to the left moving parallel with your partner.	3	Quick
5	Step R foot to the left bringing feet together.	&	Quick
6	Step L foot directly to the left completing a triple step to your left.	4	Slow
7	Step R foot directly back facing partner (Rock Step).	1	Slow
8	Step L foot forward completing the Throw-Out.	2	Slow

*Note: Precede with a Basic Step ending in Conversation Position on the Rock Step.

Bootnote: Steps 1-3 comprise a run-run-run shuffle movement that progresses past the man.

Steps 4-6   Steps 7 and 8

Western Swing

Sugar Push (triple time)
Man's Footwork

Step	Description	Timing	Rhythmic Cue	Lead
	Position: Open Swing Position with double hand hold (his left holding her right, his right holding her left).*			
1	Step L foot diagonally forward and to the left beginning to progress clockwise around your partner. Lead your partner to progress clockwise around you into Sugar Push Position. Extend the R hand hold keeping the L hand hold near chest level.	1	Quick	R hand hold extends to right
2	Step R foot forward bringing feet together continuing to progress into Sugar Push Position.	&	Quick	R hand hold extended
3	Step L foot diagonally to the right into Sugar Push Position beginning to turn clockwise toward your partner.	2	Slow	R hand hold extended
4	Step R foot directly to your right to face your partner and move parallel with her. Return double hand hold to chest level as you face your partner.	3	Quick	R and L hand hold chest level
5	Step L foot directly to the right bringing feet together and leading the lady to move parallel to your right.	&	Quick	R and L hand hold chest level
6	Step R foot directly to the right completing a triple step to your right.	4	Slow	R and L hand hold chest level
7	Step L foot directly back facing your partner (Rock Step).	1	Slow	R and L hand hold pushes
8	Step R foot directly forward completing the Sugar Push Step.	2	Slow	R and L hand hold pulls

 *Note: Retain a double hand hold throughout the entire Sugar Push movement.

Bootnote: Steps 1-3 comprise the Sugar Push movement. Steps 4-6 move parallel with your parner to your right (small steps). Steps 7-8 comprise the Rock Step that moves directly away from your partner.

Open Swing Position   Step 1   Step 3

Western Swing

Sugar Push (triple step)
Lady's Footwork

Step	Description	Timing	Rhythmic Cue
	Position: Open Swing Position with double hand hold (his left holding her right, his right holding her left).*		
1	Step R foot diagonally forward and to the left beginning to progress around your partner into Sugar Push Position.	1	Quick
2	Step L foot forward bringing feet together continuing to progress into Sugar Push Position.	&	Quick
3	Step R foot forward into Sugar Push Position pivoting approximately 1/4 turn to face your partner.	2	Slow
4	Step L foot directly to the left moving parallel with your partner. Double hand hold is at chest level.	3	Quick
5	Step R foot directly to the left bringing feet together.	&	Quick
6	Step L foot directly to the left completing a triple step to your left.	4	Slow
7	Step R foot directly back facing partner (Rock Step).	1	Slow
8	Step L foot directly forward completing the Sugar Push.	2	Slow

*Note: Retain a double hand hold throughout the entire Sugar Push movement.

Bootnote: In Sugar Push Position partners are side by side with right shoulders adjacent. Retain a double hand hold with right arms extended to the right and left arms at chest level (left elbows bent).

Steps 4-6   Steps 7-8

Western Swing

Underarm Turn Right (triple time)
Man's Footwork

Step	Description	Timing	Rhythmic Cue	Lead
	Position: Open Swing Position with single hand hold (his left holding her right).			
1	Step L foot diagonally forward and to the left as you begin to progress clockwise around your partner leading her to your right. The L hand hold encircles the lady's head counter clockwise as you change sides.	1	Quick	L hand hold pulls and raises
2	Step R foot forward bringing feet together continuing to progress around your partner leading the lady into an Underarm Turn Right.	&	Quick	L hand hold encircles
3	Step L foot diagonally to the right continuing around your partner and completing a half turn to face your partner. Begin to lower the left hand hold to waist level.	2	Slow	L hand hold lowers
4	Step R foot directly to the right moving parallel with your partner.	3	Quick	L hand hold lowers
5	Step L foot to the right bringing feet together.	&	Quick	L hand hold waist level
6	Step R foot to the right completing a triple step to your right.	4	Slow	L hand hold
7	Step L foot directly back facing partner (Rock Step).	1	Slow	L hand hold pushes
8	Step R foot directly forward completing the Underarm Turn Right.	2	Slow	L hand hold pulls

Bootnote: Steps 1-3 comprise the Underarm Turn Right movement. Steps 4-6 move parallel with your partner to your right (small steps). Steps 7-8 comprise the Rock Step that moves directly away from your partner.

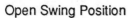

Open Swing Position   Steps 1-3   Steps 7 and 8

Western Swing

Underarm Turn Right (triple time)
Lady's Footwork

Step	Description	Timing	Rhythmic Cue
	Position: Open Swing Position with single hand hold (his left holding her right).		
1	Step R foot diagonally forward and to the left beginning to turn counterclockwise past your partner and under your right hand hold.	1	Quick
2	Step L foot forward bringing feet together as you continue counterclockwise turn.	&	Quick
3	Step R foot forward completing a half turn to face your partner as the right hand hold encircles your head.	2	Slow
4	Step L foot directly to the left moving parallel with your partner and lowering the right hand hold to waist level.	3	Quick
5	Step R foot directly to the left bringing feet together.	&	Quick
6	Step L foot directly to the left completing a triple step to your left.	4	Slow
7	Step R foot directly back facing partner (Rock Step).	1	Slow
8	Step L foot forward completing the Underarm Turn Right.	2	Slow

Bootnote: In executing the Underarm Turn Right the partners will change sides as the man's left hand hold encircles the lady's head with the free hands remaining at waist level.

Western Swing

Side Pass/Neck Pass (triple time)
Man's Footwork

Step	Description	Timing	Rhythmic Cue	Lead
	Position: Open Swing Position with single hand hold (his left holding her right).*			
1	Step L foot diagonally forward and to the left beginning to turn counterclockwise while leading the lady to progress around you clockwise. Begin the lead by placing the L hand hold on the right side at waist level. Keep the right arm above the L hand hold.	1	Quick	L hand hold pulls and places R hand held above left
2	Step R foot forward bringing feet together continuing to lead the lady to your right side. Continue to turn counterclockwise changing sides with your partner.	&	Quick	L hand hold placed R hand held above left
3	Step L foot forward pivoting to complete 1/2 turn to face your partner as you release the L hand hold. The lady will progress around you clockwise to face you.	2	Slow	L hand hold releases R hand waist level
4	Step R foot directly to the right moving parallel with your partner. Retake the L hand hold at waist level.	3	Quick	L hand hold waist level R hand held waist level
5	Step L foot to the right bringing feet together.	&	Quick	L hand hold waist level
6	Step R foot directly to the right completing a triple step to your right.	4	Slow	L hand hold waist level
7	Step L foot directly back facing your partner (Rock Step).	1	Slow	L hand hold pushes
8	Step R foot directly forward completing the Side Pass.	2	Slow	L hand hold pulls

*Note: Amalgamate Side Pass/Neck Pass with Underarm Turn Right.

Open Swing Position

Steps 1-3

Steps 4-6

Western Swing

Side Pass/Neck Pass (triple time)
Lady's Footwork

Step	Description	Timing	Rhythmic Cue
	Position: Open Swing Position with single hand hold (his left holding her right).*		
1	Step R foot diagonally forward and to the left as you begin to progress clockwise around your partner. The man will place your R hand hold near his right side at waist level leading you into the Side Pass as he begins 1/2 turn counterclockwise.	1	Quick
2	Step L foot forward bringing feet together as you progress clockwise around your partner to change sides.	&	Quick
3	Step R foot forward completing a half turn to face your partner as the man releases your R hand hold.	2	Slow
4	Step L foot directly to the left moving parallel with your partner. Retake the R hand hold at waist level.	3	Quick
5	Step R foot to the left bringing feet together.	&	Quick
6	Step L foot directly to the left completing a triple step to your left.	4	Slow
7	Step R foot directly back facing your parnter (Rock Step).	1	Slow
8	Step L foot directly forward completing the Side Pass.	2	Slow

*Note: Amalgamate Side Pass/Neck Pass with Underarm Turn Right.

Western Swing

Side Pass/Neck Pass (triple time)
Man's Footwork

Step	Description	Timing	Rhythmic Cue	Lead

NECK PASS—to execute a Neck Pass substitute the following for Step #1.

Step	Description	Timing	Rhythmic Cue	Lead
1	Step L foot diagonally forward and to the left beginning to turn counterclockwise while leading the lady to progress around you clockwise. Begin the lead by placing the L hand hold above your right shoulder at neck level. Keep the right hand at waist level.	1	Quick	L hand hold pulls and places R hand held waist level

Bootnote: Steps 1-3 comprise the Side Pass or Neck Pass movement. Steps 4-6 move parallel with your partner to your right (small steps). Steps 7-8 comprise the Rock Step that moves directly away from your partner.

Western Swing

Side Pass/Neck Pass (triple time)
Lady's Footwork

Step	Description	Timing	Rhythmic Cue

NECK PASS—to execute a Neck Pass substitute the following for Step #1.

Step	Description	Timing	Rhythmic Cue
1	Step R foot diagonally forward and to the left as you begin to progress clockwise around your partner. The man will place your R hand hold above his shoulder at neck level leading you into the Neck Pass as he begins 1/2 turn counter-clockwise.	1	Quick

Bootnote: In executing the Side Pass or Neck Pass the partners will change sides during the movement.

Western Swing

Layover (triple time)
Man's Footwork

Step	Description	Timing	Rhythmic Cue	Lead
	Position: Open Swing Position with double hand hold (his left holding her right, his right holding her left).*			
1	Step L foot directly forward beginning to lead the lady to your right side into Layover Position. Keeping your L hand hold at waist level lead the lady into position by encircling your head with your R hand hold.	1	Quick	R hand hold pulls and encircles
2	Step R foot forward bringing feet together continuing to lead the lady into Layover Position.	&	Quick	R hand hold encircles
3	Step L foot directly forward (small step) as you place your R hand hold on your left shoulder into Layover Position. The R hand hold consists of your right arm crossed in front of your chest with the lady's left arm wrapped around your shoulders, your right hand holding her left. The L hand hold is at waist level.	2	Slow	L hand hold waist level R hand hold placed
4	Step R foot directly backward (small step) in Layover Position. Double hand hold in Layover Position will initiate a body lead.	3	Quick	Double hand hold
5	Step L foot directly backward bringing feet together.	&	Quick	Double hand hold
6	Step R foot directly backward completing a triple step in Layover Position.	4	Slow	Double hand hold
7	Step L foot directly back (Rock Step).	1	Slow	Double hand hold
8	Step R foot forward completing the movement into Layover Position.	2	Slow	Double hand hold
9	Step L foot directly forward (small step) beginning to lead the lady out of Layover Position into Open Position. Release the R hand hold as the L hand hold pulls the lady forward.	3	Quick	R hand hold releases L hand hold pulls
10	Step R foot forward bringing feet together continuing to lead the lady forward, passing you, into Open Position.	&	Quick	L hand hold pulls
11	Step L foot directly forward completing a triple step and leading the lady to turn into Open Swing Position. Keep the right arm at waist level or take a double hand hold.	4	Slow	L hand hold pulls

Western Swing

Layover (triple time)
Lady's Footwork

Step	Description	Timing	Rhythmic Cue
	Position: Open Swing Position with double hand hold (his left holding her right, his right holding her left).*		
1	Step R foot diagonally forward to the left as the man begins to lead you in a clockwise turn into Layover Position. Keeping your R hand hold at waist level he will lead you into position by encircling his head with your L hand hold.	1	Quick
2	Step L foot forward bringing feet together as the man leads you to his right side continuing to turn you in a clockwise turn.	&	Quick
3	Step R foot diagonally to the right as the man leads you into Layover Position. Your L hand hold encircles his head and is placed on his left shoulder with his right arm crossed in front of his chest. Your R hand hold is at waist level.	2	Slow
4	Step L foot directly backward (small step) in Layover Position. Double hand hold in Layover Position will initiate a body lead.	3	Quick
5	Step R foot directly backward bringing feet together.	&	Quick
6	Step L foot directly backward completing a triple step in Layover Position.	4	Slow
7	Step R foot directly back (Rock Step).	1	Slow
8	Step L foot forward completing the movement into Layover Position.	2	Slow
9	Step R foot diagonally to the left (shuffle step) as the man begins to lead you out of Layover Position into Open Position. Release the L hand hold as the man leads you forward retaining the R hand hold.	3	Quick
10	Step L foot diagonally to the left passing right foot (shuffle step) as you progress past your partner beginning to turn counterclockwise 1/2 turn.	&	Quick
11	Step R foot forward pivoting to face your partner ending in Open Swing Position with a single hand hold (your right, his left).	4	Slow

Western Swing

Layover (triple time)
Man's Footwork cont'd

Step	Description	Timing	Rhythmic Cue	Lead
12	Step R foot directly to the right moving parallel with your parnter in Open Swing Position. The L hand hold leads the lady to your right as you step to the right.	1	Quick	L hand hold pressure
13	Step L foot directly to the right bringing feet together.	&	Quick	L hand hold pressure
14	Step R foot directly to the right completing a triple step to your right facing your partner.	2	Slow	L hand hold pressure
15	Step L foot directly back (Rock Step).	3	Slow	L hand hold pushes
16	Step R foot forward completing the movement out of Layover Position.	4	Slow	L hand hold pulls

*Note: Retain a double hand hold throughout the entire Layover. In the Side-by-Side position (steps 4,5,6) a triple step is executed forward and back instead of to the side.

Bootnote: Steps 1-3 take your partner into Layover Position. Steps 4-6 execute a triple step (progressing backward) in Layover Position. Steps 9-11 take your partner out of Layover Position. Steps 12-14 execute a triple step in Open Swing Position.

Open Swing Position

Steps 1-3

Steps 4-6

Steps 7-8

WESTERN SWING
Layover (triple time)
Lady's Footwork, cont'd

Step	Description	Timing	Rhythmic Cue
12	Step L foot directly to the left moving parallel with your partner.	1	Quick
13	Step R foot to the left bringing feet together.	&	Quick
14	Step L foot directly to the left completing a triple step to your left facing your partner.	2	Slow
15	Step R foot directly back (Rock Step).	3	Slow
16	Step L foot forward completing the movement out of Layover Position.	4	Slow

*Note: Retain a double hand hold throughout the entire Layover. In a Side-by-Side position the triple step is executed forward and back instead of to the side.

Bootnote: Steps 1-3 take you into Layover Position. Steps 4-6 execute a triple step (progressing backward) in Layover Position. Steps 9-11 take you out of LayoverPosition. Steps 12-14 execute a triple step in Open Swing Position.

Steps 9-11   Steps 12-14   Steps 15 and 16

Western Swing

Layover with Basic Step (triple time)
Man's Footwork

Step	Description	Timing	Rhythmic Cue	Lead
	Position: Open Swing Position with double hand hold (his left holding her right, his right holding her left).*			
1-8	Steps 1-8 in the Layover with a Basic Step are the same as steps 1-8 in the Layover.			
9	Step L foot directly forward in Layover Position. Double hand hold will initiate a body lead.	3	Quick	Double hand hold
10	Step R foot forward bringing feet together.	&	Quick	Double hand hold
11	Step L foot directly forward completing a triple step (progressing forward) in Layover Position.	4	Slow	Double hand hold
12	Step R foot directly backward in Layover Position. Double hand hold will initiate a body lead.	1	Quick	Double hand hold
13	Step L foot backward bringing feet together.	&	Quick	Double hand hold
14	Step R foot directly backward completing a triple step in Layover Position.	2	Slow	Double hand hold
15	Step L foot directly back (Rock Step).	3	Slow	Double hand hold
16	Step R foot forward completing a Basic Step in Layover Position.	4	Slow	Double hand hold
17-24	Steps 17-24 in the Layover with Basic Step are the same as steps 9-16 in the Layover.			

*Note: Retain a double hand hold throughout the entire Layover. In a Side-by-Side position a triple step is executed forward and back instead of to the side.

Bootnote: Steps 1-3 take your partner into Layover Position. Steps 4-6 execute a triple step (progressing backward) in Layover Position. Steps 9-14 execute a Basic Step in Layover Position with steps 9-11 progressing forward and steps 12-14 progressing backward. Steps 17-19 take your partner out of Layover Position. Steps 20-22 execute a triple step in Open Swing Position.

Steps 9-11   Steps 15 and 16

Western Swing

Layover with Basic Step (triple time)
Lady's Footwork

Step	Description	Timing	Rhythmic Cue
	Position: Open Swing Position with double hand hold (his left holding her right, his right holding her left).*		
1-8	Steps 1-8 in the Layover with a Basic Step are the same as steps 1-8 in the Layover.		
9	Step R foot directly forward in Layover Position. Double hand hold will initiate a body lead.	3	Quick
10	Step L foot forward bringing feet together.	&	Quick
11	Step R foot directly forward completing a triple step (progressing forward) in Layover Position.	4	Slow
12	Step L foot directly backward in Layover Position. Double hand hold will initiate a body lead.	1	Quick
13	Step R foot backward bringing feet together.	&	Quick
14	Step L foot directly backward completing a triple step (progressing backward) in Layover Position.	2	Slow
15	Step R foot directly back (Rock Step).	3	Slow
16	Step L foot forward completing a Basic Step in Layover Position.	4	Slow
17-24	Steps 17-24 in the Layover with Basic Step are the same as steps 9-16 in the Layover.		

*Note: Retain a double hand hold throughout the entire Layover. In a Side-by-Side position a triple step is executed forward and back instead of to the side.

 Bootnote: Steps 1-3 take you into Layover Position. Steps 4-6 execute a triple step (progressing backward) in Layover Position. Steps 9-14 execute a Basic Step in Layover Position with steps 9-11 progressing forward and steps 12-14 progressing backward. Steps 17-19 take you out of Layover Position. Steps 20-22 execute a triple step in Open Swing Position.

Western Swing

Sweetheart (triple time)
Man's Footwork

Step	Description	Timing	Rhythmic Cue	Lead
	Position: Open Swing Position with double hand hold (his left holding her right, his right holding her left) into Sweetheart Wrap Position.*			
1	Step L foot directly forward (small step) beginning to lead the lady into 1/2 turn counterclockwise to your right side. Pull the lady toward you with double hand hold and encircle the lady's head with your L hand hold. Your R hand hold remains at waist level.	1	Quick	R hand hold pulls L hand hold pulls and encircles
2	Step R foot directly forward bringing feet together continuing to lead the lady into Sweetheart Wrap Position.	&	Quick	L hand hold encircles
3	Step L foot directly forward (small step) completing the lead into Sweetheart Wrap Position beginning to lower the L hand hold over the lady's head. The R hand hold is at waist level.	2	Slow	L hand hold lowers
4	Step R foot directly backward (small step) in Sweetheart Wrap Position. The L hand hold is at waist level with the R hand hold wrapped behind the lady's back at waist level. The R hand hold pulls the lady backward.	3	Quick	R hand hold pulls
5	Step L foot backward bringing feet together.	&	Quick	R hand hold pulls
6	Step R foot directly backward (small step) completing a triple step in Sweetheart Wrap Position.	4	Slow	R hand hold pulls
7	Step L foot directly back (Rock Step).	1	Slow	R hand hold pulls
8	Step R foot forward completing the Sweetheart.	2	Slow	Double hand hold
9	Step L foot directly forward (small step) beginning to lead the lady out of Sweetheart Wrap Position into Open Position. The lead is executed by raising the L hand hold over the lady's head leading her to move forward from the pressure of your right forearm.	3	Quick	L hand hold raises and encircles R forearm pressure
10	Step R foot forward bringing feet together continuing to lead the lady to turn clockwise out of Sweetheart Wrap Position. Keep the R hand hold at waist level.	&	Quick	L hand hold encircles

Western Swing

Sweetheart (triple time)
Lady's Footwork

Step	Description	Timing	Rhythmic Cue
	Position: Open Swing Position with double hand hold (his left holding her right, his right holding her left) into Sweetheart Wrap Position.*		
1	Step R foot diagonally forward and to the left beginning 1/2 turn counterclockwise under your R hand hold into Sweetheart Wrap Position. Your L hand hold will remain at waist level.	1	Quick
2	Step L foot forward bringing feet together continuing to turn counterclockwise under your R hand hold to his right side.	&	Quick
3	Step R foot diagonally forward and to the left pivoting to complete 1/2 turn counterclockwise into Sweetheart Wrap Position. Your R hand hold will encircle your head and lower to waist level.	2	Slow
4	Step L foot directly backward (small step) in Sweetheart Wrap Position. You are on the man's right side.	3	Quick
5	Step R foot backward bringing feet together.	&	Quick
6	Step L foot directly backward (small step) completing a triple step in Sweetheart Wrap Position.	4	Slow
7	Step R foot directly back (Rock Step).	1	Slow
8	Step L foot forward completing the movement into Sweetheart.	2	Slow
9	Step R foot directly forward under your R hand hold beginning to move out of Sweetheart Wrap Position.	3	Quick
10	Step L foot directly forward bringing feet together beginning to turn 1/2 turn clockwise into Open Position with a double hand hold. Your L hand hold will remain at waist level.	&	Quick

Western Swing

Sweetheart (triple time)
Man's Footwork, cont'd

Step	Description	Timing	Rhythmic Cue	Lead
11	Step L foot directly forward (small step) completing a triple step and leading the lady to face you in Open Position with a double hand hold. Begin to lower the L hand hold to waist level.	4	Slow	L hand hold lowers
12	Step R foot directly to the right moving parallel with your partner in Open Swing Position. Double hand hold leads the lady to your right as you step to the right.	1	Quick	Double hand hold
13	Step L foot to the right bringing feet together.	&	Quick	Double hand hold
14	Step R foot directly to the right completing a triple step to your right facing your partner.	2	Slow	Double hand hold
15	Step L foot directly back (Rock Step).	3	Slow	Double hand hold
16	Step R foot forward completing the Sweetheart.	4	Slow	Double hand hold pulls

*Note: Retain a double hand hold throughout the entire Sweetheart. In a Side-by-Side position the triple step is executed forward and back instead of to the side.

 Boonote: Steps 1-3 take your partner into Sweetheart Wrap Position. Steps 4-6 execute a triple step (progressing backward) in Sweetheart Wrap Position. Steps 9-11 take your partner out of Sweetheart Wrap Position. Steps 12-14 execute a triple step in Open Swing Position.

Open Swing Position   Steps 1-3   Steps 7 and 8

Western Swing

Sweetheart (triple time)
Lady's Footwork, cont'd

Step	Description	Timing	Rhythmic Cue
11	Step R foot diagonally forward and to the right pivoting to complete 1/2 turn clockwise out of Sweetheart Wrap Position into Open Position with double hand hold. Your R hand hold will encircle your head and lower to waist level.	4	Slow
12	Step L foot directly to the left moving parallel with your partner in Open Swing Position.	1	Quick
13	Step R foot to the left bringing feet together.	&	Quick
14	Step L foot directly to the left completing a triple step to your left facing your partner.	2	Slow
15	Step R foot directly back (Rock Step).	3	Slow
16	Step L foot forward completing the Sweetheart.	4	Slow

*Note: Retain a double hand hold throughout the entire Sweetheart. In a Side-by-Side position the triple step is executed forward and back instead of to the side.

Bootnote: Steps 1-3 take you into Sweetheart Wrap Position. Steps 4-6 execute a triple step (progressing backward) in Sweetheart Wrap Position. Steps 9-11 take you out of Sweetheart Wrap Position. Steps 12-14 execute the a triple step in Open Swing Position.

Steps 9-11   Steps 12-14

Western Swing

Sweetheart with Basic Step (triple time)
Man's Footwork

Step	Description	Timing	Rhythmic Cue	Lead
	Position: Open Swing Position with double hand hold (his left holding her right, his right holding her left) into Sweetheart Wrap Position.*			
1-8	Steps 1-8 in the Sweetheart with a Basic Step are the same as steps 1-8 in the Sweetheart.			
9	Step L foot directly forward in Sweetheart Wrap Position. The right forearm will lead the lady forward.	3	Quick	R forearm pressure
10	Step R foot forward bringing feet together.	&	Quick	R forearm pressure
11	Step L foot directly forward completing a triple step (progressing forward) in Sweetheart Wrap Position.	4	Slow	R forearm pressure
12	Step R foot directly backward in Sweetheart Wrap Position. The R hand hold will pull the lady backward.	1	Quick	R hand hold pulls
13	Step L foot backward bringing feet together.	&	Quick	R hand hold pulls
14	Step R foot directly backward completing a triple step in Sweetheart Wrap Position.	2	Slow	R hand hold pulls
15	Step L foot directly back (Rock Step).	3	Slow	R hand hold pulls
16	Step R foot forward completing a Basic Step in Sweetheart Wrap Position.	4	Slow	R forearm pressure
17-24	Steps 17-24 in the Sweetheart with Basic Step are the same as steps 9-16 in the Sweetheart.			

*Note: Retain a double hand hold throughout the entire Sweetheart. In a Side-by-Side position a triple step is executed forward and back instead of to the side.

Bootnote: Steps 1-3 take your partner into Sweetheart Wrap Position. Steps 4-6 execute a triple step (progressing backward) in Sweetheart Wrap Position. Steps 9-14 execute a Basic Step in Sweetheart Wrap Position with steps 9-11 progressing forward and steps 12-14 progressing backward. Steps 17-19 take your partner out of Sweetheart Wrap Position. Steps 20-22 execute a triple step in Open Swing Position.

Steps 9-11   Steps 15-16

Western Swing

Sweetheart with Basic Step (triple time)
Lady's Footwork

Step	Description	Timing	Rhythmic Cue
	Position: Open Swing Position with double hand hold (his left holding her right, his right holding her left) into Sweetheart Wrap Position.*		
1-8	Steps 1-8 in the Sweetheart with a Basic Step are the same as steps 1-8 in the Sweetheart.		
9	Step R foot directly forward in Sweetheart Wrap Position. The man's right forearm will lead you forward.	3	Quick
10	Step L foot forward bringing feet together.	&	Quick
11	Step R foot directly forward completing a triple step (progressing forward) in Sweetheart Wrap Position.	4	Slow
12	Step L foot directly backward in Sweetheart Wrap Position. His R hand hold will lead you backward.	1	Quick
13	Step R foot backward bringing feet together.	&	Quick
14	Step L foot directly backward completing a triple step in Sweetheart Wrap Position.	2	Slow
15	Step R foot directly back (Rock Step).	3	Slow
16	Step L foot forward completing a Basic Step in Sweetheart Wrap Position.	4	Slow
17-24	Steps 17-24 in the Sweetheart with Basic Step are the same as steps 9-16 in the Sweetheart.		

*Note: Retain a double hand hold throughout the entire Sweetheart. In a Side-by-Side position a triple step is executed forward and back instead of to the side.

 Bootnote: Steps 1-3 take you into Sweetheart Wrap Position. Steps 4-6 execute a triple step (progressing backward) in Sweetheart Wrap Position. Steps 9-14 execute a Basic Step in Sweetheart Wrap Position with steps 9-11 progressing forward and steps 12-14 progressing backward. Steps 17-19 take you out of Sweetheart Wrap Position. Steps 20-22 execute a triple step in Open Swing Position.

Western Swing

Wringer (triple time)
Man's Footwork

Step	Description	Timing	Rhythmic Cue	Lead
	Position: Open Swing Position with double hand hold (his left holding her right, his right holding her left) into Wringer Position.*			
1	Step L foot in place (next to right foot) beginning to lead the lady to turn clockwise under your L hand hold.	1	Quick	L hand hold lifts and encircles R hand hold waist level
2	Step R foot in place continuing to lead the lady in a counterclockwise turn.	&	Quick	L hand hold encircles
3	Step L foot in place beginning to turn counterclockwise into Wringer Position. The L hand hold encircles the lady's head as the R hand hold places the lady's right arm behind her back.	2	Slow	L hand hold encircles R hand hold waist level
4	Step R foot to the right continuing to lead the lady into the Wringer. The L hand hold will begin to lower to chest level.	3	Quick	L hand hold lowers
5	Step L foot to the right bringing feet together, continuing to lower the L hand hold into Wringer Position.	&	Quick	L hand hold lowers
6	Step R foot to the right as you complete the movement into Wringer Position. The L hand hold is at chest level with the R hand hold wrapped behind the lady's back at waist level.	4	Slow	L hand hold lowers
7	Step L foot directly back (Rock Step) in Wringer Position leading the lady to rock back.	1	Slow	R hand hold pushes
8	Step R foot directly forward completing the movement into the Wringer.	2	Slow	R hand hold pushes
9	Step L foot in place beginning 1/4 turn clockwise while leading the lady to turn counterclockwise under your L hand hold.	3	Quick	L hand hold lifts and encircles R hand hold waist level
10	Step R foot in place continuing to turn the lady counterclockwise.	&	Quick	L hand hold encircles
11	Step L foot in place completing 1/4 turn clockwise leading the lady out of the Wringer.	4	Slow	L hand hold lowers

*Note: Retain a double hand hold throughout entire Wringer.

Western Swing

Wringer (triple time)
Lady's Footwork

Step	Description	Timing	Rhythmic Cue
	Position: Open Swing Position with double hand hold (his left holding her right, his right holding her left) into Wringer Position.*		
1	Step R foot diagonally to the right from Open Swing Position as the man begins to lead you under your R hand hold (clockwise) into Wringer Position.	1	Quick
2	Step L foot forward bringing feet together continuing clockwise turn under your R hand hold.	&	Quick
3	Step R foot diagonally to the right pivoting clockwise into Wringer Position. Your R hand hold will encircle your head with the L hand hold remaining at waist level.	2	Slow
4	Step L foot directly to the left moving parallel with your partner in Wringer Position. The man will lower your R hand hold to chest level with your L hand hold at waist level.	3	Quick
5	Step R foot directly to the left bringing feet together in Wringer Position.	&	Quick
6	Step L foot directly to the left (small step) completing a triple step to your left.	4	Slow
7	Step R foot directly back (Rock Step) in Wringer Position.	1	Slow
8	Step L foot directly forward completing the movement into the Wringer.	2	Slow
9	Step R foot diagonally to the left beginning to turn counterclockwise under your R hand hold.	3	Quick
10	Step L foot forward bringing feet together while continuing to turn counterclockwise. Your R hand hold will encircle your head while your L hand hold will remain at waist level.	&	Quick
11	Step R foot diagonally to the left pivoting to turn counterclockwise out of the Wringer to face your partner.	4	Slow

*Note: Retain a double hand hold throughout the entire Wringer.

Western Swing

Wringer (triple time)
Man's Footwork, cont'd

Step	Description	Timing	Rhythmic Cue	Lead
12	Step R foot directly to the right moving parallel with your partner. Double hand hold is at waist level.	1	Quick	Double hand hold
13	Step L foot to the right bringing feet together.	&	Quick	Double hand hold
14	Step R foot directly to the right completing a triple step to your right.	2	Slow	Double hand hold
15	Step L foot directly back (Rock Step).	3	Slow	Double hand hold pushes
16	Step R foot directly forward completing the Wringer.	4	Slow	Double hand hold pulls

Bootnote 1: The movement in and out of the Wringer is similar to the movements into the Underarm Turn Left and the Reverse Underarm Turn. Small steps must be executed because of the double hand hold.

Bootnote 2: Steps 1-6 take your partner into the Wringer. Steps 7-8 execute the rock step. Steps 9-14 take your partner out of the Wringer. Steps 15-16 execute the rock step.

Open Swing Position   Steps 1-3   Steps 4-6

Western Swing

Wringer (triple time)
Lady's Footwork, cont'd

Step	Description	Timing	Rhythmic Cue
12	Step L foot directly to the left moving parallel with your partner. Double hand hold is at waist level.	1	Quick
13	Step R foot to the left bringing feet together.	&	Quick
14	Step L foot to the left completing a triple step to your left.	2	Slow
15	Step R foot directly back (Rock Step).	3	Slow
16	Step L foot directly forward completing the Wringer.	4	Slow

Bootnote: Steps 1-6 take you into Wringer Position. Steps 7-8 execute the rock step. Steps 9-14 take you out of the Wringer Position. Steps 15-16 execute the rock step.

Steps 7 and 8   Steps 9-11   Steps 12-14

Western Swing

Wringer with Basic Step (triple time)
Man's Footwork

Step	Description	Timing	Rhythmic Cue	Lead
	Position: Open Swing Position with double hand hold (his left holding her right, his right holding her left) into Wringer Position.*			
1-8	Steps 1-8 in the Wringer with Basic Step are the same as steps 1-8 in the Wringer.			
9	Step L foot directly to the left in Wringer Position.	3	Quick	Double hand hold
10	Step R foot to the left bringing feet together.	&	Quick	Double hand hold
11	Step L foot directly to the left completing a triple step to your left in Wringer Position.	4	Slow	Double hand hold
12	Step R foot directly to the right in Wringer Position.	1	Quick	Double hand hold
13	Step L foot to the right bringing feet together.	&	Quick	Double hand hold
14	Step R foot directly to the right completing a triple step to your right in Wringer Position.	2	Slow	Double hand hold
15	Step L foot directly back (Rock Step).	3	Slow	Double hand hold
16	Step R foot forward completing a basic step in Wringer Position.	4	Slow	Double hand hold
17-24	Steps 17-24 in the Wringer with Basic Step are the same as the steps 9-16 in Wringer.			

*Note: Retain a double hand hold throughout the entire Wringer.

Bootnote 1: Steps 1-6 take your partner into Wringer Position. Steps 7-8 execute the rock step. Steps 9-14 execute a Basic Step in Wringer Position. Steps 15-16 execute a rock step. Steps 17-22 take your partner out of Wringer Position. Steps 23-24 execute a rock step.

Bootnote 2: A double hand hold throughout steps 9-16 initiates the lead without additional pressure.

Steps 12-14   Steps 15 and 16

Western Swing

Wringer with Basic Step (triple time)
Lady's Footwork

Step	Description	Timing	Rhythmic Cue
	Position: Open Position with double hand hold (his left holding her right, his right holding her left) into Wringer Position.*		
1-8	Steps 1-8 in the Wringer with Basic Step are the same as steps 1-8 in the Wringer.		
9	Step R foot directly to the right in Wringer Position.	1	Quick
10	Step L foot to the right bringing feet together.	&	Quick
11	Step R foot directly to the right completing a triple step to your right in Wringer Position.	2	Slow
12	Step L foot directly to the left in Wringer Position.	3	Quick
13	Step R foot to the left bringing feet together.	&	Quick
14	Step L foot directly to the left completing a triple step to your left in Wringer Position.	4	Slow
15	Step R foot directly back (Rock Step).	1	Slow
16	Step L foot forward completing a basic step in Wringer Position.	2	Slow
17-24	Steps 17-24 in the Wringer with Basic Step are the same as Steps 9-16 in Wringer.		

*Note: Retain a double hand hold throughout the entire Wringer.

 Bootnote: Steps 1-6 take you into Wringer Position. Steps 7-8 execute the rock step. Steps 9-14 execute a Basic Step in Wringer Position. Steps 15-16 execute the rock step. Steps 17-22 take you out of Wringer Position. Steps 23-24 execute a rock step.

Western Swing

Sweetheart Turns (triple time)
Man's Footwork

Step	Description	Timing	Rhythmic Cue	Lead
	Position: Open Swing Position with double hand hold (his left holding her right, his right holding her left) into Sweetheart Wrap Position.*			
1-3	Steps 1-3 in the Sweetheart Turns are the same as steps 1-3 in the Sweetheart.			
4	Step R foot diagonally forward and to the right leading the lady to step backwards to circle clockwise in Sweetheart Wrap Position. The R hand hold pulls the lady to circle backwards while the L hand hold remains at waist level.	3	Slow	R hand hold pulls
5	Step L foot diagonally forward and to the right continuing to lead the lady to step backwards in a clockwise circle.	4	Slow	R hand hold pulls
6	Step R foot diagonally forward and to the right continuing to lead the lady to step backwards in a clockwise circle.	1	Slow	R hand hold pulls
7	Step L foot diagonally forward and to the right continuing to lead the lady to step backwards in a clockwise circle.	2	Slow	R hand hold pulls
8	Step R foot diagonally forward and to the right continuing to lead the lady to step backwards in a clockwise circle.	3	Slow	R hand hold pulls
9	Step L foot diagonally forward (small step) and to the right leading the lady out of Sweetheart Wrap Position to face you. The lead is executed by lifting the L hand hold up to encircle the lady's head while the R hand hold pulls the lady to turn clockwise in place to face you.	4	Slow	L hand hold lifts and encircles R hand hold pulls

*Note: Retain a double hand hold throughout the entire Sweetheart Turns.

WESTERN SWING

Sweetheart Turns (triple time)
Lady's Footwork

Step	Description	Timing	Rhythmic Cue
	Position: Open Swing Position with double hand hold (his left holding her right, his right holding her left) into Sweetheart Wrap Position.*		
1-3	Steps 1-3 in the Sweetheart Turns are the same as steps 1-3 in the Sweeteart.		
4	Step L foot diagonally backward and to the left as the man leads you to circle clockwise in Sweetheart Wrap Position. The man will progress forward in a clockwise circle.	3	Slow
5	Step R foot diagonally backward and to the left continuing to step backwards in a clockwise circle.	4	Slow
6	Step L foot diagonally backward and to the left continuing to step backwards in a clockwise circle.	1	Slow
7	Step R foot diagonally backward and to the left continuing to step backwards in a clockwise circle.	2	Slow
8	Step L foot diagonally backward and to the left continuing to step backwards in a clockwise circle.	3	Slow
9	Step R foot diagonally backward (small step) and to the left as you pivot out of Sweetheart Wrap Position to face your partner. The lead is executed by the man lifting your R hand hold over your head while pulling your L hand hold to turn you clockwise in place to face him.	4	Slow

*Note: Retain a double hand hold throughout the entire Sweetheart Turns.

Western Swing

Sweetheart Turns (triple time)
Man's Footwork, cont'd

Step	Description	Timing	Rhythmic Cue	Lead

10-14 Steps 10-14 in the Sweetheart Turns are the
same as steps 12-16 in the Sweetheart.

Bootnote 1: Steps 4-9 require a firm pull with the R hand hold to lead the lady to circle backwards in a clockwise movement.

Bootnote 2: Steps 1-3 lead your partner into Sweetheart Wrap Position. Steps 4-8 execute the Sweetheart Turns. Step 9 leads your partner out of Sweetheart Wrap Position. Steps 10-14 execute a triple step and a rock step.

Open Swing Position   Steps 1-3   Steps 4-6

Western Swing

Sweetheart Turns (triple time)
Lady's Footwork, cont'd

Step	Description	Timing	Rhythmic Cue
10-14	Steps 10-14 in the Sweetheart Turns are the same as steps 12-16 in the Sweetheart.		

 Bootnote: Steps 1-3 lead you into Sweetheart Wrap Position. Steps 4-8 execute the Sweetheart Turns. Step 9 leads you out of Sweetheart Wrap Position. Steps 10-14 execute a triple step and a rock step.

Steps 7 and 8   Step 9   Steps 13-14

Western Swing

Kick 'N (triple time)
Man's Footwork

Step	Description	Timing	Rhythmic Cue	Lead
	Position: Closed Swing Position*			
1	Kick L foot directly forward (lead with bent knee).	1	Slow	R hand pressure
2	Step L foot in place beside right foot.	2	Slow	R hand pressure
3	Kick R foot directly forward (lead with bent knee).	3	Slow	R hand pressure
4	Step R foot in place as you turn 1/4 turn to face your partner. Lead the lady to face you with your right hand placed on her left shoulder blade.	4	Slow	R hand pressure
5	Kick L foot directly forward (lead with bent knee) outside your partners right foot.	1	Slow	R hand pressure
6	Step L foot in place beside right foot.	2	Slow	R hand pressure
7	Kick R foot directly forward (lead with bent knees) between partner's feet.	3	Slow	R hand pressure
8	Step R foot in place beside left foot.	4	Slow	R hand pressure
9	Step L foot diagonally back (Rock Step) into Fall-a-Way Position.	1	Slow	R hand pressure
10	Step R foot forward completing the Kick 'N.	2	Slow	R hand pressure

*Note: Precede with a Basic Step in Closed Position. Following the Rock Step remain in Conversation Position (side by side) to execute the Kick 'N.

 Bootnote: To execute steps 1-4 keep the lady in Conversation Position by holding her firmly with your right hand placed on her left shoulder blade. The L hand hold is held inward at waist level. Return to Closed Position facing your partner during steps 5-8 by turning her to face you as you face her. Steps 8 and 9 comprise the rock step.

Basic Swing Step

Step 1

Step 3

Western Swing

Kick 'N (triple time)
Lady's Footwork

Step	Description		Timing	Rhythmic Cue
	Position: Closed Swing Position*			
1	Kick R foot directly forward (lead with bent knee).	1	Slow	
2	Step R foot in place beside left foot.	2	Slow	
3	Kick L foot directly forward (lead with bent knee).	3	Slow	
4	Step L foot in place as you turn 1/4 turn counterclockwise to face your partner in Closed Dance Position.	4	Slow	
5	Kick R foot directly forward (lead with bent knee) between partner's feet.	1	Slow	
6	Step R foot in place beside left foot.	2	Slow	
7	Kick L foot directly forward (lead with bent knee) outside your partner's right foot.	3	Slow	
8	Step L foot in place beside right foot.	4	Slow	
9	Step R foot diagonally back (Rock Step) into Fall-a-Way Position.	1	Slow	
10	Step L foot forward completing the Kick 'N.	2	Slow	

*Note: Precede with a Basic Step in Closed Position. Following the Rock Step remain in Conversation Position (side by side) to execute the Kick 'N.

Bootnote: Steps 1-4 are executed in Conversation Position. Steps 5-8 are executed in Closed Dance Position facing your partner. Steps 9-10 comprise the rock step.

| Step 5 | Step 7 | Steps 9 and 10 |

Western Swing

Back to Back (triple time)
Man's Footwork

Step	Description	Timing	Rhythmic Cue	Lead
	Position: Closed Swing Position.*			
1	Step L foot to the left (facing your partner). To begin the lead into Back to Back turn the L hand hold inward (slightly).	1	Quick	L hand hold twist and lower R palm pressure
2	Step R foot to the left bringing feet together beginning to turn clockwise into Back to Back Position.	&	Quick	R hand palm pressure
3	Step L foot to the left turning 1/2 turn clockwise into Back to Back Position. Release the right hand contact keeping arm extended at chest level. Retain the L hand hold as you twist it inward letting the arms begin to move behind your back.	2	Slow	L hand hold twist
4	Step R foot directly to the right (back to partner).	3	Quick	L hand hold twist
5	Step L foot to the right bringing feet together continuing to turn clockwise in Back to Back Position.	&	Quick	L hand hold twist
6	Step R foot to the right turning 1/4 turn clockwise into a side-by-side position. Place the L hand hold behind your back at waist level. Extend the right hand outward (palm down) at waist level so your partner may rest her right hand on top of it.	4	Slow	R hand extended L hand hold twist
7	Step L foot directly forward (Rock Step) in a side-by-side position.	1	Slow	R hand extended L hand hold twist
8	Step R foot directly backward beginning to turn 1/4 turn counterclockwise into Back to Back Position.	2	Slow	L hand hold reverse twist
9	Step L foot directly to the left (back to partner).	3	Quick	L hand hold reverse twist
10	Step R foot to the left bringing feet together. Keep the right hand extended outward at chest level as the L hand hold twists out of Back to Back Position.	&	Quick	L hand hold reverse twist
11	Step L foot to the left turning 1/2 turn counter-clockwise to face your partner returning to Closed Position.	4	Slow	L hand hold reverse twist
12	Step R foot to the right (facing partner) as you take Closed Dance Position.	1	Quick	R finger pressure

*Note: Precede with a Basic Step in Closed Swing Position.

Western Swing

Back to Back (triple time)
Lady's Footwork

Step	Description	Timing	Rhythmic Cue
	Position: Closed Swing Position*		
1	Step R foot directly to the right (facing partner).	1	Quick
2	Step L foot to the right bringing feet together beginning to turn counterclockwise into Back to Back Position.	&	Quick
3	Step R foot to the right turning 1/2 turn counterclockwise into Back to Back Position.	2	Slow
4	Step L foot directly to the left (back to partner).	3	Quick
5	Step R foot to the left bringing feet together continuing to turn counterclockwise in Back to Back Position.	&	Quick
6	Step L foot to the left turning 1/4 turn counterclockwise into a side-by-side position. Extend the left hand outward placing it on top of the man's right hand at waist level (palm down).	4	Slow
7	Step R foot directly forward (Rock Step) in a side-by-side position.	1	Slow
8	Step L foot backward and pivot 1/4 turn clockwise into Back to Back Position.	2	Slow
9	Step R foot directly to the right (back to partner).	3	Quick
10	Step L foot to the right bringing feet together. Keep the left hand extended outward at chest level as your R hand hold twists out of Back to Back Position.	&	Quick
11	Step R foot to the right turning 1/2 turn clockwise to face your partner returning to Closed Position.	4	Slow
12	Step L foot to the left (facing partner) as you return to Closed Dance Position.	1	Quick

*Note: Precede with a Basic Step in Closed Swing Position.

Western Swing

Back to Back (triple time)
Man's Footwork, cont'd

Step	Description	Timing	Rhythmic Cue	Lead
13	Step L foot to the right bringing feet together.	&	Quick	R finger pressure
14	Step R foot to the right completing a triple step to your right.	2	Slow	R finger pressure
15	Step L foot directly back (Rock Step) into Fall-a-Way Position.	3	Slow	R hand pressure
16	Step R foot forward completing the Back to Back.	4	Slow	R hand pressure

Bootnote: Steps 1-3 execute a triple step facing your partner. Steps 4-6 execute a triple step in Back to Back Position. Steps 7-8 execute a Rock Step *forward* in a side-by-side position. Steps 9-11 execute a triple step in Back to Back Position. Steps 12-14 execute a triple step facing your partner. Steps 15-16 execute a Rock Step in Closed Swing Position.

| Basic Swing Step | Steps 1-3 | Steps 4-6 | Steps 7 and 8 |

Western Swing

Back to Back (triple time)
Lady's Footwork, cont'd

Step	Description	Timing	Rhythmic Cue
13	Step R foot to the left bringing feet together.	&	Quick
14	Step L foot to the left completing a triple step to your left.	2	Slow
15	Step R foot directly back (Rock Step) into Fall-a-Way Position.	3	Slow
16	Step L foot forward completing the Back to Back.	4	Slow

Bootnote: Steps 1-3 execute a triple step facing your partner. Steps 4-6 execute a triple step in Back to Back Position. Steps 7-8 execute a Rock Step *forward* in a side-by-side position. Steps 9-11 execute a triple step in Back to Back Position. Steps 12-14 execute a triple step facing your partner. Steps 15-16 execute a Rock Step in Closed Swing Position.

Steps 9-11   Steps 12-14   Steps 15 and 16

Western Swing

Shuttle (triple time)
Man's Footwork

Step	Description	Timing	Rhythmic Cue	Lead
	Position: Open Swing Position with crossed double hand hold (right hands over left hands) into Shuttle Position.*			
1	Step L foot diagonally to the right beginning to turn clockwise 1/2 turn into Shuttle Position while raising your double hand hold up and over the lady's head.	1	Quick	Double hand hold pulls and lifts
2	Step R foot to the left bringing feet together.	&	Quick	Double hand hold encircles
3	Step L foot to the left continuing to turn clockwise into the Shuttle. Lower the L hand hold to waist level keeping the R hand hold above head level.	2	Slow	L hand hold lowered R hand hold held high
4	Step R foot directly back (Rock Step) facing your partner in Shuttle Position.	3	Slow	R hand hold held high L hand hold waist level
5	Step L foot directly forward completing the movement into the Shuttle.	4	Slow	R hand hold held high L hand hold waist level
6	Step R foot diagonally to the left beginning to turn 1/2 turn counterclockwise into Reverse Shuttle Position. Pull slightly to lead the lady to change sides as you lift your double hand hold up and over the lady's head.	1	Quick	L hand hold pulls and lifts R hand hold encircles
7	Step L foot to the right bringing feet together.	&	Quick	Double hand hold encircles
8	Step R foot to the right continuing to turn counterclockwise into Reverse Shuttle Position. Lower the R hand hold to waist level and raise the L hand hold above head level.	2	Slow	R hand hold lowered L hand hold held high
9	Step L foot directly back (Rock Step) facing your partner in Reverse Shuttle Position.	3	Slow	L hand hold held high R hand hold waist level
10	Step R foot directly forward completing the movement into Reverse Shuttle Position.	4	Slow	R hand hold waist level L hand hold held high

*Note: Precede with a Basic Step in Open Position changing to hand hold above during steps 1-6.

Bootnote 1: Steps 1-10 may be repeated or you may return to the Basic Step in Open Position or you may execute Thread the Needle.

Bootnote 2: The Shuttle refers to the curved shape of the arms. Steps 1-3 execute a triple step into Shuttle Position. Steps 4-5 execute a Rock Step in Shuttle Position. Steps 6-8 execute a triple step into Reverse Shuttle Position. Steps 9-10 execute a Rock Step in Reverse Shuttle Position.

Western Swing

Shuttle (triple time)
Lady's Footwork

Step	Description	Timing	Rhythmic Cue
	Position: Open Swing Position with crossed double hand hold (right hands over left hands) into Shuttle Position.*		
1	Step R foot diagonally to the left beginning 1/2 turn counterclockwise into Shuttle Position. The lead will lift your double hand hold up and over your head.	1	Quick
2	Step L foot to the right bringing feet together.	&	Quick
3	Step R foot to the right continuing to turn counterclockwise into the Shuttle. The L hand hold will lower to waist level while the R hand hold remains above head level.	2	Slow
4	Step L foot directly back (Rock Step) facing your partner in Shuttle Position.	3	Slow
5	Step R foot directly forward completing the movement into the Shuttle.	4	Slow
6	Step L foot diagonally to the right beginning 1/2 turn clockwise into Reverse Shuttle Position. The lead will lift double hand hold up and over your head.	1	Quick
7	Step R foot to the right bringing feet together.	&	Quick
8	Step L foot to the right continuing to turn counterclockwise into the Reverse Shuttle. Lower the R hand hold to waist level and raise the L hand hold above head level.	2	Slow
9	Step R foot directly back (Rock Step) facing your partner in Reverse Shuttle Position.	3	Slow
10	Step L foot directly forward completing the movement into Reverse Shuttle Position.	4	Slow

*Note: Precede with a Basic Step in Open Position changing to hand hold above during steps 1-6.

Bootnote 1: Steps 1-10 may be repeated or you may return to the Basic Step in Open Position or you may execute Thread the Needle.

Bootnote 2: The Shuttle refers to the curved shape of the arms. Steps 1-3 execute a triple step into Shuttle Position. Steps 4-5 execute a Rock Step in Shuttle Position. Steps 6-8 execute a triple step in Reverse Shuttle Position. Steps 9-10 execute a Rock Step in Reverse Shuttle Position.

Western Swing

Shuttle (triple time)

Open Swing
Position

Steps 1-3

Steps 4 and 5

Western Swing

Shuttle (triple time)

Steps 6-8   Steps 9 and 10

Western Swing

Thread the Needle (triple time)
Man's Footwork

Step	Description	Timing	Rhythmic Cue	Lead
	Position: Open Swing Position with crossed double hand hold (right hands over left hands).			
1	Step L foot diagonally to the right beginning a 1-1/2 turn clockwise into Thread the Needle Position. Lift your double hand hold up and over the lady's head as you change sides into position.	1	Quick	R hand hold pulls and lifts L hand hold lifts
2	Step R foot to the left bringing feet together continuing clockwise turn.	&	Quick	L hand hold lowers R hand hold held high
3	Step L foot to the left completing 1/2 of the 1-1/2 turn clockwise. As you begin to turn under your R hand hold lower your L hand hold to rotate behind your back at waist level.		Slow	R hand hold lowers L hand hold wraps behind back
4	Step R foot diagonally to the right continuing to turn into Thread the Needle Position.	3	Quick	L hand hold wraps behind back R hand hold lowers
5	Step L foot around right foot continuing movement into a 1-1/2 turn clockwise.	&	Quick	R hand hold lowers L hand hold wraps behind back
6	Step R foot diagonally to the right completing 1-1/2 turn to face your partner in Thread the Needle Position. L hand hold is wrapped behind your back at waist level. R hand hold is held at waist level with elbow held upward to form the eye of the needle.	4	Slow	L hand hold wraps behind back R hand hold waist level with elbow extended to form eye
7	Step L foot in place beside the right foot beginning to lead the lady to bend at the hips and step into the eye of the Needle on your right side. Pull the L hand hold slightly to lead the lady while keeping the right elbow raised and extended to the right.	1	Slow	R hand hold at waist level L hand hold pulls
8	Step R foot in place continuing to lead the lady through the eye of the Needle on your right side.	2	Slow	L hand hold pulls
9	Step L foot in place completing the lady's movement through the eye of the Needle. The lady will stand up straight as you begin to lead her to step behind you (back to back) from your right side to your left side.	3	Slow	L hand hold pulls R hand hold waist level

Western Swing

Thread the Needle (triple time)
Lady's Footwork

Step	Description	Timing	Rhythmic Cue
	Position: Open Swing Position with crossed double hand hold (right hands over left hands).		
1	Step R foot diagonally forward and to the left beginning 1/2 turn counterclockwise changing sides with your partner. The lead will raise double hand hold up and over your head.	1	Quick
2	Step L foot to the right bringing feet together continuing counterclockwise turn.	&	Quick
3	Step R foot to the right continuing to turn into Thread the Needle Position. Your L hand hold will begin to lower to waist level with your R hand hold held above head level.	2	Slow
4	Step L foot to the right bringing feet together, facing your partner, as he begins to move into Thread the Needle Position. The man will turn clockwise under your R hand hold with your L hand hold wrapping behind his back at waist level.	3	Quick
5	Step R foot in place, retaining a double hand hold, as the man continues to execute a full turn clockwise in place moving into position.	&	Quick
6	Step L foot in place as the man completes his movement into Thread the Needle Position. You will end facing your partner with your double hand hold held at waist level on his right side. His right elbow is held upward to form the eye of the needle.	4	Slow
7	Step R foot diagonally forward and to the left as you bend forward at the hips beginning to progress into the eye of the needle.	1	Slow
8	Step L foot forward continuing to progress through the eye of the needle formed by the double hand hold.	2	Slow
9	Step R foot to the right behind the man's back while in a back to back position. Stand upright while executing step 9.	3	Slow

Western Swing

Thread the Needle (triple time)
Man's Footwork, cont'd

Step	Description	Timing	Rhythmic Cue	Lead
10	Step R foot in place beginning to lead the lady out of the eye of the needle. The R hand hold is wrapped at waist level behind your back. L hand hold is held at waist level with elbow held upward to form the eye of the needle.	4	Slow	L hand hold pulls
11	Step L foot in place leading the lady to step backward out of the eye of the needle on your left side.	1	Slow	L hand hold pulls
12	Step R foot in place as the lady completes movement out of Thread the Needle. Release your double hand hold to take a single hand hold, your left holding her right.	2	Slow	R hand hold releases L hand hold releases and takes her right hand
13	Step L foot directly backward (Rock Step).	3	Slow	
14	Step R foot directly forward completing Thread the Needle.	4	Slow	

*Note: One may precede with a Basic Step in Open Position or with the Shuttle.

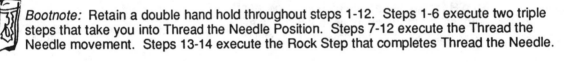

Bootnote: Retain a double hand hold throughout steps 1-12. Steps 1-6 execute two triple steps that take you into Thread the Needle Position. Steps 7-12 execute the Thread the Needle movement. Steps 13-14 execute the Rock Step that completes Thread the Needle.

Western Swing

Thread the Needle (triple time)
Lady's Footwork, cont'd

Step	Description	Timing	Rhythmic Cue
10	Step L foot diagonally backward and to the right as you bend forward at the hips to progress out of the eye of the needle on the man's left side.	4	Slow
11	Step R foot backward continuing to move out of the eye of the needle.	1	Slow
12	Step L foot backward completing movement out of the eye of the needle. Release your double hand hold and take a single hand hold, his left holding your right.	2	Slow
13	Step R foot directly back (Rock Step).	3	Slow
14	Step L foot directly forward completing Thread the Needle.	4	Slow

*Note: One may precede with a Basic Step in Open Position or with the Shuttle.

Bootnote: Steps 1-6 execute two triple steps that take you into Thread the Needle Position. Steps 7-12 execute the Thread the Needle movement. Steps 13-14 execute the Rock Step that completes Thread the Needle.

262

Western Swing
Thread the Needle (Triple Time)

Opening Swing
Position

Step 1

Step 3

Step 6

Step 7

Step 9

Western Swing
Thread the Needle (Triple Time)

Step 4

Step 5

Step 11

Step 12

Step 13 and 14

Western Swing

Twin Cities (triple time)
Man's Footwork

Step	Description	Timing	Rhythmic Cue	Lead
	Position: Open Swing Position with crossed double hand hold (right over left).*			
1	Step L foot directly to the left beginning to raise your double hand hold up and over the lady's head to turn her 1-1/4 turn clockwise.	1	Quick	R and L hand hold lifts and encircles
2	Step R foot to the left bringing feet together continuing to encircle the lady's head with your double hand hold.	&	Quick	R and L hand hold encircles
3	Step L foot directly to the left continuing to lead the lady into a clockwise turn.	2	Slow	R and L hand hold encircles
4	Step R foot directly to the right encircling the lady's head with your R hand hold as the L hand hold prepares to lower behind your head in Twin Cities position.	3	Quick	R hand hold encircles lady L hand hold raised
5	Step L foot to the right bringing feet together continuing to encircle the lady's head with the R hand hold as the L hand hold is held above your head.	&	Quick	R hand hold encircles lady L hand hold raised
6	Step R foot to the right turning 1/4 turn counterclockwise into Twin Cities position. The R hand hold will lower behind the lady's head to shoulder level as the L hand hold lowers behind your head to shoulder level.	4	Slow	R hand hold lowers L hand hold lowers
7	Step L foot directly back (Rock Step) in Twin Cities position. The lady is on your right side facing the same direction.	1	Slow	Double hand hold in Twin Cities Position
8	Step R foot forward completing the movement into Twin Cities position.	2	Slow	Double hand hold in Twin Cities Position
9	Step L foot to the left turning 1/4 turn clockwise to face your partner as you release the L hand hold. The R hand hold (remaining at shoulder level) will begin to lead the lady into 3/4 turn clockwise to face you.	3	Quick	R hand hold turns lady L hand hold releases
10	Step R foot to the left bringing feet together as you continue to lead the lady with the R hand hold out of Twin Cities position into 3/4 turn clockwise to face you.	&	Quick	R hand hold turns lady

*Note: Precede with a Basic Step in Open Swing Position changing to hand hold above during steps 1-6. Retain a double hand hold throughout the movement into Twin Cities (steps 1-8) Position.

Western Swing

Twin Cities (triple time)
Lady's Footwork

Step	Description	Timing	Rhythmic Cue
	Position: Open Swing Position with crossed double hand hold (right over left).*		
1	Step R foot diagonally to the right beginning 1/4 turn clockwise. The double hand hold will encircle your head to lead you into Twin Cities Position.	1	Quick
2	Step L foot forward bringing feet together as you continue clockwise turn into Twin Cities position.	&	Quick
3	Step R foot diagonally to the right as your double hand hold continues to encircle your head.	2	Slow
4	Step L foot diagonally forward as your R hand hold encircles your head to complete a clockwise turn with the L hand hold preparing to lower into Twin Cities Position.	3	Quick
5	Step R foot forward bringing feet together as your R hand hold completes a clockwise turn.	&	Quick
6	Step L foot diagonally forward completing 1-1/4 turn clockwise into Twin Cities Position. The man is on your left side facing the same direction. Your R hand hold lowers behind your head to shoulder level and your L hand hold lowers behind his head to shoulder level.	4	Slow
7	Step R foot directly back (Rock Step) in Twin Cities Position.	1	Slow
8	Step L foot forward completing the movement into Twin Cities Position.	2	Slow
9	Step R foot diagonally to the right beginning a 3/4 turn clockwise. Release the L hand hold and lower it to waist level as the R hand hold remains at shoulder level.	3	Quick
10	Step L foot forward bringing feet together continuing 3/4 turn clockwise to face your partner.	&	Quick

*Note: Precede with a Basic Step in Open Swing Position changing to hand hold above during steps 1-6. Retain a double hand hold throughout movement into Twin Cities (steps 1-8) Position.

Western Swing

Twin Cities (triple time)
Man's Footwork, cont'd

Step	Description	Timing	Rhythmic Cue	Lead
11	Step L foot to your left completing a triple step to the man's left. The R hand hold will complete the lead turning the lady 3/4 turn to face you as you lower the R hand hold to waist level.	4	Slow	R hand hold lowers
12	Step R foot directly to the right beginning to execute the second part of a basic step facing your partner. Retake the original hand hold, his right holding her right on top, his left holding her left on bottom at waist level.	1	Quick	R hand hold on top L hand hold on bottom
13	Step L foot to the right bringing feet together.	&	Quick	Double hand hold
14	Step R foot to the right completing a triple step to your right.	2	Slow	Double hand hold
15	Step L foot directly back (Rock Step).	3	Slow	Double hand hold pushes
16	Step R foot directly forward completing the movement into and out of Twin Cities.	4	Slow	Double hand hold pulls

 Bootnote: Steps 1-6 take you into Twin Cities position. Steps 7-8 execute a Rock Step in Twin Cities Position. Steps 9-11 take you out of Twin Cities position (release L hand hold). Steps 12-14 execute a triple step to the man's right facing your partner. Steps 15-16 execute a Rock Step facing your partner.

Open Swing Position   Step 1   Step 3   Step 5

Western Swing

Twin Cities (triple time)
Lady's Footwork, cont'd

Step	Description	Timing	Rhythmic Cue
11	Step R foot diagonally to the right completing a 3/4 turn clockwise to face your partner.	4	Slow
12	Lower the R hand hold to waist level and retake the original hand hold, his right holding her right on top, his left holding her left on bottom. Step L foot directly to the left beginning to execute the second part of a basic step facing your partner.	1	Quick
13	Step R foot to the left bringing feet together.	&	Quick
14	Step L foot to the left completing a triple step to your left.	2	Slow
15	Step R foot directly back (Rock Step).	3	Slow
16	Step L foot directly forward completing the movement into and out of Twin Cities.	4	Slow

Bootnote: Steps 1-6 take you into Twin Cities Position. Steps 7-8 execute a Rock Step in Twin Cities Position. Steps 9-11 take you out of Twin Cities Position. Steps 12-14 execute a triple step to the lady's left facing your partner. Steps 15-16 execute a Rock Step facing your partner.

Steps 7 and 8   Steps 9-11   Steps 12-14

Western Swing

Continuous Layover (triple time)
Man's Footwork

Step	Description	Timing	Rhythmic Cue	Lead
	Position: Open Swing Position with double hand hold (his right holding her right on top, his left holding her left on bottom).*			
1	Step L foot in place raising the R hand hold up and over the lady's head to place hand hold behind the lady's head at shoulder level.	1	Quick	R hand hold lifts
2	Step R foot in place continuing to place the R hand hold behind the lady's head at shoulder level.	&	Quick	R hand hold up and over
3	Step L foot in place completing a triple step in place and completing the R hand layover movement. The L hand hold remains at waist level.	2	Slow	R hand hold placed
4	Step R foot in place beginning to raise the L hand hold up and over the lady's head. Release the R hand hold and lower to waist level.	3	Quick	R hand hold releases & lowers L hand hold lift
5	Step L foot in place continuing to raise the L hand hold up and over the lady's head.	&	Quick	L hand hold up and over
6	Step R foot in place completing a triple step and completing the L hand hold layover movement. Retake the R hand hold at waist level.	4	Slow	L hand hold placed R hand hold at waist level
7	Step L foot in place raising the R hand hold up and over your head to place the L hand hold behind your head at shoulder level. Release the L hand hold behind the lady's head and lower to waist level.	1	Quick	R hand hold lifts L hand hold releases and loweres
8	Step R foot in place continuing to place the R hand hold behind your head at shoulder level.	&	Quick	R hand hold up and over
9	Step L foot in place completing a triple step and completing a R hand hold layover movement. Retake the L hand hold at waist level.	2	Slow	R hand hold placed L hand hold at waist level
10	Step R foot in place beginning to raise the L hand hold up and over your head. Release the R hand hold behind your head and begin to retake Closed Position.	3	Quick	L hand hold lifts R hand hold at waist level
11	Step L foot in place continuing to raise the L hand hold up and over your head.	&	Quick	L hand hold lifts R hand hold releases and lowers

*Note: Precede with Twin Cities movement into Continuous Layover.

Western Swing

Continuous Layover (triple time)
Lady's Footwork

Step	Description	Timing	Rhythmic Cue
	Position: Open Swing Positon with double hand hold (his right holding her right on top, his left holding her left on bottom).*		
1	Step R foot in place as the R hand hold is raised up and over your head to place L hand hold behind your head at shoulder level.	1	Quick
2	Step L foot in place continuing to place the R hand hold behind your head at shoulder level.	&	Quick
3	Step R foot in place completing a triple step in place and completing a right hand layover movement. The L hand hold remains at waist level.	2	Slow
4	Step L foot in place beginning to raise the L hand hold up and over your head. Release the R hand hold and lower to waist level.	3	Quick
5	Step R foot in place continuing to raise the L hand hold up and over your head.	&	Quick
6	Step L foot in place completing a triple step and completing the L hand hold layover movement. Retake the R hand hold at waist level.	4	Slow
7	Step R foot in place raising the R hand hold up and over the man's head to place the hand hold behind the man's head at shoulder level. Release the L hand hold behind your head and lower to waist level.	1	Quick
8	Step L foot in place continuing to place the R hand hold behind the man's head at shoulder level.	&	Quick
9	Step R foot in place completing a triple step and completing a R hand hold layover movement. Retake the L hand hold at waist level.	2	Slow
10	Step L foot in place beginning to raise the L hand hold up and over the man's head. Release the R hand hold behind the man's head and begin to retake Closed Position.	3	Quick
11	Step R foot in place continuing to raise the L hand hold up and over the man's head.	&	Quick

*Note: Precede with Twin Cities movement into Continuous Layover.

Western Swing

Continuous Layover (triple time)
Man's Footwork, cont'd

Step	Description	Timing	Rhythmic Cue	Lead
12	Step R foot in place completing a triple step and completing the L hand hold layover movement. Place the right hand on the lady's left shoulder blade in Closed Dance Position.	4	Slow	L hand hold placed behind head R hand hold placed on shoulder blade
13	Step L foot diagonally back into Fall-a-Way Position (Rock Step). Release the L hand hold returning to Closed Dance Position.	1	Slow	L hand hold releases
14	Step R foot forward completing the Continuous Layover movement.	2	Slow	

Bootnote: Steps 1-3 execute a triple step in place and a R hand hold layover movement placed behind the lady's head. Steps 4-6 execute a triple step in place and a L hand hold layover movement place behind the lady's head. Steps 7-9 execute a triple step in place and a R hand hold layover movement placed behind the man's head. Steps 10-12 execute a triple step in place and a L hand hold layover movement placed behind the man's head. Steps 13-14 execute a Rock Step in Closed Dance Position completing the Continuous Layover.

Open Swing Position

Step 1

Step 3

Step 7

Step 9

Western Swing

Continuous Layover (triple time)
Lady's Footwork, cont'd

Step	Description	Timing	Rhythmic Cue
12	Step L foot in place completing a triple step and completing the L hand hold layover movement as you begin to retake Closed Dance Position.	4	Slow
13	Step R foot diagonally back into Fall-a-Way Position (Rock Step). Release the L hand hold and retake Closed Dance Position.	1	Slow
14	Step L foot forward completing the Continuous Layover movement.	2	Slow

Bootnote: Steps 1-3 execute a triple step in place and a R hand hold layover movement placed behind the lady's head. Steps 4-6 execute a triple step in place and a L hand hold layover movement placed behind the lady's head. Steps 7-9 execute a triple step in place and a R hand hold layover movement placed behind the man's head. Steps 13-14 execute a Rock Step in Closed Dance Position completing the Continuous Layover.

Step 4

Step 6

Step 10

Step 12

Step 13 and 14

WESTERN SWING
AMALGAMATIONS

1 Basic Step
   Basic Step Turning
   Underarm Turn Left
   Reverse Underarm Turn

2 Sugar Push (twice)
   Underarm Turn Right
   Side Pass
   Underarm Turn Right
   Neck Pass

3 Sugar Push
   Sweetheart
   Sugar Push
   Wringer
   Sugar Push
   Sweetheart Turns

4 Basic Step
   Basic Step Turning
   Kick 'N (twice)
   Back to Back (twice)

5 Sugar Push
   Layover
   Back to Back
   Kick 'N

6 Sugar Push
   Shuttle (twice)
   Thread the Needle

7 Sugar Push
   Twin Cities
   Continuous Layover

 Bootnote: For the Western Swing amalgamations to flow use the Basic Step Turning between variations in Closed Swing Position and the Sugar Push between variations requiring a double hand hold.

FAVORITE WESTERN SWING SELECTIONS

"A Six Pack to Go" (medium) by Hank Thompson

"Baby's Got Her Blue Jeans On" (medium) by Mel McDaniel

"Betty's Bein' Bad" (fast) by Sawyer Brown

"Black Sheep" (medium fast) by John Anderson

"Bombed,Boozed, and Busted" (medium fast) by Joe Sun

"Bop" (medium) by Dan Seals

"Cheap Love" (medium) by Juice Newton

"Choo-Choo Ch'Boogie (medium fast) by Asleep at the Wheel

"Don't It Make You Wanna Dance (medium) by Bonnie Raitt

"Feel Alright" (medium) by Tanya Tucker

"Honey (Open That Door)" (medium) by Ricky Skaggs

"Honky Tonk" (medium slow) by Bill Doggett or by Roy Clark

"I Just Can't Leave Those Honky Tonks Alone" (medium) by Moe Bandy

"I'll Pass" (medium) by Gus Hardin

"I'm a Honky Tonk Man" (medium fast) by Dwight Yoakum

"Is Anybody Going to San Antone" (medium) by Charley Pride

"Jose Cuervo" (medium) by Shelly West

"Let it Roll" (medium) by Mel McDaniel

"Mama, This One's For You" (medium) by Jerry Lee Lewis

"Milk Cow Blues" (medium slow) by Adolph Hofner or by Bob Wills and the Texas Playboys

"Mountain of Love" (medium) by Charley Pride

"Somewhere My Love (medium) by Red Stegall

"Super Love" (medium) by Exile

"Swinging" (medium slow) by John Anderson

"Texas Honky Tonk (medium) by David Houston

"The South is Gonna Do It Again" (fast) by the Charley Daniel's Band

"Tulsa Time" (medium) by Mel Tillis

"Two Dollars in the Jukebox" (medium) by Eddie Rabbitt

"Whiskey River (medium fast) by Johnny Bush

"Women I've Never Had (medium) by Hank Williams, Jr.

Western Polka

Western Polka

The Polka originated as a Bohemian folk dance in the 1830s. It is believed by dance historians that a Czechoslovakian musician was inspired as he watched a young peasant girl sing and dance to an improvised melody. He noted the music, and the dance was later performed as a round dance at village festivals. Beliefs differ on the origin of the name with some people believing that the name Polka came from the Czech word "Pulka", meaning half, and referring to the half-step found in the step-close-step foot pattern. Others believe the name signified Polish girl.

The Polka gained popularity in the ballroom after it was introduced as part of a ballet sequence in Paris. Using the same intimate closed dance position as the Waltz, it created immediate attention as it moved throughout Europe and across the Atlantic to the remote areas of Western America. The pioneers and American cowboy used foot-tapping, hand-clapping melodies of the Polka to add excitement and adventure to the wild west. Today, the Polka has found popularity around the world with variations differing from one area to another. From an exaggerated hop to a lively smoothness, the Polka in 2/4 time can be danced in closed position, shoulder-waist position, Varsouvienne position, open position, and in a line of three or more.

The Polish form of Polka, very similar to the original Bohemian folk dance, is the most popular variation in the Country-Western dance halls. The basic step of Western Polka is known to folk dancers as a "two-step" because of the musical timing "1 & 2". Ballroom dancers refer to the movement as a "triple-step" because the footwork requires you to change weight three times during the step-close-step pattern.

Single Time Polka

"Single Time Polka" also known as "Western Whip" or "Country Swing", uses many of the same arm movements as "Triple Time Polka" but the foot pattern is a shuffle step in even rhythm. Single Time Polkas may be danced to medium or fast tempos, but most people prefer the faster music.

Western Polka

1. Basic Step Forward

2. Conversation Step

3. Polka Flare

4. Underarm Turn

5. Continuous Underarm Turn

6. Windmill

7. Heel 'n' Toe

8. Push 'n' Pull (Clockwise)

9. Whip (Alternate Underarms)

10. String-A-Long

11. Sweetheart

12. Wringer

13. Sweetheart into Wringer

14. Pretzel

15. Lariat to Double Wringer

16. Advanced Polka Turns

Rhythmical Analysis

WESTERN POLKA----Time Signature 2/4

Step Pattern, Man:	Step forward,	Step together,	Step forward,	Step forward,	Step together,	Step forward
Lady:	Step backward	Step together,	Step backward	Step backward,	Step together,	Step backward
Count: Notation:	1 —	& —	2 —	1 —	& —	2 —
Rhythmic Cue:	Quick	Quick	Slow	Quick	Quick	Slow

To complete a basic step in Western Polka one will use two measures of music in 2/4 time.

Western Polka

Basic Step Forward (Triple Time)
Man's Footwork

Step	Description	Timing	Rhythmic Cue	Lead
	Position: Closed Dance Position			
1	Step L foot directly forward.	1	Quick	R Heel pressure
2	Step R foot directly forward bringing feet together (3rd position, L foot forward). The weight is placed on the ball of the foot.	&	Quick	R Heel pressure
3	Step L foot directly forward.	2	Slow	R Heel pressure
4	Step R foot directly forward passing L foot.	1	Quick	R Heel pressure
5	Step L foot directly forward bringing feet together (3rd position, R foot forward). The weight is placed on the ball of the foot.	&	Quick	R Heel pressure
6	Step R foot directly forward.	2	Slow	R Heel pressure

Closed Dance Position   Step 1   Step 2   Step 3

Western Polka

Basic Step Forward (Triple Time)
Lady's Footwork

Step	Description	Timing	Rhythmic Cue
	Position: Closed Dance Position		
1	Step R foot directly backward.	1	Quick
2	Step L foot directly backward bringing feet together (3rd position, L foot forward). The weight is placed on the ball of the foot.	&	Quick
3	Step R foot directly backward.	2	Slow
4	Step L foot directly backward passing R foot.	1	Quick
5	Step R foot directly backward bringing feet together (3rd position, R foot forward). The weight is placed on the ball of the foot.	&	Quick
6	Step L foot directly backward.	2	Slow

Step 4

Step 5

Step 6

Western Polka

Conversation Step (Triple Time)
Man's Footwork

Step	Description	Timing	Rhythmic Cue	Lead
	Position: Closed Dance Position into Conversation Position.			
	Steps 1-5 are the same as Basic Step Forward			
6	Step R foot directly forward beginning to lead the lady into Conversation Position and continuing to move down the line of dance.	2	Slow	R Palm pressure
7	Step L foot directly forward passing R foot and completing the lead into Conversation Position.	1	Quick	R Hand pressure
8	Step R foot directly forward bringing feet together (3rd position, L foot forward) in Conversation Position.	&	Quick	R Hand pressure
9	Step L foot directly forward. (Conversation Position).	2	Slow	R Hand pressure
10	Step R foot directly forward, passing L foot. (Conversation Position).	1	Quick	R Hand pressure
11	Step L foot directly forward bringing the feet together (3rd position, R foot forward).	&	Quick	R Hand pressure
12	Step R foot directly forward. (Conversation Position).	2	Slow	R Hand pressure

Note: Steps 6 through 12 may be repeated or return to closed dance position after step #12. The man will lead the lady to face him as she pivots 1/2 turn left (counterclockwise).

Closed Dance
Position

Steps 7-9

Steps 10-12

Western Polka

Conversation Step (Triple Time)
Lady's Footwork

Step	Description	Timing	Rhythmic Cue
	Position: Closed Dance Position into Conversation Position.		
	Steps 1-5 are the same as Basic Step Forward (Lady's Footwork).		
6	Step L foot directly backward pivoting into 1/2 turn clockwise (right) as the man leads you into Conversation Position.	2	Slow
7	Step R foot directly forward as the man completes the lead into Conversation Position.	1	Quick
8	Step L foot directly forward bringing feet together (3rd position, R foot forward) in Conversation Position.	&	Quick
9	Step R foot directly forward. (Conversation Position).	2	Slow
10	Step L foot directly forward, passing R foot. (Conversation Position).	1	Quick
11	Step R foot directly forward bringing the feet together (3rd position, L foot forward).	&	Quick
12	Step L foot directly forward. (Conversation Position).	2	Slow

Note: To return to Closed Position following Step #12 the man leads the lady to face him as she pivots 1/2 turn counterclockwise (left).

Western Polka

Polka Flare (Triple Time)
Man's Footwork

Step	Description	Timing	Rhythmic Cue	Lead
	Position: Conversation Position			
	Steps 1-5 (Polka Flare) are the same as steps 7-12 of the Conversation Step (man's footwork).			
6	Step R foot directly forward pivoting 1/4 turn to the right to face your partner as you lead the lady to face you from Conversation Position.	2	Slow	R Finger pressure
7	Step L foot directly to the left progressing down the line of dance (sideways) facing your partner.	1	Quick	R Hand pressure
8	Step R foot directly to the left bringing feet together.	&	Quick	R Hand pressure
9	Step L foot directly to the left; then pivot 1/4 turn to the left returning to Conversation Position as you lead the lady to turn 1/4 turn.	2	Slow	R Hand pressure
10	Step R foot directly forward, passing L foot. (Conversation Position).	1	Quick	R Hand pressure
11	Step L foot directly forward bringing feet together (3rd position, R foot forward).	&	Quick	R Hand pressure
12	Step R foot directly forward. (Conversation Position).	2	Slow	R Hand pressure

Note: Polka Flare may be repeated by substituting step #6 for step #12 and repeating steps 7-11. The man will lead the lady to face him as she pivots 1/2 turn left (counterclockwise).

Closed Dance Position	Step 1	Step 4

Western Polka

Polka Flare (Triple Time)
Lady's Footwork

Step	Description	Timing	Rhythmic Cue
	Position: Conversation Position		
	Steps 1-5 (Polka Flare) are the same as steps 7-12 of the Conversation Step (lady's footwork).		
6	Step L foot directly forward pivoting 1/4 turn to the left to face your partner from Conversation Position into a Polka Flare.	2	Slow
7	Step R foot directly to the right progressing down the line of dance (sideways) facing your partner.	1	Quick
8	Step L foot directly to the right bringing feet together.	&	Quick
9	Step R foot directly to the right pivoting 1/4 turn to the right into Conversation Position.	2	Slow
10	Step L foot directly forward, passing R foot. (Conversation Position).	1	Quick
11	Step R foot directly forward bringing feet together (3rd position, L foot forward).	&	Quick
12	Step L foot directly forward. (Conversation Position).	2	Slow

Note: Polka Flare may be repeated by substituting step #6 for step #12 and repeating steps 7-11. The man will lead the lady to face him as she pivots 1/2 turn left (counterclockwise).

Step 7   Step 10

Western Polka

Underarm Turn (Triple Time)
Man's Footwork

Step	Description	Timing	Rhythmic Cue	Lead
	Position: Closed Dance Position			
	Steps 1-6 are the same as Basic Step Forward (man's footwork).			
7	Step L foot directly forward as you begin to lead the lady to turn clockwise under your L hand hold.	1	Quick	L Hand hold encircling
8	Step R foot directly forward bringing feet together (3rd position, L foot forward). Continue to encircle the L hand hold over the lady's head.	&	Quick	L Hand hold encircling
9	Step L foot directly forward.	2	Slow	L Hand hold encircling
10	Step R foot directly forward, passing L foot and returning to Closed Dance Position as the lady completes the Underarm Turn (clockwise).	1	Quick	L Hand hold lowers
11	Step L foot directly forward bringing feet together (3rd position, R foot forward) as you complete movement into Closed Dance Position.	&	Quick	R Heel pressure
12	Step R foot directly forward completing the Underarm Turn.	2	Slow	R Heel pressure

Closed Dance Position   Steps 7-9   Steps 10-12

Western Polka

Underarm Turn (Triple Time)
Lady's Footwork

Step	Description	Timing	Rhythmic Cue
	Position: Closed Dance Position		
	Steps 1-6 are the same as Basic Step Forward (man's footwork).		
7	Turning 1/2 turn clockwise, Step R foot directly forward progressing down your line of dance into an Underarm Turn.	1	Quick
8	Step L foot directly forward bringing feet together (3rd position, R foot forward) continuing Underarm Turn Clockwise.	&	Quick
9	Step R foot directly forward continuing Underarm Turn clockwise pivoting 1/2 turn to face your partner.	2	Slow
10	Step L foot directly backward as you return to Closed Dance Position.	1	Quick
11	Step R foot directly backward bringing the feet together (3rd position, R foot forward).	&	Quick
12	Step L foot directly backward completing the Underarm Turn.	2	Slow

Western Polka

Continuous Underarm Turn (Triple Time)
Man's Footwork

Step	Description	Timing	Rhythmic Cue	Lead
	Position: Closed Dance Position			
	Steps 1-6 are the same as Basic Step Forward (man's footwork).			
7	Step L foot directly forward as you begin to lead the lady to turn clockwise under your L hand hold.	1	Quick	L Hand hold encircling
8	Step R foot directly forward bringing feet together (3rd position, L foot forward). Continue to encircle lady's head with L hand hold.	&	Quick	L Hand hold encircling
9	Step L foot directly forward continuing Underarm lead with L hand hold placing free hand (right) on your right hip.	2	Slow	L Hand hold encircling
10	Step R foot directly forward, passing left foot and leading the lady to face you. Remain in Open Dance Position with a single hand hold (his left holding her right).	1	Quick	L Hand hold
11	Step L foot directly forward bringing feet together (3rd position, R foot forward) as you complete the lead for the lady to face you.	&	Quick	L Hand hold
12	Step R foot directly forward facing your partner remaining in Open Dance Position with a single hand hold, free hand (right) resting on your hip.	2	Slow	L Hand hold

Note: Repeat steps 7-12 twice giving the Continuous Underarm Turn a total of eight measures and a total of three Underarm Turns (steps 13-18 and 19-24). Return to Closed Position after 3rd turn.

Closed
Dance Position

Steps 7-9, 13-15

Steps 10-12, 16-18

Western Polka

Continuous Underarm Turn (Triple Time)
Lady's Footwork

Step	Description	Timing	Rhythmic Cue
	Position: Closed Dance Position		
	Steps 1-6 are the same as Basic Step Forward (lady's footwork).		
7	Turning 1/2 turn clockwise, step R foot directly forward progressing down your line of dance as the man begins the lead for the Underarm Turn.	1	Quick
8	Step L foot directly forward bringing feet together (3rd position, R foot forward) continuing Underarm Turn clockwise. Rest free hand (left) on your left hip.	&	Quick
9	Step R foot directly forward continuing Underarm Turn clockwise by pivoting 1/2 turn to face your partner.	2	Slow
10	Step L foot directly backward as you return to face your partner with a single hand hold (his left holding her right). Free hand is on left hip.	1	Quick
11	Step R foot directly backward bringing feet together (3rd position, R foot forward) remaining in open dance position with a single hand hold.	&	Quick
12	Step L foot directly backward remaining in Open Dance Position with a single hand hold. Free hand is on left hip.	2	Slow

Note: Repeat steps 7-12 twice giving the Continuous Underarm Turn a total of eight measures and three Underarm turns (steps 13-18 and 19-24). Return to closed position after the 3rd turn.

Steps 19-21   Steps 22-24

Western Polka

Windmill (Triple Time)
Man's Footwork

Step	Description	Timing	Rhythmic Cue	Lead
	Position: Closed Dance Position into Windmill			
	Steps 1-9 are the same as Underarm Turns (man's footwork)			
10-12	Execute a Step-Together-Step (4th Triple step beginning with the right foot) as you turn clockwise 3/4 of a turn moving into Windmill Position. Lower L hand hold placing the left arm behind your back as you execute the 3/4 turn.	1 & 2	Q,Q,S	L Hand hold movement
13-15	Execute a Step-Together-Step (5th Triple Step beginning with the left foot) while circling clock wise with your partner for the Windmill movement. Left arm is behind your back with your left hand holding her right. With right shoulders adjacent, your right arm will circle up and over her right arm.	1 & 2	Q,Q,S	L Hand hold movement
16-18	Execute a Step-Together-Step (6th Triple step beginning with the right foot) continuing to circle clockwise with your partner for a Windmill movement. Your right arm having circled over her right arm will now reach under her right arm, behind her back so that your right hand may take her left hand. This will complete the movement into Windmill Position.	1 &2	Q,Q,S	L Hand hold pulls
19-21	Execute a Step-Together-Step (7th Triple step beginning with the left foot) continuing to circle clockwise with your partner in Windmill Position.	1 & 2	Q,Q,S	L Hand hold pulls
22-24	Execute a Step-Together-Step (8th Triple step beginning with the right foot) continuing to circle clockwise with your partner in Windmill Position. Movement should end with your facing down the line of dance.	1 & 2	Q,Q,S	L Hand hold pulls
25-36	Execute four Step-Together-Steps (9th,10th,11th, 12th Triple Steps beginning with the left foot) in place as you release your R hand hold. Your L hand hold remaining at waist level will lead the lady to circle clockwise around you. Lady should end facing you, with your facing down your line of dance.	1 & 2	Q,Q,S	L Hand hold pulls

Western Polka

Windmill (Triple Time)
Lady's Footwork

Step	Description	Timing	Rhythmic Cue
	Position: Closed Dance Position into Windmill		
	Steps 1-8 are the same as Underarm Turns (lady's footwork)		
9	Step R foot diagonally to the right completing 3/4 turn with your right shoulder facing your partner.	2	Slow
10-12	Execute a Step-Together-Step (4th Triple step beginning with the L foot) in place as man moves into Windmill Position.	1 & 2	Q,Q,S
13-15	Execute a Step-Together-Step (5th Triple step beginning with the right foot) while circling clockwise with your partner for the Windmill movement. Man's right arm will begin to circle up and over your right arm to complete Windmill Position.	1 & 2	Q,Q,S
16-18	Execute a Step-Together-Step (6th Triple step beginning with the left foot) continuing to circle clockwise with your partner for a Windmill movement. His right arm will reach over and then under your right arm as his right hand takes your left hand behind your back completing the movement into Windmill Position.	1 & 2	Q,Q,S
19-21	Execute a Step-Together-Step (7th Triple step beginning with the right foot) continuing to circle clockwise with your partner in Windmill Position.	1 & 2	Q,Q,S
22-24	Execute a Step-Together-Step (8th Triple step beginning with the left foot) continuing to circle clockwise with your partner in Windmill Position. Movement should end with your backing the line of dance.	1 & 2	Q,Q,S
25-36	Execute four Step-Together-Steps (9th, 10th, 11th, 12th Triple steps beginning with the right foot) as the man releases your L hand hold and moves you around him clockwise to face him. His L hand hold will initiate the lead as he executes his four Triple steps in place.	1 & 2	Q,Q,S

Western Polka

Windmill (Triple Time)
Man's Footwork, cont'd

Step	Description	Timing	Rhythmic Cue	Lead
37-48	Execute four Step-Together-Steps (13th, 14th, 15th, 16th Triple steps beginning with the left foot) as you lead the lady under your L hand hold into a double underarm turn. (Same as Steps #7-#12 in the Continuous Underarm Turns). Return to Closed Dance Position on 16th triple step.	1 & 2	Q,Q,S	L Hand hold encircles

Closed Dance Position

Steps 7-9

Steps 10-12

Steps 13-15

Steps 22-24

Steps 25-27

Western Polka

Windmill (Triple Time)
Lady's Footwork, cont'd

Step	Description	Timing	Rhythmic Cue
37-48	Execute four Step-Together-Steps (13th,14th, 15th,16th Triple steps beginning with the left foot) as the man leads you under his L hand hold into a double underarm turn. (Same as Steps 7-12 in Continuous Underarm Turns). Return to Closed Dance Position.	1 & 2	Q,Q,S

Steps 16-18

Steps 19-21

Steps 31-33

Steps 37-39, 43-45

Steps 46-48

Western Polka
Heel 'n' Toe (Triple Time)
Man's Footwork

Step	Description	Timing	Rhythmic Cue	Lead
	Position: Closed Dance Position			
	Steps 1-6 are the same as Basic Step Forward (man's footwork).			
7	Extend L foot (heel touching floor, toe upward) to the left as you lean slightly to the left leading the lady into Heel 'n' Toe Polka. Concentrate on lifting the right side rather than lowering the left side of the body.	1	Slow	Slight body lean left
8	Touch toe of left foot beside right foot (knee turned out) continuing to lean slightly to your left.	2	Slow	Slight body lean left
9	Step L foot directly to the left facing partner in Closed Dance Position.	1	Quick	R Palm pressure
10	Step R foot directly to the left bringing feet together.	&	Quick	R Palm pressure
11	Step L foot directly to the left completing a triple step.	2	Slow	R Palm pressure
12	Extend R foot (heel touching floor, toe upward) to your right as you lean slightly to the right leading the lady into Heel 'n' Toe Polka. Concentrate on lifting the left side rather than lowering the right side of the body.	1	Slow	Slight body lean right
13	Touch toe of right foot beside left foot (knee turned out) continuing to lean slightly to your right.	2	Slow	Slight body lean right
14	Step R foot directly to the right facing partner in Closed Dance Position.	1	Quick	R Finger pressure
15	Step L foot directly to the right bringing feet together.	&	Quick	R Finger pressure
16	Step R foot directly to the right completing a triple step.	2	Slow	R Finger pressure

Note: Heel 'n' Toe Polka (steps 7-16) may be repeated or you may return to the basic step.

Closed Dance Position   Step 7   Step 8

Western Polka
Heel 'n' Toe (Triple Time)
Lady's Footwork

Step	Description	Timing	Rhythmic Cue
	Position: Closed Dance Position		
	Steps 1-6 are the same as Basic Step Forward (lady's footwork).		
7	Extend R foot (heel touching floor, toe upward) to your right leaning slightly to your right into Heel 'n' Toe Polka. Concentrate on lifting the left side rather than lowering the right side of the body.	1	Slow
8	Touch toe of right foot beside left foot (knee turned out) continuing to lean slightly to your right.	2	Slow
9	Step R foot directly to the right facing partner in Closed Dance Position.	1	Quick
10	Step L foot directly to the right bringing feet together.	&	Quick
11	Step R foot directly to the right completing a triple step.	2	Slow
12	Extend L foot (heel touching floor, toe upward) to your left leaning slightly to the left into Heel 'n' Toe Polka. Concentrate on lifting the right side rather than lowering the left side of the body.	1	Slow
13	Touch toe of left foot beside right foot (knee turned out) continuing to lean slightly to your left.	2	Slow
14	Step L foot directly to the left facing partner in Closed Dance Position.	1	Quick
15	Step R foot directly to the left bringing feet together.	&	Quick
16	Step L foot directly to the left completing a triple step.	2	Slow

Note: Heel 'n' Toe Polka (steps 7-12) may be repeated or you may return to the basic step.

Step 12   Step 13

Western Polka

Push 'n' Pull (Triple Time)
Man's Footwork

Step	Description	Timing	Rhythmic Cue	Lead
	Position: Open Position with Double Hand Hold. *			
1	Step L foot directly forward (small step) toward your partner as you lead her forward (Pull).	1	Quick	L and R Hand holds pull
2	Step R foot directly forward bringing feet together (3rd position, L foot forward).	&	Quick	L and R Hand holds pull
3	Step L foot directly forward (small step) completing a triple step (Pull) toward your partner.	2	Slow	L and R Hand holds pull
4	Step R foot directly backward (small step) away from your partner as you lead her backward (Push).	1	Quick	L and R Hand holds push
5	Step L foot directly backward bringing feet together (3rd position, L foot forward).	&	Quick	L and R Hand holds push
6	Step R foot directly backward (small step) completing a triple step (Push) away from your partner.	2	Slow	L and R Hand holds push

* Note: This step consists of a triple step toward your partner (Pull) and a triple step away from your partner (Push). The step usually preceeds variations in Open Position with a double hand hold.

 Bootnote: The Push 'n' Pull with proper resistance gives you a "rubber band" effect. This enables you to execute a proper lead in variations from Open Positions. Examples: Whip, String-A-Long, and Pretzel.

Open Dance
Position

Steps 1-3

Steps 4-6

Western Polka

Push 'n' Pull (Triple Time)
Lady's Footwork

Step	Description	Timing	Rhythmic Cue
	Position: Open Position with Double Hand Hold. *		
1	Step R foot directly forward (small step) toward your partner as he leads you forward (Pull).	1	Quick
2	Step L foot directly forward bringing feet together (3rd position, R foot forward).	&	Quick
3	Step R foot directly forward (small step) completing a triple step (Pull) toward your partner.	2	Slow
4	Step L foot directly backward (small step) away from your partner as he moves away from you (Push).	1	Quick
5	Step R foot directly backward bringing feet together (3rd position, R foot forward).	&	Quick
6	Step L foot directly backward (small step) completing a triple step (Push) away from your partner.	2	Slow

* Note: This step consists of a triple step toward your partner (Pull) and a triple step away from your partner (Push). The step usually preceeds variations in Open Position with a double hand hold.

 Bootnote: The Push 'n' Pull with proper resistance gives you a "rubber band" effect. This enables you to follow the lead in variations from Open Positions. Examples: Whip, String-a-Long, and Pretzel.

Western Polka

Whip
Man's Footwork

Step	Description	Timing	Rhythmic Cue	Lead
	Position: Open Position with Double Hand Hold.			
	Steps 1-6 are the same as Push 'n' Pull.			
7	Step L foot directly forward beginning to lead the lady past your right side. Raise your R hand hold over your head and keep your L hand hold at waist level.	1	Quick	L Hand hold pulls R Hand hold pulls and lifts
8	Step R foot directly forward bringing feet together (3rd position, L foot forward) continuing to encircle your head with the R hand hold. L hand hold remains at waist level.	&	Quick	L Hand hold pulls R Hand hold lifts and encircles
9	Step L foot diagonally to the left beginning to turn left (counterclockwise) to face your partner. R Hand hold encircles your head and begins to lower as you release L hand hold.	2	Slow	L Hand hold releases R Hand hold encircles and lowers
10	Step R foot to the right and slightly backward facing your partner as you retake a double hand hold.	1	Quick	L and R Hand holds
11	Step L foot to the right bringing feet together.	&	Quick	L and R Hand holds
12	Step R foot to the right and slightly backward completing a triple step.	2	Slow	L and R Hand holds
13	Step L foot directly forward beginning to lead the lady past your right side. Raise your L hand hold over her head and keep your R hand hold at waist level.	1	Quick	R Hand hold pulls L Hand hold pulls and lifts
14	Step R foot forward bringing feet together (3rd position, L foot forward) continuing to encircle her head with L hand hold. Keep your R hand hold at waist level.	&	Quick	R Hand hold pulls L Hand hold lifts and encircles
15	Step L foot diagonally to the right beginning 1/2 turn right (clockwise) to face your partner. L hand hold encircles her head and begins to lower as you release R hand hold at waist level.	2	Slow	R Hand hold releases L Hand hold encircles and lowers
16	Step R foot to the right and slightly backward facing your partner as you retake double hand hold.	1	Quick	L and R Hand holds

Western Polka

Whip
Lady's Footwork

Step	Description	Timing	Rhythmic Cue
	Position: Open Position with Double Hand Hold.		
	Steps 1-6 are the same as Push 'n' Pull.		
7	Step R foot forward as the man begins to lead you past his right side. Your L hand hold begins to move over his head as the R hand hold remains at waist level.	1	Quick
8	Step L foot directly forward bringing feet together (3rd position, R foot forward) continuing to move past his right side. Your L hand hold encircles his head with the R hand hold remaining at waist level.	&	Quick
9	Step R foot diagonally to the right beginning to turn right (clockwise) to face your partner. The L hand hold encircles his head and begins to lower as you release the R hand hold.	2	Slow
10	Step L foot to the left and slightly backward facing your partner as you retake a double hand hold.	1	Quick
11	Step R foot to the left bringing feet together.	&	Quick
12	Step L foot to the left and slightly backward completing a triple step.	2	Slow
13	Step R foot directly forward as the man begins to lead you past his right side. The R hand hold begins to move over your head as the L hand hold remains at waist level.	1	Quick
14	Step L foot forward bringing feet together (3rd position, R foot forward) continuing to move past the man's right side. The R hand hold encircles your head as the L hand hold remains at waist level.	&	Quick
15	Step R foot diagonally to the left beginning 1/2 turn left (counterclockwise) to face your partner. The R hand hold encircles your head and begins to lower as you release the L hand hold.	2	Slow
16	Step L foot to the left and slightly backward facing your partner as you retake a double hand hold.	1	Quick

Western Polka

Whip
Man's Footwork, cont'd

Step	Description	Timing	Rhythmic Cue	Lead
17	Step L foot to the right bringing feet together.	&	Quick	L and R Hand holds
18	Step R foot to the right and slightly backward completing a triple step.	2	Slow	L and R Hand holds

Bootnote: You may repeat the Whip (steps 7-18), return to the Basic Step in Closed Dance Position or execute other variations with a double hand hold.

Open Dance
Position

Steps 7-9

Steps 10-12

Western Polka

Whip
Lady's Footwork, cont'd

Step	Description	Timing	Rhythmic Cue
17	Step R foot to the left bringing feet together.	&	Quick
18	Step L foot to the left and slightly backward completing a triple step.	2	Slow

Bootnote: You may repeat the Whip (steps 7-18), return to the Basic Step in Closed Dance Position or execute other variations with a double hand hold.

Steps 13-15   Steps 16-18

Western Polka

String-A-Long
Man's Footwork

Step	Description	Timing	Rhythmic Cue	Lead
	Position: Open Position with Double Hand Hold.			
	Steps 1-6 are the same as Push 'n' Pull.			
7	Step L foot directly forward beginning to lead the lady past your right side. Raise your L hand hold over your head keeping your R hand hold at waist level.	1	Quick	L Hand hold pulls and lifts R Hand hold pulls
8	Step R foot directly forward bringing feet together (3rd position, L foot forward) continuing to encircle your head with the L hand hold.	&	Quick	L Hand hold lifts and encircles R Hand hold pulls
9	Step L foot diagonally to the left beginning 1/2 turn left (counterclockwise) to face your partner. The L hand hold encircles your head and begins to lower as you release the R hand hold.	2	Slow	L Hand hold encircles and lowers R Hand hold releases
10	Step R foot to the right and slightly backward facing your partner as you retake a double hand hold.	1	Quick	L and R Hand holds
11	Step L foot to the right bringing feet together.	&	Quick	L and R Hand holds
12	Step R foot to the right and slightly backward completing a triple step.	2	Slow	L and R Hand holds
13	Step L foot directly forward beginning to lead the lady past your right side. Raise the R hand hold over her head and keep the L hand hold at waist level.	1	Quick	R Hand hold pulls and lifts L Hand hold pulls
14	Step R foot forward bringing feet together (3rd position, L foot forward) continuing to encircle her head with the R hand hold.	&	Quick	R Hand hold lifts and encircles L Hand hold pulls
15	Step L foot diagonally to the right beginning 1/2 turn (clockwise) to face your partner. The R hand hold encircles her head and begins to lower as you release the L hand hold.	2	Slow	R Hand hold encircles and lowers L Hand hold releases
16	Step R foot to the right and slightly backward facing your partner as you retake a double hand hold.	1	Quick	L and R Hand holds

Western Polka

String-A-Long
Lady's Footwork

Step	Description	Timing	Rhythmic Cue
	Position: Open Position with Double Hand Hold.		
	Steps 1-6 are the same as Push 'n' Pull.		
7	Step R foot forward as the man begins to lead you past his right side. Your R hand hold begins to move over his head with the L hand hold remaining at waist level.	1	Quick
8	Step L foot forward bringing feet together (3rd position, R foot forward) continuing to move past his right side.	&	Quick
9	Step R foot diagonally to the right beginning 1/2 turn right (clockwise) to face your partner. The R hand hold encircles your partner's head and begins to lower as you release the L hand hold.	2	Slow
10	Step L foot to the left and slightly backward as you retake a double hand hold facing your partner.	1	Quick
11	Step R foot to the left bringing feet together.	&	Quick
12	Step L foot to the left and slightly backward completing a triple step.	2	Slow
13	Step R foot forward as the man begins to lead you past his right side. Your L hand hold begins to move over your head as the R hand hold remains at waist level.	1	Quick
14	Step L foot forward bringing feet together (3rd position, R foot forward) as the L hand hold continues to encircle your head.	&	Quick
15	Step R foot diagonally to the left beginning 1/2 turn left (counterclockwise) to face your partner. The L hand hold encircles your head and begins to lower as you release the R hand hold.	2	Slow
16	Step L foot to the left and slightly backward facing your partner as you retake a double hand hold.	1	Quick

Western Polka

String-A-Long
Man's Footwork, cont'd

17	Step L foot to the right bringing feet together.	&	Quick	L and R Hand holds
18	Step R foot to the right and slightly backward completing a triple step.	2	Slow	L and R Hand holds

Bootnote: You may repeat the String-A-Long (Steps 7-18), return to the Basic Step in Closed Dance Position or execute other variations with a double hand hold.

Open Dance
Position

Steps 7-9

Steps 10-12

Western Polka

String-A-Long
Lady's Footwork, cont'd

17	Step R foot to the left bringing feet together.	&	Quick
18	Step L foot to the left and slightly backward completing a triple step.	2	Slow

Bootnote: You may repeat the String-A-Long (Steps 7-18), return to the Basic Step in Closed Dance Position or execute other variations with a double hand hold.

Steps 13-15   Steps 16-18

Western Polka

Sweetheart
Man's Footwork

Step	Description	Timing	Rhythmic Cue	Lead
	Position: Open Position with double hand hold into Sweetheart Wrap Position. *			
1	Step L foot diagonally to the left beginning to move clockwise around your partner. The L hand hold begins to encircle the lady's head as the R hand hold remains at waist level.	1	Quick	L Hand hold pulls and raises R Hand hold pulls
2	Step R foot forward bringing feet together (3rd position, L foot forward) continuing to move around your partner.	&	Quick	L Hand hold raises.
3	Step L foot diagonally to the left as you move around your partner into Sweetheart Wrap Position. The L hand hold continues to encircle her head as the R hand hold remains at waist level.	2	Slow	L Hand hold raises
4	Step R foot diagonally to the right as you begin to lower the L hand hold to waist level.	1	Quick	L Hand hold encircles and lowers
5	Step L foot forward bringing feet together (3rd position, R foot forward) as you lower the L hand hold to waist level.	&	Quick	L and R Hand holds
6	Step R foot diagonally to the right as you complete a triple step into Sweetheart Wrap Position.	2	Slow	L and R Hand holds
7	Step L foot diagonally to the right beginning to circle clockwise with your partner in Sweetheart Wrap Position. The R hand hold leads the lady to circle backward as you circle forward.	1	Quick	R Hand hold pulls
8	Step R foot forward bringing feet together (3rd position, L foot forward) continuing clockwise circle.	&	Quick	R Hand hold pulls
9	Step L foot diagonally to the right completing approximately 1/4 circle clockwise.	2	Slow	R Hand hold pulls
10	Step R foot to the right (clockwise) turning 1/4 turn to face your partner as you lead her out of Sweetheart Wrap Position. The R hand hold pulls at waist level as the L hand hold begins to encircle the lady's head to turn her clockwise.	1	Quick	R Hand hold pulls L Hand hold raises and encircles

Western Polka

Sweetheart
Lady's Footwork

Step	Description	Timing	Rhythmic Cue
	Position: Open Position with double hand hold into Sweetheart Wrap Position. *		
1	Step R foot directly forward as the man moves to your right side and begins to encircle your head with the R hand hold.	1	Quick
2	Step L foot forward bringing feet together (3rd position, R foot forward) as the man continues to move around you.	&	Quick
3	Step R foot directly forward (small step) as the man continues to move into Sweetheart Wrap Position. The R hand hold encircles your head as the L hand hold remains at waist level.	2	Slow
4	Step L foot in place as the R hand hold encircles and begins to lower to waist level.	1	Quick
5	Step R foot in place continuing to lower the R hand hold.	&	Quick
6	Step L foot in place completing the movement into Sweetheart Wrap Position.	2	Slow
7	Step R foot diagonally to the left (backward) beginning to circle clockwise with your partner in Sweetheart Wrap Position.	1	Quick
8	Step L foot backward bringing feet together (3rd position, L foot forward) continuing clockwise circle.	&	Quick
9	Step R foot diagonally to the left (backward) completing approximately 1/4 circle clockwise.	2	Slow
10	Step L foot diagonally to the right as the man begins to lead you out of Sweetheart Wrap Position. The L hand hold pulls at waist level as the R hand hold encircles your head to turn you clockwise.	1	Quick

Western Polka

Sweetheart -
Man's Footwork, cont'd

11   Step left foot beside right foot as you continue   L Hand hold encircles
      to lead the lady out of Sweetheart Wrap Position.   &   Quick   and lowers

12   Step R foot slightly backward as you lower
      double hand hold to waist level to complete
      the Sweetheart.   2   Slow   L and R Hand holds

* Note: Precede with Push 'n' Pull. Retain a double hand hold throughout entire Sweetheart.

Bootnote 1:   Steps 1-3 (1st triple step) take your partner into Sweetheart Wrap Position. Steps 4-6 (2nd triple step) circle clockwise in Sweetheart Wrap Position. Steps 7-9 (3rd triple step) take your partner out of Sweetheart Wrap Position into Open Dance Position with a double hand hold. Steps 10-12 (4th triple step) complete the Sweetheart.

Bootnote 2: To continue Sweetheart movement execute additional triple steps in Sweetheart Wrap Position.

Open Dance
Position

Steps 1-3

Steps 4-6

Western Polka

Sweetheart
Lady's Footwork

11	Step R foot forward bringing feet together (3rd position, L foot forward) continuing to turn out of Sweetheart Wrap Position.	&	Quick
12	Step L foot around right foot to face you partner completing the Sweetheart.	2	Slow

* Note: Retain a double hand hold throughout the entire Sweetheart.

Bootnote 1: Steps 1-3 (1st triple step) take you into Sweetheart Wrap Position. Steps 4-6 (2nd triple step) circle clockwise in Sweetheart Wrap Position. Steps 7-9 (3rd triple step) take you out of Sweetheart Wrap Position into Open Dance Position with a double hand hold. Steps 10-12 (4th triple step) complete the Sweetheart.

Bootnote 2: To continue Sweetheart movement execute additional triple steps in Sweetheart Wrap Position.

Steps 7-9	Step 10	Steps 11-12

Western Polka

Wringer
Man's Footwork

Step	Description	Timing	Rhythmic Cue	Lead
	Position: Open Position with double hand hold. *			
1	Step L foot in place as the L hand hold begins to encircle the lady's head to turn her 3/4 turn clockwise. The R hand hold remains at waist level.	1	Quick	L Hand hold lifts and encircles
2	Step R foot in place continuing to turn your partner clockwise.	&	Quick	L Hand hold encircles
3	Step L foot diagonally to the left (small step) beginning 1/4 turn counterclockwise. The L hand hold continues to encircle the lady's head as you complete a triple step.	2	Slow	L Hand hold encircles
4	Step R foot beside the left foot completing 1/4 turn counterclockwise in place. The L hand hold begins to lower to chest level as you place the R hand hold behind the lady's back.	1	Quick	L Hand hold lowers
5	Step L foot in place continuing movement into Wringer Position.	&	Quick	L Hand hold lowers
6	Step R foot in place completing movement into Wringer Position. The L hand hold is at your chest level and the R hand hold is behind the lady's back at waist level.	2	Slow	L Hand hold lowers
7	Step L foot diagonally to the right beginning to circle clockwise with your partner in Wringer Position. With the R hand hold on the lady's back, lead her to circle forward as you circle forward.	1	Quick	R Hand pressure
8	Step R foot forward bringing feet together (3rd position, L foot forward) continuing to lead the lady in a clockwise circle.	&	Quick	R Hand pressure
9	Step L foot diagonally to the right completing approximately 1/2 circle clockwise.	2	Slow	L Hand hold encircles
10	Step R foot diagonally to the right beginning to lead the lady out of Wringer Position. The R hand hold pulls as the L hand hold begins to encircle the lady to turn her counterclockwise.	1	Quick	R Hand hold pulls L Hand hold lifts and encircles

Western Polka

Wringer
Lady's Footwork

Step	Description	Timing	Rhythmic Cue
	Position: Open Position with double hand hold. *		
1	Step R foot diagonally to the right (small step) beginning 3/4 turn clockwise into Wringer Position. Your R hand hold encircles your head as your L hand hold remains at waist level.	1	Quick
2	Step L foot forward bringing feet together (3rd position, R foot forward) continuing clockwise turn.	&	Quick
3	Step R foot diagonally to the right (small step) continuing to move into Wringer Position. The R hand hold continues to encircle your head as you complete a triple step.	2	Slow
4	Step left foot around right foot completing 3/4 turn clockwise. The R hand hold begins to lower to chest level and the L hand hold is placed behind your back.	1	Quick
5	Step R foot forward bringing feet together (3rd position, L foot forward) continuing movement into Wringer Position.	&	Quick
6	Step L foot in place completing movement into Wringer Position. The R hand hold is extended to the right at the man's chest level and the L hand hold is placed behind your back at waist level.	2	Slow
7	Step R foot diagonally to the right beginning to circle clockwise with your partner in Wringer Position.	1	Quick
8	Step L foot forward bringing feet together (3rd position, R foot forward) continuing clockwise circle.	&	Quick
9	Step R foot diagonally to the right completing approximately 1/2 circle clockwise.	2	Slow
10	Step L foot diagonally to the left beginning to move out of Wringer Position. The R hand hold encircles your head to turn you counter-clockwise to face your partner.	1	Quick

Western Polka

Wringer
Man's Footwork, cont'd

Step	Description	Timing	Rhythmic Cue	Lead
11	Step L foot forward bringing feet together (3rd position, R foot forward) as you continue to lead the lady out of Wringer Position.	&	Quick	L Hand hold encircles
12	Step R foot diagonally to the right lowering double hand hold to waist level to complete the Wringer.	2	Slow	L Hand hold lowers

*Note: Precede with Push 'n' Pull. Retain a double hand hold throughout entire Wringer.

Bootnote 1: Steps 1-6 (1st and 2nd triple steps) take your partner into Wringer Position. Steps 7-9 (3rd triple step) circle clockwise in Wringer Position. Steps 10-12 (4th triple step) take your partner out of Wringer Position into Open Position with a double hand hold.

Bootnote 2: To continue Wringer movement execute additional triple steps in Wringer Position. Wringer should end with the man facing down the line of dance.

Open Dance Position   Steps 1-3   Step 4   Steps 5-6

Western Polka

Wringer
Lady's Footwork, cont'd

Step	Description	Timing	Rhythmic Cue
11	Step R foot into 3rd position (L foot forward) as you continue to move out of Wringer Position.	&	Quick
12	Step L foot diagonally to the left as double hand hold lowers to waist level to complete the Wringer.	2	Slow

* Note: Retain a double hand hold throughout entire Wringer.

Bootnote 1: Steps 1-6 (1st and 2nd triple steps) take you into Wringer Position. Steps 7-9 (3rd triple step) circle clockwise in Wringer Position. Steps 10~12 (4th triple step) take you out of Wringer Position into Open Position with a double hand hold.

Bootnote 2: To continue Wringer movement execute additional triple steps in Wringer Position.

Steps 7-9

Step 10

Steps 11-12

Western Polka

Sweetheart into Wringer
Man's Footwork

Step	Description	Timing	Rhythmic Cue	Lead
	Position: Open Position with double hand hold into Sweetheart Wrap Position. *			
1-9	Same as steps 1-9 in the Sweetheart.			
10	Step R foot in place as you begin to lead the lady from Sweetheart Wrap Position into Wringer Position. The L hand hold begins to encircle the lady's head to turn her 1-1/2 turns in place clockwise.	1	Quick	L Hand lifts and encircles
11	Step L foot in place continuing to encircle the lady with the L hand hold. The R hand hold remains at waist level.	&	Quick	L Hand hold encircles
12	Step R foot in place as you complete a triple step and the movement out of Sweetheart Wrap Position. The L hand hold continues to encircle the lady's head.	2	Slow	L Hand hold encircles
13	Step L foot in place as the L hand hold continues to encircle the lady's head leading her from Sweetheart Wrap into Wringer Position.	1	Quick	L Hand hold encircles
14	Step R foot in place continuing to turn the lady clockwise into the Wringer.	&	Quick	L Hand hold encircles and lowers
15	Step L foot in place as the L hand hold lowers to chest level completing the lead into Wringer Position.	2	Slow	L Hand hold lowers
16-18	Execute a Step-Together-Step (triple step beginning with the right foot) as you circle clockwise with your partner in Wringer Position.	1 & 2	Q,Q,S	R Hand pressure

Western Polka

Sweetheart into Wringer
Lady's Footwork

Step	Description	Timing	Rhythmic Cue
	Position: Open Position with double hand hold into Sweetheart Wrap Position. *		
1-9	Same as steps 1-9 in the Sweetheart.		
10	Step L foot around right foot beginning to move from Sweetheart Wrap Position into Wringer Position. The R hand hold begins to encircle your head to turn you 1-1/2 turns in place clockwise.	1	Quick
11	Step R foot into 3rd position (L foot forward) as you continue to turn clockwise. The L hand hold remains at waist level.	&	Quick
12	Step L foot diagonally to the right completing the movement out of Sweetheart Wrap Position. The R hand hold continues to encircle your head.	2	Slow
13	Step R foot diagonally to the right as the R hand hold moves you from Sweetheart Wrap into the Wringer.	1	Quick
14	Step L foot into 3rd position (R foot forward) continuing to turn clockwise into Wringer Position.	&	Quick
15	Step R foot diagonally to the right as the R hand hold lowers to chest level completing the movement into Wringer Position.	2	Slow
16-18	Execute a Step-Together-Step (triple step beginning with the left foot) as you circle clockwise with your partner in Wringer Position.	1 & 2	Q,Q,S

Western Polka

Sweetheart into Wringer
Man's Footwork, Cont'd

19-21 Execute a Step-Together-Step (triple step
beginning with the left foot) as you continue
to circle clockwise with your partner. 1 & 2 Q,Q,S R Hand pressure

22-24 Same as steps 10-12 in the Wringer. 1 & 2 Q,Q,S

* Note: Retain a double hand hold throughout entire Sweetheart to Wringer.

Bootnote 1: Steps 1-6 (1st and 2nd triple steps) take your partner into Sweetheart Wrap Position. Steps 7-9 (3rd triple step) circle clockwise in Sweetheart Wrap Position. Steps 10-15 (4th and 5th triple steps) take your partner from Sweetheart Wrap Position into Wringer Position. Steps 16-21 (6th and 7th triple steps) circle clockwise in Wringer Position. Steps 22-24 (8th triple step) take your partner out of Wringer Position into Open Position.

Bootnote 2: The circle clockwise in Sweetheart Wrap Position and in Wringer Position may be repeated as many times as you wish before taking your partner back to Open Position. Sweetheart into Wringer should end with the man facing down his line of dance.

Open Dance Position

Steps 1-3

Steps 4-6

Steps 13-14

Step 15

Western Polka

Sweetheart into Wringer
Lady's Footwork, Cont'd

19-21 Execute a Step-Together-Step (triple step
beginning with the right foot) as you continue
to circle clockwise with your partner.   1 & 2   Q,Q,S

22-24 Same as steps 10-12 in the Wringer.   1 & 2   Q,Q,S

* Note: Retain a double hand hold throughout entire Sweetheart to Wringer.

Bootnote 1: Steps 1-6 (1st and 2nd triple steps) take you into Sweetheart Wrap Position.
Steps 7-9 (3rd triple step) circle clockwise in Sweetheart Wrap Position. Steps 10-15 (4th and 5th
triple steps) take you from Sweetheart Wrap Position into Wringer Position. Steps 16-21
(6th and 7th triple steps) circle clockwise in Wringer Position. Steps 22-24 (8th triple step) take
you out of Wringer Position into Open Position.

Bootnote 2: The circle clockwise in Sweetheart Wrap Position and in Wringer Position may be
repeated as many times as you wish before going back to Open Position.

Steps 7-9

Step 10

Steps 11-12

Steps 16-18

Step 22

Steps 23-24

Western Polka

Pretzel (Triple Time)
Man's Footwork

Step	Description	Timing	Rhythmic Cue	Lead
	Position: Open Position with double hand hold (his left holding her right, his right hand holding her left). *			
1-3	Execute a Step-Together-Step (1st triple step beginning with the left foot) as you raise your L hand hold to turn under it 1/2 turn counter-clockwise. Lower the R hand hold to prepare for next movement. (Lady will execute steps 1-6 facing you).	1 & 2	Q,Q,S	L Hand hold lifts and encircles
4-6	Execute a Step-Together-Step (2nd triple step beginning with the right foot) as you continue to circle counterclockwise under your L hand hold to face your partner (left shoulders adjacent). Lower the L hand hold as you extend it to your left placing your right arm behind your back.	1 & 2	Q,Q,S	L Hand hold encircles and lowers
7-9	Execute a Step-Together-Step (3rd triple step beginning with the left foot) as you turn clockwise raising the L hand hold up and over the lady's head turning her clockwise. End in back-to-back position with hand holds lowered below waist level.	1 & 2	Q,Q,S	L Hand hold lifts and encircles
10-12	Execute a Step-Together-Step (4th triple step beginning with the right foot) as you turn clockwise raising the R hand hold up and over the lady's head turning her clockwise. End facing your partner (right shoulders adjacent) with your R hand hold extended to the right and the left arm behind your back.	1 & 2	Q,Q,S	R Hand hold lifts and encircles
13-15	Execute a Step-Together-Step (5th triple step beginning with the left foot) turning a full turn clockwise under your R hand hold to face your partner. Lower the R hand hold to waist level near the L hand hold. (Lady executes a triple step in place).	1 & 2	Q,Q,S	R Hand hold lifts and encircles
16-18	Execute a Step-Together-Step (6th triple step beginning with the right foot) leading the lady into Sweetheart Wrap Position. Move your L hand hold up and over her head leading the lady into a counterclockwise turn to your right side.	1 & 2	Q,Q,S	L Hand hold lifts and encircles

Western Polka

Pretzel (Triple Time)
Lady's Footwork

Step	Description	Timing	Rhythmic Cue
	Position: Open Position with double hand hold (his left hand holding her right hand, his right hand holding her left hand) *		
	Note: Lady will execute steps 1-6 in place facing her partner.		
1-3	Execute a Step-Together-Step (1st triple step beginning with the right foot) as you R hand hold moves up and over your partner's head counterclockwise as he begins a full turn.	1 & 2	Q,Q,S
4-6	Execute a Step-Together-Step (2nd triple step beginning with the left foot) in place as the man continues to turn counterclockwise to face you (left shoulders adjacent). Lower your right arm to chest level with your left hand holding his right hand behind his back.	1 & 2	Q,Q,S
7-9	Execute a Step-Together-Step (3rd triple step beginning with the right foot) turning clockwise into back-to-back position. Your R hand hold will move up and over your head as you move into position. End in back-to-back position with hand holds lowered below waist level.	1 & 2	Q,Q,S
10-12	Execute a Step-Together-Step (4th triple step beginning with the left foot) turning clockwise to face your partner (right shoulders adjacent) Your L hand hold will move up and over your head lowering to chest level. Your right hand will hold his left hand behind his back.	1 & 2	Q,Q,S
13-15	Execute a Step-Together-Step (5th triple step beginning with the right foot) in place as the man turns counterclockwise under your L hand hold to face you. Lower your L hand hold to waist level near R hand hold.	1 & 2	Q,Q,S
16-18	Execute a Step-Together-Step (6th triple step beginning with the left foot) as you move into Sweetheart Wrap Position. Your R hand hold will move up and over your head as you turn counterclockwise to his right side.	1 & 2	Q,Q,S

Western Polka

Pretzel (Triple Time)
Man's Footwork, cont'd

Step	Description	Timing	Rhythmic Cue	Lead
19-21	Execute a Step-Together-Step (7th triple step beginning with the left foot) in place as you lead the lady out of Sweetheart Wrap Position. Move your L hand hold up and over her head leading the lady to turn clockwise to face you.	1 & 2	Q,Q,S	L Hand hold lifts and encircles
22-24	Execute a Step-Together-Step (8th triple step beginning with the right foot) as you return to Closed Dance Position.	1 & 2	Q,Q,S	L and R Hand movements

* Note:Triple steps are executed very small and almost in place. Emphasis is on arm action instead of footwork. Retain a double hand hold throughout entire Pretzel movement. Steps 22-24 may be substituted with an Underarm Turn instead of a Basic Step Forward. The lady will turn clockwise under the man's left arm and then return to Closed Dance Position.

Open Dance Position

Steps 1-3

Step 4

Steps 5-6

Steps 11-12

Step 13

Step 14

Step 15

Western Polka

Pretzel (Triple Time)
Lady's Footwork,cont'd

Step	Description	Timing	Rhythmic Cue
19-21	Execute a Step-Together-Step (7th triple step beginning with the right foot) as you move out of Sweetheart Wrap Position. Your R hand hold will move up and over your head as you turn clockwise to face your partner.	1 & 2	Q,Q,S
22-24	Execute a Step-Together-Step (8th triple step beginning with the left foot) as you return to Closed Dance Position.	1 & 2	Q,Q,S

* Note:Triple steps are executed very small and almost in place. Emphasis is on arm action instead of footwork. Retain a double hand hold throughout entire Pretzel movement. Steps 22-24 may be substituted with an Underarm Turn instead of a Basic Step Forward. The lady will turn clockwise under the man's left arm and then return to Closed Dance Position.

Step 7

Steps 8-9

Step 10

Step 16

Steps 17-18

Step 19

Steps 20-21

Western Polka

Lariat into Double Wringer
Man's Footwork

Step	Description	Timing	Rhythmic Cue	Lead
	Position: Open Position with double hand hold. *			
1-3	Execute a Step-Together-Step (1st triple step beginning with the left foot) forward as you begin to lead the lady past your right side to move clockwise around you. Double hand hold will encircle your head.	1 & 2	Q,Q,S	Double hand hold pulls and lifts
4-6	Execute a Step-Together-Step (2nd triple step beginning with the right foot) in place as you lead the lady behind you.	1 & 2	Q,Q,S	Double hand hold encircles
7-9	Execute a Step-Together-Step (3rd triple step beginning with the left foot) backward as you continue to lead the lady to move clockwise around you. Double hand hold continues to encircle your head as you lead the lady past your left side.	1 & 2	Q,Q,S	Double hand hold encircles
10-12	Execute a Step-Together-Step (4th triple step beginning with the right foot) in place as you complete Lariat movement to face your partner in Open Position.	1 & 2	Q,Q,S	Double hand hold lowers slightly
13-15	Execute a Step-Together-Step (5th triple step beginning with the left foot) in place beginning to encircle the lady's head with double hand hold to turn her a 1-3/4 turn into Wringer Position.	1 & 2	Q,Q,S	Double hand hold encircles
16-18	Execute a Step-Together-Step (6th triple step beginning with the right foot) in place continuing to turn the lady clockwise into Wringer Position. The L hand hold encircles the lady's head and lowers to chest level as the R hand hold is placed behind the lady's back at waist level.	1 & 2	Q,Q,S	R Hand hold lowers L Hand hold encircles and lowers
19-21	Execute a Step-Together-Step (7th triple step beginning with the left foot) diagonally to the right beginning to circle clockwise with your partner in Wringer Position.	1 & 2	Q,Q,S	R Hand pressure
22-24	Execute a Step-Together-Step (8th triple step beginning with the right foot) diagonally to the right to continue clockwise circle.	1 & 2	Q,Q,S	R Hand pressure

Western Polka

Lariat into Double Wringer
Lady's Footwork

Step	Description	Timing	Rhythmic Cue
	Position: Open Position with double hand hold. *		
1-3	Execute a Step-Together-Step (1st triple step beginning with the right foot) diagonally to the left as you begin to move clockwise around your partner. Double hand hold will encircle his head.	1 & 2	Q,Q,S
4-6	Execute a Step-Together-Step (2nd triple step beginning with the left foot) diagonally to the right as you continue to move around your partner. Lead has positioned you behind your partner.	1 & 2	Q,Q,S
7-9	Execute a Step-Together-Step (3rd triple step beginning with the right foot) as double hand hold moves you past your partner's left side.	1 & 2	Q,Q,S
10-12	Execute a Step-Together-Step (4th triple step beginning with the left foot) as you complete Lariat movement to face your partner in Open Position.	1 & 2	Q,Q,S
13-15	Execute a Step-Together-Step (5th triple step beginning with the right foot) diagonally to the right (in place) as the double hand hold begins to encircle your head to turn you a 1-3/4 turn into Wringer Position.	1 & 2	Q,Q,S
16-18	Execute a Step-Together-Step (6th triple step beginning with the left foot) diagonally to the right (in place) continuing to turn clockwise into Wringer Position. The R hand hold encircles your head and lowers to chest level as the L hand hold is placed behind your back at waist level.	1 & 2	Q,Q,S
19-21	Execute a Step-Together-Step (7th triple step beginning with the right foot) diagonally to the right beginning to circle clockwise with your partner in Wringer Position.	1 & 2	Q,Q,S
22-24	Execute a Step-Together-Step (8th triple step beginning with the left foot) diagonally to the right to continue clockwise circle.	1 & 2	Q,Q,S

Western Polka

Lariat into Double Wringer
Man's Footwork, cont'd

Step	Description	Timing	Rhythmic Cue	Lead
25-27	Execute a Step-Together-Step (9th triple step beginning with the left foot) turning 1/4 turn right (in place) beginning to lead the lady out of Wringer into Reverse Wringer Position. The L hand hold encircles the lady's head to turn her counter-clockwise in place as the R hand hold remains at waist level.	1 & 2	Q,Q,S	L Hand hold encircles and lowers
28-30	Execute a Step-Together-Step (10th triple step beginning with the right foot) turning 1/4 turn right (in place) to lead the lady into Reverse Wringer Position. The R hand hold encircles the lady's head to turn her counterclockwise. The L hand hold lowers to waist level.	1 & 2	Q,Q,S	L Hand hold lowers R Hand hold encircles and lowers
31-42	Execute four Step-Together-Steps (11th,12th, 13th, and 14th triple steps) diagonally to the left to complete a full circle counterclockwise in Reverse Wringer Position.	1 & 2 1 & 2 1 & 2 1 & 2	Q,Q,S Q,Q,S Q,Q,S Q,Q,S	L Hand pressure
43-45	Execute a Step-Together-Step (15th triple step beginning with the left foot) diagonally to the left (in place) leading the lady out of Reverse Wringer Position. The R hand hold encircles the lady's head to turn her clockwise to face you. The L hand hold pulls at waist level.	1 & 2	Q,Q,S	R Hand hold encircles and lowers
46-48	Execute a Step-Together-Step (16th triple step beginning with the right foot) in place completing the Lariat to Double Wringer.	1 & 2	Q,Q,S	L and R Hand holds

* Note: Retain double hand hold throughout entire Lariat into Double Wringer

Bootnote: Steps 1-12 (1st, 2nd, 3rd, and 4th triple steps) execute the Lariat movement. Steps 13-18 (5th and 6th triple steps) take your partner from the Lariat into Wringer Position. Steps 19-24 (7th and 8th triple steps) circle clockwise in Wringer Position. Steps 25-30 (9th and 10th triple steps) take your partner from Wringer Position into Reverse Wringer Position. Steps 31-42 (11th, 12th, 13th, and 14th triple steps) circle counterclockwise in Reverse Wringer Position. Steps 43-45 (15th triple step) take your partner from Reverse Wringer Position into Open Position.

Western Polka

Lariat into Double Wringer
Lady's Footwork, cont'd

Step	Description	Timing	Rhythmic Cue
25-27	Execute a Step-Together-Step (9th triple step beginning with the right foot) diagonally to the left (in place) turning out of Wringer into Reverse Wringer Position. The R hand hold encircles your head as the L hand hold remains at waist level.	1 & 2	Q,Q,S
28-30	Execute a Step-Together-Step (10th triple step beginning with the left foot) diagonally to the left (in place) completing the turn into Reverse Wringer. The L hand hold encircles your head and lowers to chest level as the R hand hold lowers to waist level.	1 & 2	Q,Q,S
31-42	Execute four Step-Together-Steps (11th,12th, 13th, and 14th triple steps) diagonally to the left to complete a full circle counterclockwise in Reverse Wringer Position.	1 & 2 1 & 2 1 & 2 1 & 2	Q,Q,S Q,Q,S Q,Q,S Q,Q,S
43-45	Execute a Step-Together-Step (15th triple step beginning with the right foot) diagonally to the right moving out of Reverse Wringer Position. The L hand hold encircles your head turning you clockwise to face your partner.	1 & 2	Q,Q,S
46-48	Execute a Step-Together-Step (16th triple step beginning with the left foot) in place completing the Lariat to Double Wringer.	1 & 2	Q,Q,S

* Note: Retain a double hand hold throughout entire Lariat into Double Wringer.

Bootnote: Steps 1-12 (1st, 2nd, 3rd, and 4th triple steps) execute the Lariat movement. Steps 13-18 (5th and 6th triple steps) take you from the Lariat into Wringer Position. Steps 19-24 (7th and 8th triple steps) circle clockwise in Wringer Position. Steps 25-30 (9th and 10th triple steps) take you from Wringer Position into Reverse Wringer Position. Steps 31-42 (11th, 12th, 13th, and 14th triple steps) circle counterclockwise in Reverse Wringer Position. Steps 43-45 (15th triple step) take you from Reverse Wringer Position into Open Position.

Lariat into Double Wringer

Open Dance
Position

Steps 1-3

Steps 4-6

Steps 7-9

Step 16

Steps 17-18

Steps 19-24

Steps 29-30

Steps 31-36

Steps 37-42

Lariat into Double Wringer

Steps 10-12

Step 13

Steps 14-15

Steps 25-26

Step 27

Step 28

Step 43

Steps 44-45

Steps 46-48

Western Polka
Advanced Polka Turns Left (clockwise)
Man's Footwork

Step	Description	Timing	Rhythmic Cue	Lead
	Position: Closed Dance Position *			
	Steps 1-3 are the same as Basic Step Forward (man's footwork)			
4	Step R foot diagonally to the right beginning to turn 1/4 turn clockwise.	1	Quick	R Palm pressure
5	Step L foot directly forward bringing feet together (3rd position, R foot forward).	&	Quick	R Palm pressure
6	Step R foot diagonally forward completing 1/4 turn clockwise preparing you for the Advanced Polka Turns.	2	Slow	R Palm pressure
7	Step L foot directly to the left traveling sideways down your line of dance.	1	Quick	R Hand pressure
8	Step R foot to the left bringing feet together.	&	Quick	R Hand pressure
9	Step L foot to the left around your partner pivoting 1/2 turn clockwise (right) remaining in Closed Position. (Strong lead is required to retain Closed Dance Position).	2	Slow	R Hand pressure
10	Step R foot directly to the right (small step) traveling sideways down your line of dance.	1	Quick	R Hand pressure
11	Step L foot to the right bringing feet together.	&	Quick	R Hand pressure
12	Step R foot directly to the right (between your partner's feet) pivoting 1/2 turn clockwise remaining in Closed Dance Position to complete one full Polka Turn Clockwise.	2	Slow	R Hand pressure

* Note: Advanced Polka Turns travel sideways down the line of dance. Steps 1-6 prepare you for the Advanced Turns by positioning you sideways. Momentum helps in maintaining the continuous turns.

Bootnote: Steps 7-12 (Advanced Polka Turns Clockwise) may be repeated as many times as you choose or you may return to the Basic Step Forward (man's footwork).

Closed Dance Position	Step 1	Step 6

Western Polka
Advanced Polka Turns Left (clockwise)
Lady's Footwork

Step	Description	Timing	Rhythmic Cue
	Position: Closed Dance Position *		
	Steps 1-3 are the same as Basic Step Forward (lady's footwork)		
4	Step L foot diagonally backward beginning to turn 1/4 turn clockwise (right).	1	Quick
5	Step R foot directly backward bringing feet together (3rd position, R foot forward).	&	Quick
6	Step L foot diagonally backward completing 1/4 turn clockwise preparing you for the Advanced Polka Turns Clockwise.	2	Slow
7	Step R foot directly to the right (small step) traveling sideways down your line of dance.	1	Quick
8	Step L foot to the right bringing feet together.	&	Quick
9	Step R foot to the right between your partner's feet to pivot 1/2 turn clockwise (right) remaining in Closed Dance Position.	2	Slow
10	Step L foot directly to the left traveling sideways down your line of dance.	1	Quick
11	Step R foot to the left bringing feet together.	&	Quick
12	Step L foot to the left around your partner pivoting 1/2 turn clockwise remaining in Closed Dance Position to complete a full Polka Turn Clockwise.	2	Slow

* Note: Advanced Polka Turns travel sideways down the line of dance. Steps 1-6 prepare you for the Advanced Turns by positioning you sideways. Momentum helps in maintaining the continuous turns.

Bootnote: Steps 7-12 (Advanced Polka Turns Clockwise) may be repeated as many times as you choose or you may return to the Basic Step Forward (lady's footwork).

| Step 7 | Step 9 | Step 12 | Step 1 |

Western Polka

Amalgamations

1 Basic Step Forward
Heel and Toe Polka
Basic Step Forward

2 Basic Step Forward
Conversation Step (four times)
Flare (four times)

3 Basic Step Forward
Underarm Turn (twice)
Continuous Underarm Turn
Windmill

4 Push 'n' Pull
Whip
Push 'n' Pull
String-A-Long

5 Push 'n' Pull
Sweetheart
Push 'n' Pull
Wringer
Push 'n' Pull
Sweetheart to Wringer

Favorite Western Polka Selections

"Big Mamou" (medium fast) by Frenchie Burke

"Cajun Moon" (medium) by Ricky Skaggs

"Colinda" (medium fast) by Frenchie Burke

"Crippled Turkey" (medium) by Bob Wills and The Texas Playboys

"Devils' Dream" (medium) by Frenchie Burke

"Down in Mexico" (medium) by Auggie Meyers

"Drivin' Nails in My Coffin" (medium fast) by Johnny Bush

"El Rancho Grande" (medium) by Al Dean and The All Stars

"Foggy Mountain Breakdown" (medium fast) by Al Dean and The All Stars

"Hey Joe (Hey Moe)" (medium) by Moe Bandy and Joe Stampley

"Jalisco" (medium fast) by Al Dean and by Adolph Hofner

"Jessie Polka" (medium) by Adolph Hofner

"Model "A" Polka" (medium) by Al Dean and The All Stars

"Mountain Music" (medium and fast) by Alabama

"My Baby Thinks He's a Train" (fast) by Rosanne Cash

"New Cut Road" (medium slow) by Bobby Bare

"On The Road Again" (medium slow) by Willie Nelson

"Orange Blossom Special" (fast) by Frenchie Burke or The Charley Daniel's Band

"Rocky Top" (fast) by The Osborne Brothers

"San Antonio Stroll" (medium slow) by Tanya Tucker

Put Your Little Foot

Put Your Little Foot

Put Your Little Foot was originally known as the Varsouvienne (also Varsouviana) and originated as a Polish folk dance in the mid-1800s. Adapted to the court dances of the Renaissance Period, the Varsouvienne evolved from the Minuet. Arriving in Texas with Polish immigrants during the westward migration, the Varsouvienne became known as Put Your Little Foot. Its popularity has continued to grow and it is danced by people of all ages throughout the dance halls of Texas.

Put Your Little Foot

1   Basic Step (Man's and Lady's footwork)

2   Sweetheart Crossovers

3   Sweetheart Separations

Rhythmical Analysis

PUT YOUR LITTLE FOOT --Time Signature 3/4

Step Pattern,

Man and Lady:	Cross,	Step,	Close,	Cross,	Step,	Close,	Cross,	Step,	Step,	Step,	Touch	
Count: Notation:	1 —	2 —	3 —	1 —	2 —	3 —	1 —	2 —	3 —	1 —	2 —	3 —
Rhythmical Cue:	Quick	Quick	Quick	Quick	Quick	Quick	Quick	Quick	Quick	Quick	Slow	

Repeat the above sequence once or three times, dictated by the music.

Step Pattern,

Man and Lady:	Cross,	Step,	Step,	Step,	Touch	
Count: Notation:	1 —	2 —	3 —	1 —	2 —	3 —
Rhythmical Cue:	Quick	Quick	Quick	Quick	Slow	

Repeat the above sequence three times.

Put Your Little Foot

Basic Step
Man's and Lady's Footwork

Step	Description	Timing	Rhythmic Cue	Lead
	Position: Sweetheart Position			
	Part 1A-Moving to the left diagonally, begin with weight on the R foot, L foot extended diagonally to the left with the heel touching the floor and the toe pointed upward.			
1	Cross L foot in front of the right leg.	1	Quick	L and R hand holds with right forearm pressure.
2	Step L foot diagonally to the left.	2	Quick	"
3	Step R foot forward bringing feet together (3rd position, L foot forward).	3	Quick	"
4	Cross L foot in front of the right leg.	1	Quick	"
5	Step L foot diagonally to the left.	2	Quick	"
6	Step R foot forward bringing feet together (3rd position, left foot forward).	3	Quick	"
7	Cross L foot in front of the right leg.	1	Quick	"
8	Step L foot diagonally to the left.	2	Quick	"
9	Step R foot forward passing L foot (small step).	3	Quick	"
10	Step L foot forward passing R foot (small step) and pivoting 1/4 turn to face right diagonal.	1	Quick	"
11	Extend R leg diagonally to the right, heel touching the floor, toe pointed upward.	2	Slow	"
12	Hold position.	3		

Put Your Little Foot, Basic Step: Part IA

Sweetheart Position

Steps 1 and 4

Steps 2 and 5

Steps 3 and 6

Step 7

Step 8

Step 9

Step 10

Steps 11 and 12

Put Your Little Foot

Basic Step
Man's and Lady's Footwork

Step	Description	Timing	Rhythmic Cue	Lead
	Part 1B-Moving to the right diagonally, begin with weight on the L foot, R foot extended diagonally to the right with the heel touching the floor and the toe pointed upward.			
1	Cross R foot in front of the left leg.	1	Quick	L and R Hand holds with right forearm pressure.
2	Step R foot diagonally to the right.	2	Quick	"
3	Step L foot forward bringing feet together (3rd position, right foot forward).	3	Quick	"
4	Cross R foot in front of the left leg.	1	Quick	"
5	Step R foot diagonally to the right.	2	Quick	"
6	Step L foot forward bringing feet together (3rd position, right foot forward).	3	Quick	"
7	Cross R foot in front of the left leg.	1	Quick	"
8	Step R foot diagonally to the right.	2	Quick	"
9	Step L foot forward passing R foot (small step).	3	Quick	"
10	Step R foot forward passing L foot (small step) and pivoting 1/4 turn to face left diagonal.	1	Quick	"
11	Extend L leg diagonally to the left, heel touching the floor, toe pointed upward.	2	Slow	"
12	Hold position.	3		

Put Your Little Foot, Basic Step: Part IB

Sweetheart Position

Steps 1 and 4

Steps 2 and 5

Steps 3 and 6

Step 7

Step 8

Step 9

Step 10

Steps 11 and 12

Put Your Little Foot
Basic Step
Man's and Lady's Footwork

Step	Description	Timing	Rhythmic Cue	Lead
	Position: Sweetheart Position			
	Part 2A-Moving to the left diagonally, begin with weight on the R foot, L foot extended diagonally to the left with the heel touching the floor and the toe pointed upward.			
1	Cross L foot in front of the right leg.	1	Quick	L and R Hand holds with right forearm pressure
2	Step L foot diagonally to the left.	2	Quick	"
3	Step R foot forward passing L foot (small step).	3	Quick	"
4	Step L foot forward passing R foot (small step) and pivoting 1/4 turn to face R diagonal.	1	Quick	"
5	Extend R leg diagonally to the right, heel touching the floor, toe pointed upward.	2	Slow	"
6	Hold position.	3		

Sweetheart Position

Step 1

Step 2

Step 3

Step 4

Steps 5 and 6

Put Your Little Foot
Basic Step
Man's and Lady's Footwork, Cont'd

Part 2B-Moving to the right diagonally, begin with weight on the L foot, R foot extended diagonally to the right with the heel touching the floor and the toe pointed upward.

1	Cross R foot in front of the left leg.	1	Quick	L and R hand holds with right forearm pressure
2	Step R foot diagonally to the right.	2	Quick	"
3	Step L foot forward passing R foot (small step).	3	Quick	"
4	Step R foot forward passing L foot (small step) and pivoting 1/4 turn to face left diagonal.	1	Quick	"
5	Extend L leg diagonally to the left, heel touching the floor, toe pointed upward.	2	Slow	"
6	Hold position.	3		

Repeat 2A, Steps 1-6 and 2B, Steps 1-6.

Bootnote : Musical arrangements may vary in dictating the number of times parts 2A and 2B should be repeated.

Sweetheart Position

Step 1

Step 2

Step 3

Step 4

Steps 5 and 6

Put Your Little Foot

Sweetheart Crossovers
Man's Footwork

Step	Description	Timing	Rhythmic Cue	Lead
	Position: Sweetheart Position into Reverse Sweetheart Position. *			
	Part 1A-Begin with weight on the R foot, L foot extended diagonally to the left, heel touching the floor, toe pointed upward.			
1	Cross L foot in front of the right leg.	1	Quick	L and R hand holds with right forearm pressure
2	Step L foot diagonally to the left.	2	Quick	"
3	Step R foot forward bringing feet together (3rd position, left foot forward).	3	Quick	"
4	Cross L foot in front of the right leg.	1	Quick	"
5	Step L foot diagonally to the left.	2	Quick	"
6	Step R foot forward bringing feet together (3rd position, left foot forward).	3	Quick	"
7	Cross L foot in front of right leg.	1	Quick	"
8	Step L foot diagonally to the left beginning to lead the lady from your right side to your left side.	2	Quick	L Hand hold pulls
9	Step R foot forward passing L foot (small step) continuing to lead the lady from Sweetheart Position into Reverse Sweetheart Position.	3	Quick	"
10	Step L foot forward passing R foot (small step) and pivoting 1/4 turn to face R diagonal completing the movement into Reverse Sweetheart Position.	1	Quick	"
11	Extend R leg diagonally to the right, heel touching the floor, toe pointed upward.	2	Slow	R and L Hand holds
12	Hold position.	3		

* Note: Retain a double hand hold throughout Sweetheart Crossovers.

Put Your Little Foot

Sweetheart Crossovers
Lady's Footwork

Step	Description	Timing	Rhythmic Cue
	Position: Sweetheart Position into Reverse Sweetheart Position. *		
	Part 1A-Begin with weight on the R foot, L foot extended diagonally to the left, heel touching the floor, toe pointed upward.		
1	Cross L foot in front of the right leg.	1	Quick
2	Step L foot diagonally to the left.	2	Quick
3	Step R foot forward bringing feet together (3rd position, left foot forward).	3	Quick
4	Cross L foot in front of the right leg.	1	Quick
5	Step L foot diagonally to the left.	2	Quick
6	Step R foot forward bringing feet together (3rd position, left foot forward).	3	Quick
7	Cross L foot in front of right leg.	1	Quick
8	Step L foot diagonally to the left as you begin to move from the man's right side to his left side.	2	Quick
9	Step R foot forward passing L foot (large step) continuing to move from Sweetheart Position into Reverse Sweetheart Position.	3	Quick
10	Step L foot forward passing R foot (large step) and pivoting 1/4 turn to face R diagonal completing the movement into Reverse Sweetheart Position.	1	Quick
11	Extend R leg diagonally to the right, heel touching the floor, toe pointed upward.	2	Slow
12	Hold position.	3	

* Note: Retain a double hand hold throughout Sweetheart Crossover Position.

Put Your Little Foot

Sweetheart Crossovers
Man's Footwork

Step	Description	Timing	Rhythmic Cue	Lead
	Position: Reverse Sweetheart Position into Sweetheart Position.			
	Part 1B-Begin with weight on the L foot, R foot extended diagonally to the right, heel touching the floor, toe pointed upward.			
1	Cross R foot in front of the left leg.	1	Quick	R and L hand hold with L forearm pressure
2	Step R foot diagonally to the right.	2	Quick	"
3	Step L foot forward bringing feet together (3rd position, right foot forward).	3	Quick	"
4	Cross R foot in front of the left leg.	1	Quick	"
5	Step R foot diagonally to the right.	2	Quick	"
6	Step L foot forward bringing feet together (3rd position, right foot forward).	3	Quick	"
7	Cross R foot in front of the left leg.	1	Quick	"
8	Step R foot diagonally to the right beginning to lead the lady from your left side to your right side.	2	Quick	R Hand hold pulls
9	Step L foot forward passing R foot (small step) continuing to lead the lady from Reverse Sweetheart Position into Sweetheart Position.	3	Quick	R Hand hold pulls
10	Step R foot forward passing L foot (small step) and pivoting 1/4 turn to face L diagonal completing the movement into Sweetheart Position.	1	Quick	R Hand hold pulls
11	Extend L leg diagonally to the left, heel touching the floor, toe pointed upward.	2	Slow	L and R hand holds
12	Hold position.	3		L and R hand holds

Put Your Little Foot

Sweetheart Crossovers
Lady's Footwork

Step	Description	Timing	Rhythmic Cue
	Position: Reverse Sweetheart Position into Sweetheart Position.		
	Part 1B-Begin with weight on the L foot, R foot extended diagonally to the right, heel touching the floor, toe pointed upward.		
1	Cross R foot in front of the left leg.	1	Quick
2	Step R foot diagonally to the right.	2	Quick
3	Step L foot forward bringing feet together (3rd position, right foot forward).	3	Quick
4	Cross R foot in front of the left leg.	1	Quick
5	Step R foot diagonally to the right.	2	Quick
6	Step L foot forward bringing feet together (3rd position, right foot forward).	3	Quick
7	Cross R foot in front of the left leg.	1	Quick
8	Step R foot diagonally to the right beginning to move from the man's left side to his right side.	2	Quick
9	Step L foot forward passing R foot (large step) continuing to move from Reverse Sweetheart Position into Sweetheart Position.	3	Quick
10	Step R foot forward passing L foot (large step) and pivoting 1/4 turn to face L diagonal completing the movement into Sweetheart Position.	1	Quick
11	Extend L leg diagonally to the left, heel touching the floor, toe pointed upward.	2	Slow
12	Hold position.	3	

Sweetheart Crossovers: Part IA

Sweetheart Position

Steps 1 and 4

Steps 2 and 5

Steps 3 and 6

Step 7

Step 8

Step 9

Step 10

Steps 11 and 12

Sweetheart Crossovers: Part IB

Reverse Sweetheart Position

Steps 1 and 4

Steps 2 and 5

Steps 3 and 6

Step 7

Step 8

Step 9

Step 10

Steps 11 and 12

Put Your Little Foot

Sweetheart Crossovers
Man's Footwork

Step	Description	Timing	Rhythmic Cue	Lead
	Position: Sweetheart Position into Reverse Sweetheart Position.			
	Part 2A-Begin with weight on the R foot, L foot extended diagonally to the left, heel touching the floor, toe pointed upward.			
1	Cross L foot in front of the right leg.	1	Quick	L and R Hand holds
2	Step L foot diagonally to the left beginning to lead the lady from your right side to your left side.	2	Quick	L Hand hold pulls
3	Step R foot forward passing L foot (small step) continuing to lead the lady from Sweetheart Position into Reverse Sweetheart Position.	3	Quick	L Hand hold pulls
4	Step L foot forward passing R foot (small step) and pivoting 1/4 turn to face R diagonal completing the movement into Reverse Sweetheart Position.	1	Quick	L Hand hold pulls
5	Extend R leg diagonally to the right, heel touching the floor, toe pointed upward.	2	Slow	R and L hand holds
6	Hold Position.	3		R and L hand holds

Sweetheart Position

Step 1

Step 2

Put Your Little Foot

Sweetheart Crossovers
Lady's Footwork

Step	Description	Timing	Rhythmic Cue
	Position: Sweetheart Position into Reverse Sweetheart Position		
	Part 2A-Begin with weight on the R foot, L foot extended diagonally to the left, heel touching the floor, toe pointed upward.		
1	Cross L foot in front of the right leg.	1	Quick
2	Step L foot diagonally to the left beginning to move from the man's right side to his left side.	2	Quick
3	Step R foot forward passing L foot (large step) continuing to move from Sweetheart Position into Reverse Sweetheart Position.	3	Quick
4	Step L foot forward passing R foot (large step) and pivoting 1/4 turn to face R diagonal completing the movement into Reverse Sweetheart Position.	1	Quick
5	Extend R leg diagonally to the right, heel touching the floor, toe pointed upward.	2	Slow
6	Hold position.	3	

Step 3

Step 4

Steps 5 and 6

Put Your Little Foot

Sweetheart Crossovers
Man's Footwork

Step	Description	Timing	Rhythmic Cue	Lead
	Position: Reverse Sweetheart Position into Sweetheart Position.			
	Part 2B-Begin with weight on the L foot, R foot extended diagonally to the right, heel touching the floor, toe pointed upward.			
1	Cross R foot in front of the left leg.	1	Quick	R and L hand holds
2	Step R foot diagonally to the right beginning to lead the lady from your left side to your right side.	2	Quick	R Hand hold pulls
3	Step L foot forward passing R foot (small step) continuing to lead the lady from Reverse Sweetheart Position into Sweetheart Position.	3	Quick	R Hand hold pulls
4	Step R foot forward passing L foot (small step) and pivoting 1/4 turn to face L diagonal completing the movement into Sweetheart Position.	1	Quick	R Hand hold pulls
5	Extend L leg diagonally to the left, heel touching the floor, toe pointed upward.	2	Slow	L and R hand holds
6	Hold position.	3		L and R hand holds

Repeat 2A, Steps 1-6 and 2B, Steps 1-6.

 Bootnote: Musical arrangements may vary in dictating the number of times Parts 2A and 2B should be repeated.

Reverse Sweetheart Position

Step 1

Step 2

Put Your Little Foot

Sweetheart Crossovers
Lady's Footwork

Step	Description	Timing	Rhythmic Cue
	Position: Reverse Sweetheart Position into Sweetheart Position.		
	Part 2B-Begin with weight on the L foot, R foot extended diagonally to the right, heel touching the floor, toe pointed upward.		
1	Cross R foot in front of the left leg.	1	Quick
2	Step R foot diagonally to the right beginning to move from the man's left side to his right side.	2	Quick
3	Step L foot forward passing R foot (large step) continuing to move from Reverse Sweetheart Position into Sweetheart Position.	3	Quick
4	Step R foot forward passing L foot (large step) and pivoting 1/4 turn to face L diagonal completing the movement into Sweetheart Position.	1	Quick
5	Extend L leg diagonally to the left, heel touching the floor, toe pointed upward.	2	Slow
6	Hold Position.	3	

Repeat 2A, Steps 1-6 and 2B, Steps 1-6.

Bootnote: Musical arrangements may vary in dictating the number of times Parts 2A and 2B should be repeated.

Step 3   Step 4   Steps 5 and 6

Put Your Little Foot

Sweetheart Separations
Man's Footwork

Step	Description	Timing	Rhythmic Cue	Lead
	Position: Sweetheart Position into Reverse Sweetheart Separation Position. *			
	Part 1A-Begin with weight on the R foot, L foot extended diagonally to the left, heel touching the floor, toe pointed upward.			
1	Cross L foot in front of the right leg.	1	Quick	L and R hand holds with right forearm pressure
2	Step L foot diagonally to the left.	2	Quick	"
3	Step R foot forward bringing feet together (3rd position, left foot forward).	3	Quick	"
4	Cross L foot in front of the right leg.	1	Quick	"
5	Step L foot diagonally to the left.	2	Quick	"
6	Step R foot forward bringing feet together (3rd position, left foot forward).	3	Quick	"
7	Cross L foot in front of the right leg.	1	Quick	"
8	Step L foot diagonally to the left beginning to lead the lady from your right side to your left side.	2	Quick	L Hand hold pulls
9	Step R foot forward passing L foot (small step) continuing to lead the lady from Sweetheart Position into Reverse Sweetheart Separation Position.The L hand hold begins to lift up and over the lady's head as you move into position.	3	Quick	"
10	Step L foot forward passing R foot (small step) and pivoting 1/4 turn to face R diagonal completing the movement into Reverse Sweetheart Separation Position. The L hand hold lowers to chest level.	1	Quick	"
11	Extend R leg diagonally to the right, heel touching the floor, toe pointed upward.	2	Slow	R and L hand holds
12	Hold position.	3		R and L hand holds

* Note: Retain a double hand hold throughout Sweetheart Separations.

Put Your Little Foot

Sweetheart Separations
Lady's Footwork

Step	Description	Timing	Rhythmic Cue
	Position: Sweetheart Position into Reverse Sweetheart Separation Position. *		
	Part 1A-Begin with weight on the R foot, L foot extended diagonally to the left, heel touching the floor, toe pointed upward.		
1	Cross L foot in front of the right leg.	1	Quick
2	Step L foot diagonally to the left.	2	Quick
3	Step R foot forward bringing feet together (3rd position, left foot forward).	3	Quick
4	Cross L foot in front of the right leg.	1	Quick
5	Step L foot diagonally to the left.	2	Quick
6	Step R foot forward bringing feet together (3rd position, left foot forward).	3	Quick
7	Cross L foot in front of the right leg.	1	Quick
8	Step L foot diagonally to the left as you begin to move from the man's right side to his left side.	2	Quick
9	Step R foot forward passing L foot (large step) continuing to move from Sweetheart Position into Reverse Sweetheart Separation Position. The man will begin to lift the L hand hold up and over your head as you move into position.	3	Quick
10	Step L foot forward passing R foot (large step) and pivoting 1/4 turn to face R diagonal) completing the movement into Reverse Sweetheart Separation Position. The man will lower the L hand hold to chest level to complete the movement.	1	Quick
11	Extend R leg diagonally to the right, heel touching the floor, toe pointed upward.	2	Slow
12	Hold position.	3	

* Note: Retain a double hand hold throughout Sweetheart Separations.

Put Your Little Foot

Sweetheart Separations
Man's Footwork

Step	Description	Timing	Rhythmic Cue	Lead
	Position: Reverse Sweetheart Separation Position into Sweetheart Separation Position.			
	Part 1B-Begin with weight on the L foot, R foot extended diagonally to the right, heel touching the floor, toe pointed upward.			
1	Cross R foot in front of the left leg.	1	Quick	R and L hand hold with left forearm pressure
2	Step R foot diagonally to the right.	2	Quick	"
3	Step L foot forward bringing feet together (3rd position, right foot forward).	3	Quick	"
4	Cross R foot in front of the left leg.	1	Quick	"
5	Step R foot diagonally to the right.	2	Quick	"
6	Step L foot forward bringing feet together (3rd position, right foot forward).	3	Quick	"
7	Cross R foot in front of the left leg.	1	Quick	"
8	Step R foot diagonally to the right beginning to lead the lady from your left side to your right side.	2	Quick	R Hand hold pulls
9	Step L foot forward passing R foot (small step) continuing to lead the lady from Reverse Sweetheart Separation Position into Sweetheart Separation Position. The R hand hold begins to lift up and over the lady's head as you move into position.	3	Quick	R Hand hold pulls
10	Step R foot forward passing L foot (small step) and pivoting 1/4 turn to face L diagonal completing the movement into Sweetheart Separation Position. The R hand hold lowers to chest level to complete the movement.	1	Quick	R Hand hold pulls
11	Extend L leg diagonally to the left, heel touching the floor, toe pointed upward.	2	Slow	L and R Hand holds
12	Hold position.	3		L and R Hand holds

Put Your Little Foot

Sweetheart Separations
Lady's Footwork

Step	Description	Timing	Rhythmic Cue
	Position: Reverse Sweetheart Separation Position into Sweetheart Separation Position.		
	Part 1B-Begin with weight on the L foot, R foot extended diagonally to the right, heel touching the floor, toe pointed upward.		
1	Cross R foot in front of the left leg.	1	Quick
2	Step R foot diagonally to the right.	2	Quick
3	Step L foot forward bringing feet together (3rd position, right foot forward).	3	Quick
4	Cross R foot in front of the left leg.	1	Quick
5	Step R foot diagonally to the right.	2	Quick
6	Step L foot forward bringing feet together (3rd position, right foot forward).	3	Quick
7	Cross R foot in front of the left leg.	1	Quick
8	Step R foot diagonally to the right beginning to move from the man's left side to his right side.	2	Quick
9	Step L foot forward passing R foot (large step) continuing to move from Reverse Sweetheart Separation Position into Sweetheart Separation Position. The man will begin to lift the R hand hold up and over your head as you move into position.	3	Quick
10	Step R foot forward passing L foot (large step) and pivoting 1/4 turn to face the L diagonal completing the movement into Sweetheart Separation Position. The man will lower the L hand hold to chest level to complete the movement.	1	Quick
11	Extend L leg diagonally to the left, heel touching the floor, toe pointed upward.	2	Slow
12	Hold position.	3	

350

Sweetheart Separations: Part IA

Sweetheart Position

Steps 1 and 4

Steps 2 and 5

Steps 3 and 6

Step 7

Step 8

Step 9

Step 10

Steps 11 and 12

Sweetheart Separations: Part IB

Reverse Sweetheart
Separation Position

Steps 1 and 4

Steps 2 and 5

Steps 3 and 6

Step 7

Step 8

Step 9

Step 10

Steps 11 and 12

Put Your Little Foot

Sweetheart Separations
Man's Footwork

Step	Description	Timing	Rhythmic Cue	Lead
	Position: Sweetheart Separation Position into Reverse Sweetheart Separation Position.			
	Part 2A-Begin with weight on the R foot, L foot extended diagonally to the left, heel touching the floor, toe pointed upward.			
1	Cross L foot in front of the right leg.	1	Quick	L and R hand holds
2	Step L foot diagonally to the left beginning to lead the lady from your right side to your left side.	2	Quick	L Hand hold pulls
3	Step R foot forward passing L foot (small step) continuing to lead the lady from Sweetheart Separation Position into Reverse Sweetheart Separation Position. The L hand hold begins to lift up and over the lady's head as you move into position.	3	Quick	L Hand hold pulls
4	Step L foot forward passing R foot (small step) and pivoting 1/4 turn to face R diagonal and completing the movement into Reverse Sweetheart Separation Position. L Hand hold lowers to chest level.	1	Quick	L Hand hold pulls
5	Extend R leg diagonally to the right, heel touching the floor, toe pointed upward.	2	Slow	R and L Hand holds
6	Hold position.	3		R and L Hand holds

Sweetheart Separation
Position

Step 1

Step 2

Put Your Little Foot

Sweetheart Separations
Lady's Footwork

Step	Description	Timing	Rhythmic Cue
	Position: Sweetheart Separation Position into Reverse Sweetheart Separation Position.		
	Part 2A-Begin with weight on the R foot, L foot extended diagonally to the left, heel touching the floor, toe pointed upward.		
1	Cross L foot in front of the right leg.	1	Quick
2	Step L foot diagonally to the left beginning to move from the man's right side to his left side.	2	Quick
3	Step R foot forward passing L foot (large step) continuing to move from Sweetheart Separation Position into Reverse Sweetheart Separation Position. The man will begin to lift the L hand hold up and over your head as you move into position.	3	Quick
4	Step L foot forward passing R foot (large step) and pivoting 1/4 turn to face R diagonal completing the movement into Reverse Sweetheart Separation Position. The man will lower the L hand hold to chest level to complete the movement.	1	Quick
5	Extend R leg diagonally to the right, heel touching the floor, toe pointed upward.	2	Slow
6	Hold position.	3	

Step 3

Step 4

Steps 5 and 6

Put Your Little Foot

Sweetheart Separations
Man's Footwork

Step	Description	Timing	Rhythmic Cue	Lead
	Position: Reverse Sweetheart Separation Position into Sweetheart Separation Position.			
	Part 2B-Begin with weight on the L foot, R foot extended diagonally to the right, heel touching the floor, toe pointed upward.			
1	Cross R foot in front of the left leg.	1	Quick	R and L hand holds
2	Step R foot diagonally to the right beginning to lead the lady from your left side to your right side.	2	Quick	R Hand hold pulls
3	Step L foot forward passing R foot (small step) continuing to lead the lady from Reverse Sweetheart Separation into Sweetheart Separation Position. The R hand hold begins to lift up and over the lady's head as you move into position.	3	Quick	R Hand hold pulls
4	Step R foot forward passing L foot (small step) and pivoting 1/4 turn to face L diagonal completing the movement into Sweetheart Separation Position. The R hand hold lowers to chest level to complete the movement.	1	Quick	R Hand hold pulls
5	Extend L leg diagonally to the left, heel touching the floor, toe pointed upward.	2	Slow	L and R Hand holds
6	Hold position.	3		L and R Hand holds

Repeat 2A, Steps 1-6 and 2B, Steps 1-6.

Bootnote: Musical arrangements may vary in dictating the number of times parts 2A and 2B should be repeated.

Reverse Sweetheart
Separation Position

Step 1

Step 2

Put Your Little Foot

Sweetheart Separations
Lady's Footwork

Step	Description	Timing	Rhythmic Cue
	Position: Reverse Sweetheart Separation Position into Sweetheart Separation Position.		
	Part 2B-Begin with weight on the left foot, right foot extended diagonally to the right, heel touching the floor, toe pointed upward.		
1	Cross R foot in front of the left leg.	1	Quick
2	Step R foot diagonally to the right beginning to move from the man's left side to his right side.	2	Quick
3	Step L foot forward passing R foot (large step) continuing to move from Reverse Sweetheart Separation Position into Sweetheart Separation Position. The man will begin to lift the R hand hold up and over your head as you move into position.	3	Quick
4	Step R foot forward passing L foot (large step) and pivoting 1/4 turn to face L diagonal completing the movement into Sweetheart Separation Position. The man will lower the R hand hold to chest level to complete the movement.	1	Quick
5	Extend L leg diagonally to the left, heel touching the floor, toe pointed upward.	2	Slow
6	Hold position.	3	

Repeat 2A, Steps 1-6 and 2B, Steps 1-6.

Bootnote: Musical arrangements may vary in dictating the number of times parts 2A and 2B should be repeated.

| Step 3 | Step 4 | Steps 5 and 6 |

FAVORITE PUT YOUR LITTLE FOOT SELECTIONS

"Put Your Little Foot" by Al Dean

"Put Your Little Foot" by Johnny Gimble

"Put Your Little Foot" by Adolph Hofner

"Put Your Little Foot" by David Houston

Ten Step Polka

Ten-Step Polka

The Ten-Step Polka is an offspring of the old-time folk dance favorite Jessie Polka. The original Jessie Polka consisted of eight counts alternating with four Polka steps that progress forward. The Ten-Step Polka, appearing on the scene after "Urban Cowboy" fame, has added an additional two counts to the verse. Because of the foot placement, the dance is sometimes called Heel and Toe Polka, which is confusing since there is an authentic folk dance by the same name.

Advanced dancers may combine the Ten-Step Polka with the Western Polka by returning to closed position with the lady then executing a fake step (change of weight) in order to get on the opposite foot. The "Ten-Step" series offers a brief period in which you may "catch your breath" while executing the more strenuous turns of the Polka.

Once you master the basic step you may enjoy such variations as "The Lasso" or "Weave the Basket" or you may prefer to create your own!

Ten-Step Polka

1. Basic Step (Man's and Lady's)
2. Lasso
3. Lady's Double Turn (clockwise)

4. Continuous Lasso
5. Weave the Basket

Rhythmical Analysis

TEN-STEP POLKA----Time Signature 2/4

Step pattern:

Man and Lady:	Touch L forward,	Step in place,	Touch R back,	Step in place,	Touch R forward,	Touch R across
Count: Notation	1 —	2 —	1 —	2 —	1 —	2 —
Rhythmical Cue:	Quick	Quick	Quick	Quick	Quick	Quick

Man and Lady:	Touch R forward,	Step in place,	Touch L forward,	Cross L in front
Count: Notation	1 —	2 —	1 —	2 —
Rhythmical Cue:	Quick	Quick	Quick	Quick

To complete the basic "Ten Step" one will use 5 measures of music in 2/4 time. For rhythmical analysis of the remainder of this dance refer to Western Polka.

Ten-Step Polka

Basic Step
Man's and Lady's Footwork

Step	Description	Timing	Rhythmic Cue	Lead
	Position: Sweetheart Position *			
1	Step L foot directly forward.	1	Quick	L and R hand holds
2	Step R foot directly forward bringing feet together (3rd position, L foot forward).	&	Quick	"
3	Step L foot directly forward.	2	Slow	"
4	Step R foot directly forward passing L foot.	1	Quick	"
5	Step L foot directly forward bringing feet together (3rd position, R foot forward).	&	Quick	"
6	Step R foot directly forward.	2	Slow	"
7-12	Repeat Steps 1-6 before executing the Ten-Step Polka.			

TEN-STEP POLKA

Step	Description	Timing	Rhythmic Cue	Lead
13	(1) Extend L foot forward, heel touching floor with toe upward.	1	Slow	L and R hand holds
14	(2) Step L foot in place bringing feet together and changing weight to the L foot.	2	Slow	"
15	(3) Extend R foot backward, toe touching floor.	1	Slow	"
16	(4) Step R foot in place bringing feet together Do not change weight.	2	Slow	"
17	(5) Extend R foot forward, heel touching floor with toe upward.	1	Slow	"
18	(6) Cross R foot in front of left leg (shin) with toe touching floor near L foot.	2	Slow	"
19	(7) Extend R foot forward, heel touching floor with toe upward.	1	Slow	"
20	(8) Step R foot in place bringing feet together and changing weight to R foot.	2	Slow	"
21	(9) Extend L foot forward, heel touching floor with toe upward.	1	Slow	"
22	(10) Cross L foot in front of right leg (shin) with L foot off floor.	2	Slow	"

* Note: Steps 1-12 (4 triple steps progressing forward) are the same as Basic Step Forward (man's footwork) in Western Polka. Lady and Man begin with the left foot.

Ten-Step

Sweetheart Position

Step 13

Step 14

Step 15

Step 16

Step 17

Step 18

Step 19

Step 20

Step 21

Step 22

Ten-Step Polka

Lasso
Man's Footwork

Step	Description	Timing	Rhythmic Cue	Lead
	Position: Lasso Position #1 (Sweetheart Position) into Lasso Position #2 into Lasso Position #3. *			
1	Step L foot directly forward.	1	Quick	L and R hand holds
2	Step R foot directly forward bringing feet together (3rd position, L foot forward).	&	Quick	"
3	Step L foot directly forward.	2	Slow	"
4	Step R foot directly forward passing L foot.	1	Quick	"
5	Step L foot directly forward bringing feet together (3rd position, R foot forward).	&	Quick	"
6	Step R foot directly forward.	2	Slow	"
7-12	Repeat Steps 1-6 before executing the Ten-Step Polka.			

*Note: Steps 1-12 (4 Triple Steps progressing forward) are the same as Basic Step Forward (man's footwork) in Western Polka. Lady and Man begin with the left foot. Lady remains in Lasso Position #1.

TEN-STEP POLKA

Step	Description	Timing	Rhythmic Cue	Lead
13	(1) Extend L foot forward, heel touching floor with toe upward.	1	Slow	L and R hand holds
14	(2) Step L foot in place bringing feet together and changing weight to the L foot.	2	Slow	"
15	(3) Extend R foot backward, toe touching floor.	1	Slow	"
16	(4) Step R foot in place bringing feet together Do not change weight.	2	Slow	"
17	(5) Extend R foot forward, heel touching floor with toe upward.	1	Slow	"
18	(6) Cross R foot in front of left leg (shin) with toe touching floor near L foot.	2	Slow	"
19	(7) Extend R foot forward, heel touching floor with toe upward.	1	Slow	"
20	(8) Step R foot in place bringing feet together and changing weight to R foot.	2	Slow	"

Ten-Step Polka

Lasso
Lady's Footwork

Step	Description	Timing	Rhythmic Cue
	Position: Lasso Position #1 (Sweetheart Position) into Lasso Position #2 into Lasso Position #3. *		
1	Step L foot directly forward.	1	Quick
2	Step R foot directly forward bringing feet together (3rd position, L foot forward).	&	Quick
3	Step L foot directly forward.	2	Slow
4	Step R foot directly foward passing L foot.	1	Quick
5	Step L foot directly forward bringing feet together (3rd position, R foot forward).	&	Quick
6	Step R foot directly forward.	2	Slow
7-12	Repeat Steps 1-6 before executing the Ten-Step Polka.		

* Note: Steps 1-12 (4 Triple Steps progressing forward) are the same as Basic Step Forward (man's footwork) in Western Polka. Lady and Man begin with the left foot. Lady remains in Position #1 during steps 1-12.

TEN-STEP POLKA

Step	Description	Timing	Rhythmic Cue
13	(1) Extend L foot forward, heel touching floor with toe upward.	1	Slow
14	(2) Step L foot in place bringing feet together and changing weight to the L foot.	2	Slow
15	(3) Extend R foot backward, toe touching floor.	1	Slow
16	(4) Step R foot in place bringing feet together Do not change weight.	2	Slow
17	(5) Extend R foot forward, heel touching floor with toe upward.	1	Slow
18	(6) Cross R foot in front of left leg (shin) with toe touching floor near L foot.	2	Slow
19	(7) Extend R foot forward, heel touching floor with toe upward.	1	Slow
20	(8) Step R foot in place bringing feet together and changing weight to R foot.	2	Slow

Ten-Step Polka

Lasso
Man's Footwork, Cont'd

21	(9) Extend L foot forward, heel touching floor with toe upward.	1	Slow	L and R hand holds
22	(10) Cross L foot in front of right leg (shin) with L foot off floor.	2	Slow	"

*Note: Steps 23-34 (4 triple steps progressing forward) are the same as Basic Step Forward (man's footwork) in Western Polka as the man leads the lady from Position #1 into Position #2 from his right side to his left side. Retain a double hand hold.

23-25 Execute a Step-Together-Step (1st Triple Step beginning with left foot) as the man leads the lady counterclockwise from his right side to his left side. Your R hand hold raises and begins to lead the lady to move in front of you. L hand hold remains at waist level.

26-28 Execute a Step-Together-Step (2nd Triple Step beginning with right foot) as the man continues to lead the lady in a counterclockwise movement in front of him by circling his R hand hold over her head.

29-31 Execute a Step-Together-Step (3rd Triple Step beginning with the left foot) as the man continues to lead the lady in a counterclockwise movement from his right side to his left side. Your R hand hold encircles her head and begins to turn the lady to face down the line of dance at your left side.

32-34 Execute a Step-Together-Step (4th Triple Step beginning with right foot) as you complete Lasso movement from Position #1 (man's right side) to Position #2 (man's left side). As you complete the Lasso movement lower the R hand hold behind your head with L hand hold extended diagonally to the left.

35-44 Execute the Ten-Step Polka in Position #2 of the Lasso.

*Note: Steps 45-56 (4 triple steps progressing forward) are the same as Basic Step Forward (man's footwork) in Western Polka as the man leads the lady from Position #2 (man's left side) into Position #3 (man's right side).

45-47 Execute a Step-Together-Step (1st Triple Step beginning with the left foot) as you begin to lead the lady from Position #2 (man's left side) into Position #3 (man's right side) by placing your L hand hold on your left shoulder. As you progress forward the lady will begin to move behind you to your right side.

48-50 Execute a Step-Together-Step (2nd Triple Step beginning with the right foot) as you continue to lead the lady behind you from your left side to your right side. L hand hold is placed on your left shoulder.

51-53 Execute a Step-Together-Step (3rd Triple Step beginning with the left foot) as you continue to lead the lady from your left side, behind you, to your right side. L hand hold is placed on your left shoulder as your R hand hold extends diagonally to the right at waist level.

54-56 Execute a Step-Together-Step (4th Triple Step beginning with the right foot) as you complete leading the lady from Position #2 into Position #3 ending with your L hand hold placed on your shoulder. Your R hand hold is extended diagonally to your right at waist level.

57-66 Execute the Ten-Step Polka in Position #3 of the Lasso.

Ten-Step Polka

Lasso
Lady's Footwork, Cont'd

21	(9) Extend L foot forward, heel touching floor with toe upward.	1	Slow
22	(10) Cross L foot in front of right leg (shin) with L foot off floor.	2	Slow

* Note: Steps 23-34 consist of 4 Triple steps progressing from Position #1 into Position #2 as the man leads the lady from his right side to his left side.

23-25 Execute a Step-Together-Step (1st Triple Step beginning with the left foot) as the man leads you counterclockwise from his right side to his left side. The R hand hold raises and begins to lead you in front of him. L hand hold remains at waist level.

26-28 Execute a Step-Together-Step (2nd Triple Step beginning with the right foot) as the man continues to lead you in a counterclockwise movement in front of him. R hand hold encircles your head with the L hand hold remaining at waist level.

29-31 Execute a Step-Together-Step (3rd Triple Step beginning with the left foot) as the man continues to lead you in a counterclockwise movement from his right side to his left side. R hand hold encircles your head and begins to turn you to face down the line of dance at the man's left side.

32-34 Execute a Step-Together-Step (4th Triple Step beginning with the right foot) as the man completes Lasso movement from Position #1 into Position #2 (man's right side to man's left side). Man will lower R hand hold behind his head. The L hand hold is extended diagonally to the left.

34-44 Execute the Ten-Step Polka in Position #2 of the Lasso.

* Note: Steps 45-56 consist of 4 triple steps beginning with the left foot as the man begins to lead the lady from his left side behind him to his right side. Man will be progressing directly forward during the movement.

45-47 Execute a Step-Together-Step (1st Triple Step beginning with the left foot) as the man begins to lead you from Position #1 (Man's left side) into Position 33 (Man's right side) by placing his L hand hold on his left shoulder. As the man progresses forward you will begin to move behind him to his right side.

48-50 Execute a Step-Together-Step (2nd Triple Step beginning with the right foot) as the man continues to lead you behind him from his left side to his right side.

51-53 Execute a Step-Together-Step (3rd Triple Step beginning with the left foot) as the man continues to lead you from his left side, behind him, to his right side by placing his L hand hold on his left shoulder and extending his R hand hold diagonally to the right at waist level.

54-56 Execute a Step-Together-Step (4th Triple Step beginning with the right foot) as the man completes leading you from Position #2 into Position #3 ending with the L hand hold placed on his left shoulder. The R hand hold is extended diagonally to the right at waist level.

57-66 Execute the Ten-Step Polka in Position #3 of the Lasso.

Ten-Step Polka

Lasso
Man's Footwork, Cont'd

*Note: Steps 67-78 (4 Triple step progressing forward) are the same as Basic Step Forward (man's footwork) in Western Polka as the man leads the lady from Position #3 (man's right side) into Position #1 (man's right side).

67-69 Execute a Step-Together-Step (1st Triple Step beginning with the left foot) as you begin to lead the lady from Position #3 into Position #1. R hand hold begins to pull at waist level as L hand hold lifts up and over your head beginning to turn the lady counterclockwise.

70-72 Execute a Step-Together-Step (2nd Triple Step beginning with the right foot) as you continue to lead the lady into Position #1. L hand hold moves over the lady's head and begins to lower to waist level.

73-75 Execute a Step-Together-Step (3rd Triple Step beginning with the left foot) as you continue to lead the lady from Position #3 into Position #1 by lowering your L hand hold to waist level. R hand hold completes the lead by turning the lady counterclockwise into Position #1.

76-78 Execute a Step-Together-Step (4th Triple Step beginning with the right foot) directly forward to complete the Lasso.

79-88 Execute the Ten-Step Polka in Position #1 of the Lasso.

*Note: The Lasso may be repeated or followed by other Ten-Step Polka variations.

Lasso Position #1   Lasso Position #2   Lasso Position #3

Ten-Step Polka

Lasso
Lady's Footwork, Cont'd

*Note: Steps 67-78 consist of 4 Triple Steps progressing from Position #3 into Position #1 as the man leads the lady to turn one full turn counterclockwise on the man's right side while progressing down the line of dance.

67-69   Execute a Step-Together-Step (1st Triple Step beginning with the left foot) as the man begins to lead your from Position #3 into Position #1. L hand hold lifts upward beginning to turn you counterclockwise in place.

70-72   Execute a Step-Together-Step (2nd Triple Step beginning with the right foot) as the man begins to lead you into Position #1. L hand hold encircles your head and begins to lower to waist level.

73-75   Execute a Step-Together-Step (3rd Triple Step beginning with the left foot) as the man continues to lead you from Position #3 into Position #1 by lowering the L hand hold at waist level.

76-78   Execute a Step-Together-Step (4th Triple Step beginning with the right foot) directly forward to complete the Lasso.

79-88   Execute the Ten-Step Polka in Position #1 of the Lasso.

* Note: The Lasso may be repeated or followed by other Ten-Step Polka variations.

Ten-Step Polka

Lady's Double Turn
Man's Footwork

Step   **Description**

Position: Sweetheart Position *

1-3   Execute a Step-Together-Step (1st Triple Step beginning with the left foot) directly forward as you begin to lead the lady into 1/2 turn clockwise under your R hand hold. Release L hand hold keeping it at waist level or placing it on your hip.

4-6   Execute a Step-Together-Step (2nd Triple Step beginning with the right foot) directly forward. Continue to turn the lady another 1/2 turn clockwise under your R hand hold. The lady will complete a full turn during steps 1-6.

7-9   Execute a Step-Together-Step (3rd Triple Step beginning with the left foot) directly forward. Lead the lady into another 1/2 turn clockwise under your R hand hold as you both progress down the line of dance.

10-12 Execute a Step-Together-Step (4th Triple Step beginning with the right foot) directly forward. Continue to lead the lady to turn clockwise completing the double turn and returning to Sweetheart Position. Lower the R hand hold around the lady's shoulder and retake the L hand hold in front at waist level.

13-22 Execute the Ten-Step Polka in Position #1 to complete the Lady's Double Turn.

* Note: The Lady's Double Turn may be preceded by any of the Ten-Step Polka variations. It is easily executed following the Lasso. Steps 1-12 consist of four triple steps progressing down the line of dance as the man leads the lady into a Double Turn Clockwise under his R hand hold.

Sweetheart Position   Step 1   Step 3

Ten-Step Polka

Lady's Double Turn
Lady's Footwork

Step	Description

Position: Sweetheart Position *

1-3   Execute a Step-Together-Step (1st Triple Step beginning with the left foot) as the man leads you into 1/2 turn clockwise under his R hand hold. Turn is executed by pivoting on the left foot on step #3.

4-6   Execute a Step-Together-Step (2nd Triple Step beginning with the right foot) as the man leads you into another 1/2 turn clockwise as you face the line of dance.

7-9   Execute a Step-Together-Step (3rd Triple Step beginning with the left foot) as the man leads you into another 1/2 turn clockwise as you face the line of dance.

10-12   Execute a Step-Together-Step (4th Triple Step beginning with the right foot) as you complete the second full turn clockwise returning to Sweetheart Position.

13-22   Execute the Ten-Step Polka in Position #1 to complete the Lady's Double Turn.

* Note: The Lady's Double Turn may be preceded by any of the Ten-Step Polka variations. It is easily executed following the Lasso. Steps 1-12 consist of four triple steps progressing down the line of dance as the man leads the Lady into a Double Turn Clockwise under his R hand hold.

Step 6

Step 9

Step 12

Ten-Step Polka

Continuous Lasso
Man's Footwork

Step	Description	Timing	Rhythmic Cue	Lead
	Position: Lasso Position #1 (Sweetheart Position) into Continuous Lasso. *			
1	Step L foot directly forward.	1	Quick	L and R hand holds
2	Step R foot directly forward bringing feet together (3rd position, L foot forward).	&	Quick	"
3	Step L foot directly forward.	2	Slow	"
4	Step R foot directly forward passing L foot.	1	Quick	"
5	Step L foot directly forward bringing feet together (3rd position, R foot forward).	&	Quick	"
6	Step R foot directly forward.	2	Slow	"

7-12 Repeat Steps 1-6 before executing the Ten-Step Polka.

*Note: Steps 1-12 (4 Triple steps progressing forward) are the same as Basic Step Forward (man's footwork) in Western Polka. Lady and Man begin with the left foot.

TEN-STEP POLKA

Step	Description	Timing	Rhythmic Cue	Lead
13	(1) Extend L foot forward, heel touching floor with toe upward.	1	Slow	L and R hand holds
14	(2) Step L foot in place bringing feet together and changing weight to the L foot.	2	Slow	"
15	(3) Extend R foot backward, toe touching floor.	1	Slow	"
16	(4) Step R foot in place bringing feet together Do not change weight.	2	Slow	"
17	(5) Extend R foot forward, heel touching floor with toe upward.	1	Slow	"
18	(6) Cross R foot in front of left leg (shin) with toe touching floor near L foot.	2	Slow	"
19	(7) Extend R foot forward, heel touching floor with toe upward.	1	Slow	"
20	(8) Step R foot in place bringing feet together and changing weight to R foot.	2	Slow	"

Ten-Step Polka

Continuous Lasso
Lady's Footwork

Step	Description	Timing	Rhythmic Cue
	Position: Lasso Position #1 (Sweetheart Position) into Continuous Lasso. *		
1	Step L foot directly forward.	1	Quick
2	Step R foot directly forward bringing feet together (3rd position, L foot forward).	&	Quick
3	Step L foot directly forward.	2	Slow
4	Step R foot directly forward passing L foot.	1	Quick
5	Step L foot directly forward bringing feet together (3rd position, R foot forward).	&	Quick
6	Step R foot directly forward.	2	Slow
7-12	Repeat Steps 1-6 before executing the Ten-Step Polka.		

* Note: Steps 1-12 (4 Triple steps progressing forward) are the same as the Basic Step Forward (man's footwork) in Western Polka. Lady and Man begin with the left foot. Lady remains in Position #1 during steps 1-12.

TEN-STEP POLKA

Step	Description	Timing	Rhythmic Cue
13	(1) Extend L foot forward, heel touching floor with toe upward.	1	Slow
14	(2) Step L foot in place bringing feet together and changing weight to the L foot.	2	Slow
15	(3) Extend R foot backward, toe touching floor.	1	Slow
16	(4) Step R foot in place bringing feet together Do not change weight.	2	Slow
17	(5) Extend R foot forward, heel touching floor with toe upward.	1	Slow
18	(6) Cross R foot in front of left leg (shin) with toe touching floor near L foot.	2	Slow
19	(7) Extend R foot forward, heel touching floor with toe upward.	1	Slow
20	(8) Step R foot in place bringing feet together and changing weight to R foot.	2	Slow

Ten-Step Polka

Continuous Lasso
Man's Footwork, Cont'd

21	(9) Extend L foot forward, heel touching floor with toe upward.	1	Slow	"
22	(10) Cross L foot in front of right leg (shin) with L foot off floor.	2	Slow	L and R hand holds

* Note: Steps 23-46 execute 8 triple steps progressing from Position #1 past Position #2 into Position #3 and returning to Position #1 as the man leads the lady counterclockwise around him for a Continuous Lasso. This movement is also used in Cotton-Eyed Joe and Schottische.

23-25 Execute a Step-Together-Step (1st Triple Step beginning with the left foot) progressing directly forward down the line of dance. Keeping the L hand hold at waist level raise your R hand hold up and over the Lady's head as she moves around you.

26-28 Execute a Step-Together-Step (2nd Triple Step beginning with the right foot) as the man continues to move the lady counterclockwise in front of him.

29-31 Execute a Step-Together-Step (3rd Triple Step beginning with the left foot) as you continue to lead the lady in a counterclockwise movement encircling your R hand hold over the lady's head as she passes past your left side. Your R hand hold begins to encircle your head with the L hand hold remaining at waist level.

32-34 Execute a Step-Together-Step (4th Triple Step beginning with the right foot) as you continue leading the lady to move counterclockwise around you as you progress forward down the line of dance. Your R hand hold will encircle your head as you begin to raise your L hand hold to place it on your left shoulder.

35-37 Execute a Step-Together-Step (5th Triple Step beginning with the left foot) as you lead the lady behind you to your right side into Position #3. The L hand hold is placed on your left shoulder with the lady's left arm wrapped around you. The R hand hold is extended diagonally to your right at waist level.

38-40 Execute a Step-Together-Step (6th Triple Step beginning with the right foot) as you continue to progress down the line of dance. Retain a double hand hold and keep your partner on your right side as you raise your L hand hold over your head and lower to chest level. R hand hold remains at waist level.

41-43 Execute a Step-Together-Step (7th Triple Step beginning with the left foot) as you raise your L hand hold up and over the lady's head turning her counterclockwise one full turn. The lady will remain on your right side moving from Position #3 into Position #1.

44-46 Execute a Step-Together-Step (8th Triple Step beginning with the right foot) as you complete the Continuous Lasso ending with the lady in Position #1.

47-50 Execute the Ten-Step Polka in Position #1 after completing the Continuous Lasso.

Bootnote: The Continuous Lasso may be repeated or followed by other Ten-Step Polka variations.

Ten-Step Polka

Continuous Lasso
Lady's Footwork, Cont'd

21 (9) Extend L foot forward, heel touching floor
with toe upward.   1   Slow

22 (10) Cross L foot in front of right leg (shin) with
L foot off floor.   2   Slow

* Note: Steps 23-46 execute 8 triple step progressing from Position #1 past Position #2 into Position #3 and returning to Position #1 as the man leads the lady counterclockwise around him for a Continuous Lasso. This movement is also used in Cotton-Eyed Joe and Schottische.

23-25 Execute a Step-Together-Step (1st Triple Step beginning with the left foot) beginning to move counterclockwise in front of your partner. Man will raise the R hand hold above your head and keep the L hand hold at waist level to initiate the lead for the Continuous Lasso.

26-28 Execute a Step-Together-Step (2nd Triple Step beginning with the right foot) continuing to move counterclockwise around your partner. The second triple step should move you in front of him from his left side to his right side.

29-31 Execute a Step-Together-Step (3rd Triple Step beginning with the left foot) as the man continues to lead you through the Continuous Lasso. The third triple step will lead you past his left side as the R hand hold encircles your head. The L hand hold remains at waist level.

32-34 Execute a Step-Together-Step (4th Triple Step beginning with the right foot) continuing to circle counterclockwise around your partner. R hand hold will encircle the man's head leading you behind him with the L hand hold placed on his left shoulder.

35-37 Execute a Step-Together-Step (5th Triple Step beginning with the left foot) moving behind the man from his left side to his right side. Your left arm will wrap around his shoulder with the R hand hold extended to the right at waist level.

38-40 Execute a Step-Together-Step (6th Triple Step beginning with the right foot) directly forward at the man's right side as he lifts your left arm up and over his head to chest level. R hand hold will remain extended to the right during the sixth triple step.

41-43 Execute a Step-Together-Step (7th Triple Step beginning with the left foot) as the man leads you to twirl counterclockwise at his right side. The L hand hold will encircle your head and lower to waist level as the R hand hold pulls to turn into Lasso Position #1.

44-46 Execute a Step-Together-Step (8th Triple Step beginning with the right foot) directly forward with the man on your left side in Sweetheart Position to complete the Continuous Lasso.

47-56 Execute the Ten-Step Polka in Position #1 after completing the Continuous Lasso.

Bootnote: The Continuous Lasso movement may be repeated or followed by other Ten-Step Polka variations.

Continuous Lasso

Sweetheart Position

Steps 26-28

Steps 32-34

Steps 35-37

Continuous Lasso

Steps 38-40

Steps 41-43

Steps 44-46

Ten-Step Polka

Weave the Basket
Man's Footwork

Step	Description	Timing	Rhythmic Cue	Lead
	Position: Sweetheart Position into Weave the Basket. *			
1	Step L foot directly forward.	1	Quick	L and R hand holds
2	Step R foot direclty forward bringing feet together (3rd position, L foot forward).	&	Quick	"
3	Step L foot directly forward.	2	Slow	"
4	Step R foot directly forward passing L foot.	1	Quick	"
5	Step L foot directly forward bringing feet together (3rd position, R foot forward).	&	Quick	"
6	Step R foot directly forward.	2	Slow	"
7-12	Repeat Steps 1-6 before executing the Ten-Step Polka.			

TEN-STEP POLKA

Step	Description	Timing	Rhythmic Cue	Lead
13	(1) Extend L foot forward, heel touching floor with toe upward.	1	Slow	L and R hand holds
14	(2) Step L foot in place bringing feet together and changing weight to the L foot.	2	Slow	"
15	(3) Extend R foot backward, toe touching floor.	1	Slow	"
16	(4) Step R foot in place bringing feet together Do not change weight.	2	Slow	"
17	(5) Extend R foot forward, heel touching floor with toe upward.	1	Slow	"
18	(6) Cross R foot in front of left leg (shin) with toe touching floor near L foot.	2	Slow	"
19	(7) Extend R foot forward, heel touching floor with toe upward.	1	Slow	"
20	(8) Step R foot in place bringing feet together and changing weight to R foot.	2	Slow	"
21	(9) Extend L foot forward, heel touching floor with toe upward.	1	Slow	"
22	(10) Cross L foot in front of right leg (shin) with L foot off the floor.	2	Slow	"

Ten-Step Polka

Weave the Basket
Lady's Footwork

Step	Description	Timing	Rhythmic Cue
	Position: Sweetheart Position into Weave The Basket. *		
1	Step L foot directly forward.	1	Quick
2	Step R foot directly forward bringing feet together (3rd position, L foot forward).	&	Quick
3	Step L foot directly forward.	2	Slow
4	Step R foot directly forward passing L foot.	1	Quick
5	Step L foot directly forward bringing feet together (3rd position, R foot forward).	&	Quick
6	Step R foot directly forward.	2	Slow
7-12	Repeat Steps 1-6 before executing the Ten-Step Polka		

TEN-STEP POLKA

Step	Description	Timing	Rhythmic Cue
13	(1) Extend L foot forward, heel touching floor with toe upward.	1	Slow
14	(2) Step L foot in place bringing feet together and changing weight to the L foot.	2	Slow
15	(3) Extend R foot backward, toe touching floor.	1	Slow
16	(4) Step R foot in place bringing feet together Do not change weight.	2	Slow
17	(5) Extend R foot forward, heel touching floor with toe upward.	1	Slow
18	(6) Cross R foot in front of left leg (shin) with toe touching floor near L foot.	2	Slow
19	(7) Extend R foot forward, heel touching floor with toe upward.	1	Slow
20	(8) Step R foot in place bringing feet together and changing weight to R foot.	2	Slow
21	(9) Extend L foot forward, heel touching floor with toe upward.	1	Slow
22	(10) Cross L foot in front of right leg (shin) with L foot off floor.	2	Slow

Ten-Step Polka

Weave the Basket
Man's Footwork, Cont'd

* Note: Steps 23-46 execute 8 triple steps as both the man and lady face directly forward progressing down the line of dance. The lady will move (Weave) counterclockwise around you.

23-25 Execute a Step-Together-Step (1st Triple Step beginning with the left foot) directly forward as you begin to lead the lady from Sweetheart Position in front of you into Reverse Sweetheart Position. Retain a double hand hold as L hand hold begins to pull the lady from your right side to your left side.

26-28 Execute a Step-Together-Step (2nd Triple Step beginning with the right foot) directly forward as you continue to lead the lady from Sweetheart Position into Reverse Sweetheart Position. Your steps will be small because the lady is passing in front of you. Both the man and lady face down the line of dance during the entire movement of Weave the Basket.

29-31 Execute a Step-Together-Step (3rd Triple Step beginning with left foot) directly forward as you complete leading the lady from Sweetheart Position on your right side into Reverse Sweetheart Position on your left side. Retain a double hand hold with your left arm around her shoulder and your R hand hold extended at waist level.

32-34 Execute a Step-Together-Step (4th Triple Step beginning with the right foot) directly forward as you progress down the line of dance releasing the R hand hold and taking the L hand hold up and over the lady's head. Extend your right hand to the right at waist level preparing to take the lady's right hand.

35-37 Execute a Step-Together-Step (5th Triple Step beginning with the left foot) directly forward as you begin to lead the lady behind you to progress from your left side to your right side. L hand hold moves up behind your back to waist level and right hand extends to the right.

38-40 Execute a Step-Together-Step (6th Triple Step beginning with the right foot) directly forward as you continue to lead the lady from your left side behind you to your right side. L hand hold is placed behind your back at waist level as you retake the R hand hold.

41-43 Execute a Step-Together-Step (7th Triple Step beginning with the left foot) directly forward as you lead the lady back into Sweetheart Position. R hand hold moves (weaves) up and over the lady's head. Release L hand hold behind your back and retake L hand hold in front at waist level.

44-46 Execute a Step-Together-Step (8th Triple Step beginning with the right foot) directly forward as you complete Weave the Basket ending in Sweetheart Position.

47-55 Execute the Ten-Step Polka in Sweetheart Position after completing the Weave the Basket.

* Note: The Weave the Basket may be repeated or followed by other Ten-Step Polka variations.

Sweetheart Position   Steps 23-25   Steps 26-28   Steps 29-31   Steps 32-34

Ten-Step Polka

Weave the Basket
Lady's Footwork, Cont'd

* Note: Steps 23-46 execute 8 triple steps progressing counterclockwise around your partner as both progress down the line of dance. Face directly forward during entire Weave The Basket.

23-25 Execute a Step-Together-Step (1st Triple Step beginning with the left foot) as the man begins to lead you from Sweetheart Position in front of him into Reverse Sweetheart Position. Retain a double hand hold.

26-28 Execute a Step-Together-Step (2nd Triple Step beginning with the right foot) as the man continues to lead you from Sweetheart Position into Reverse Sweetheart Position. Both the man and lady face down the line of dance during the entire movement of Weave the Basket.

29-31 Execute a Step-Together-Step (3rd Triple Step beginning with the left foot) as the man completes leading you from Sweetheart Position on his right side into Reverse Sweetheart Position on his left side.

32-34 Execute a Step-Together-Step (4th Triple Step beginning with the right foot) directly forward (small steps) as you progress down the line of dance. The man's left arm moves (weaves) up and over your head. Release R hand hold keeping hand at waist level.

35-37 Execute a Step-Together-Step (5th Triple Step beginning with the left foot) as the man begins to lead you behind him to progress from his left side to his right side. L hand hold moves up behind his back to waist level.

38-40 Execute a Step-Together-Step (6th Triple Step beginning with the right foot) as the man continues to lead you from his left side behind him to his right side. L hand hold is placed behind the man's back at waist level as you retake his R hand hold.

41-43 Execute a Step-Together-Step (7th Triple Step beginning with the left foot) as the man leads you back into Sweetheart Position. R hand hold moves (weaves) up and over your head. Release L hand hold behind your back and retake L hand hold at waist level.

44-46 Execute a Step-Together-Step (8th Triple Step beginning with the right foot) directly forward as you complete Weave The Basket.

47-55 Execute the Ten-Step Polka in Position #1 after completing the Weave The Basket.

* Note: The Weave The Basket may be repeated or followed by other Ten-Step Polka variations.

Steps 35-37

Steps 38-40

Steps 41-43

Steps 44-46

Favorite Ten-Step Polka Selections

"Big Mamou" (medium fast) by Frenchie Burke

"Cajun Moon" (medium) by Ricky Skaggs

"Colinda" (medium fast) by Frenchie Burke

"Crippled Turkey" (medium) by Bob Wills and The Texas Playboy

"Devil's Dream" (medium) by Frenchie Burke

"Down in Mexico" (medium) by Auggie Meyers

"Drivin' Nails in My Coffin" (medium fast) by Johnny Bush

"El Rancho Grande" (medium) by Al Dean and the Allstars

"Foggy Mountain Breakdown" (medium fast) by Al Dean and The Allstars

"Hey Joe (Hey Moe)" (medium) by Moe Bandy and Joe Stampley

"Jalisco" (medium fast) by Al Dean and by Adolph Hofner

"Jessie Polka" (medium) by Adolph Hofner

"Model "A" Polka" (medium) by Al Dean and The Allstars

"Mountain Music" (medium and fast) by Alabama

"My Baby Thinks He's a Train" (fast) by Rosanne Cash

"New Cut Road" (medium slow) by Bobby Bare

"On The Road Again" (medium slow) by Willie Nelson

"Orange Blossom Special" (fast) by Frenchie Burke or the Charley Daniel's Band

"Rocky Top" (fast) by The Osborne Brothers

"San Antonio Stroll" (medium slow) by Tanya Tucker